THE BURDEN OF VISUAL TRUTH

THE ROLE OF PHOTOJOURNALISM IN MEDIATING REALITY

LEA's Communication Series
Jennings Bryant/Dolf Zillmann, General Editors

Selected titles in Journalism (Maxwell McCombs, Advisory Editor) include:

Crespi • The Public Opinion Process: How the People Speak

Friedman/Dunwoody/Rogers • Communicating Uncertainty: Media Coverage of New and Controversial Science

Hachten • The Troubles of Journalism: A Critical Look at What's Right and Wrong With the Press

McCombs/Reynolds • The Poll With a Human Face: The National Issues Convention Experiment in Political Communication

Merritt • Public Journalism and Public Life: Why Telling the News is Not Enough, Second Edition

Perloff • Political Communication: Politics, Press, and Public in America

Wanta • The Public and the National Agenda: How People Learn About Important Issues

Weaver/Wilhoit • The American Journalist in the 1990s: U.S. News People at the End of an Era

For a complete list of other titles in LEA's Communication Series, please contact Lawrence Erlbaum Associates, Publishers

THE BURDEN OF VISUAL TRUTH
THE ROLE OF PHOTOJOURNALISM IN MEDIATING REALITY

Julianne H. Newton
The University of Oregon

Routledge
Taylor & Francis Group
New York   London

Transferred to Digital Printing 2008

Copyright © 2001 by Lawrence Erlbaum Associates, Inc.

First published by Lawrence Erlbaum Associates, Inc., Publishers
10 Industrial Avenue
Mahwah, New Jersey 07430

Reprinted 2008 by Routledge
Routledge
Taylor & Francis Group
270 Madison Avenue
New York, NY 10016

Routledge
Taylor & Francis Group
2 Park Square
Milton Park, Abingdon
Oxon OX14 4RN

Cover design by Kathryn Houghtaling Lacey
Cover Photograph by Julianne H. Newton

Library of Congress Cataloging-in-Publication Data

Newton, Julianne Hickerson, 1949–
   The burden of visual truth: the role of photojournalism in mediating reality/ Julianne
H. Newton.
   p.   cm.
   Includes bibliographical references and index.
   ISBN 0-8058-3375-7 (cloth: alk. paper)—ISBN 0-8058-3376-5 (pbk.: alk. paper)
   1. Photojournalism.   I. Title.

TR820.N44 2000
070.4'9—dc21

                                                                                  00-034769

Publisher's Note
The publisher has gone to great lengths to ensure the quality of this reprint
but points out that some imperfections in the original may be apparent

Dedication

To those who risk all so the rest of us can see—and, therefore, know.

STAKEOUT. *Washington Times* photojournalist Ken Lambert, right, rushes to get a good angle on a legislator leaving a closed meeting on Capitol Hill in January 1997. With much of the inner workings of the U.S. government conducted privately, members of the Washington, DC press corps regularly stakeout, or wait outside closed doors leading to Capitol Hill meeting rooms and offices in hopes of retrieving a quick quote, photo, or video clip when people exit. (Photo by Julie Newton.)

THE BURDEN
OF VISUAL TRUTH
THE ROLE OF PHOTOJOURNALISM IN MEDIATING REALITY

Julianne H. Newton
The University of Oregon

Routledge
Taylor & Francis Group
New York   London

Transferred to Digital Printing 2008

First published by Lawrence Erlbaum Associates, Inc., Publishers
10 Industrial Avenue
Mahwah, New Jersey 07430

Reprinted 2008 by Routledge
Routledge
Taylor & Francis Group
270 Madison Avenue
New York, NY 10016

Routledge
Taylor & Francis Group
2 Park Square
Milton Park, Abingdon
Oxon OX14 4RN

Cover design by Kathryn Houghtaling Lacey
Cover Photograph by Julianne H. Newton

Library of Congress Cataloging-in-Publication Data

Newton, Julianne Hickerson, 1949–
   The burden of visual truth: the role of photojournalism in mediating reality/ Julianne H. Newton.
      p.   cm.
   Includes bibliographical references and index.
   ISBN 0-8058-3375-7 (cloth: alk. paper)—ISBN 0-8058-3376-5 (pbk.: alk. paper)
   1. Photojournalism.   I. Title.

TR820.N44 2000
070.4'9—dc21

                                                                          00-034769

Publisher's Note
The publisher has gone to great lengths to ensure the quality of this reprint
but points out that some imperfections in the original may be apparent

CONTENTS

Preface   ix

Acknowledgments   xv

CHAPTER 1   **Introduction**   1

CHAPTER 2   **The Vision Instinct**
             The Roots of Visual Reportage   15

CHAPTER 3   **From Instinct to Practice**
             Who Are the Players and What's
             the Goal of the Game?   31

CHAPTER 4   **The Heart of the Seer**
             Photographer Concerns/Ethics   47

CHAPTER 5   **Stealing the Soul**
             Subject Concerns/Identity   61

CHAPTER 6   **Tending the Gate**
             Editor Concerns/Social Responsibility   73

CHAPTER 7   **Is Seeing Still Believing?**
             Viewer Concerns/Visual Perception Theory   81

CHAPTER 8   **Whose Truth?**
             Society and Visual Culture   93

CHAPTER 9   **Toward an Ecology of the Visual**
             The Whole Picture   105

CHAPTER 10   **Translating the Visual**
             A Typology of Visual Behavior   127

CHAPTER 11   **The Problem of Real People**
              *What Do Pictures of Real
              Life Mean to Us?*   149

CHAPTER 12   **The Future**
              *Photo+Graphic+Video+Print+Film
              +Internet+Virtual Reality+
              Visual Literacy = ???*   175

Afterword   187

References   189

Credits and Permissions   201

Author Index   203

Subject Index   207

PREFACE

Photojournalism, at the beginning of the 21st century, finds itself at the proverbial crossroads: Will image-making technologies and public cynicism lead to its demise, or will journalists rise to the challenge by practicing a new, more credible form of visual journalism? From the time of its invention in the early 19th century, photography enjoyed the unparalleled credibility assumed through a mechanistic perception of a neutral, "mirror of nature" camera. By the beginning of the 20th century, photographs were being used as irrefutable evidence of the veracity of their manifest content, a position supported by empiricism, modernism, and the scientific method. Additionally, journalism's deliberate move toward objectivity in mid-20th-century media culture underscored the value of photographic evidence. By the 1960s, photojournalism was flourishing—the 35-mm camera had made the physical challenges of picture taking easier, printing advances had made publication of photographs a simpler matter, and news publications had begun to realize the informational and economic value of photographs.

Paradoxically, however, the physical sciences had already challenged the idea of an objective world "out there." The development of quantum physics shifted all notions of reality, zooming in on the subjective nature of our comprehension of all things. Literary, art, and communication scholars echoed physicists' concerns through their critiques of the scientific method and modernism itself. The photograph as an evidentiary document began to lose face in light of increased understanding of the subjective nature of visual representation. Constructionism, semiotics, and then deconstructionism offered new ways to interpret visual culture and human visual behavior.

And if those issues were not enough to shake the ground of photo-journalism's raison d'être, digital imaging technology, with its ability to flawlessly manipulate a genre that was not supposed to be manipulated, did. Ethical blunders by such journalistic icons as *National Geographic* and *Time* magazine in the 1980s and 1990s contributed to a popular misconception that digital imaging is rapidly eroding any trust viewers or readers might still hold in journalistic media. Furthermore, such events as the paparazzi's pursuit of Princess Diana the night of her death fueled the fires of public concern about the practice of photojournalism.

Yet, human beings continue to die from war, murder, natural disasters; to be born, now in litters as large as seven or eight; to live in harmony and conflict. Newspapers and photojournalism have survived the onslaught of electronic media, continuing to report the human maelstrom of a global citizenry as if it were a vivid reality play in the midst of the nonreality of turn-of-the-millennium culture. Almost drowned within media criticism have been the voices of those professionals whose appreciation of the subjective nature of observation and reportage has led to more sensitive and sophisticated practice of visual journalism. In daily practice, digital-imaging technology has led to increased awareness of the ease of manipulating visual reportage, in turn leading to higher—not lower—ethical standards. At the same time, new technology has made visual coverage faster, easier, and more prolific via digital distribution.

As a result, photojournalism at the beginning of the 21st century finds itself maturing beyond the naive idealism of early and mid-20th-century positivism, and even beyond the dark cynicism of late-20th-century post-modernism, toward a profound sense of purpose: Good visual reportage may very well be the only credible source of reasonably true images in decades to come. The heart of photojournalism is reporting human experience accurately, honestly, and with an overriding sense of social responsibility. The key to earning and maintaining public trust is increasing awareness of the process of visual reporting and its potential to inform or misinform. Drawing on an eclectic theoretical base grounded in classical ethics, surveillance theory, social constructionism, and visual perception, this book considers the symbiotic concerns of various travelers through the visual truth labyrinth: photographers, human subjects, editors, viewers, and society at large. Using an original typology of visual ethics ranging from visual embrace to visual suicide, the book examines visual reportage as a form of human visual behavior, concluding with a proposal for an "ecology of the visual" appropriate for the 21st century.

OBJECTIVES

The primary objective of this book is to analyze the role of visual reportage in the understanding of others, the world, and ourselves. The book approaches the subject matter from several perspectives.

One perspective is to examine ideas underlying concepts of visual truth, particularly as conveyed by the news media. Chapter 2 summarizes and synthesizes a number of relevant theories, ranging from surveillance theory to visual perception theory, looking for the origins of photojournalism in human biology and culture as a way to understand the role of visual reportage in present and future life. A running theme throughout the book is that visual reportage encompasses a synergistic process involving photographers, subjects, editors, viewers, and society at large.

A second perspective, which spans chapters 3 through 7, is to synthesize and apply relevant research on photojournalism and reality imagery. Available research ranges from qualitative critiques of photography in general to quantitative experiments on the effects of camera angle on viewer perception. I have evaluated the practice of visual reportage within the context of late-20th-century understanding of ways of knowing.

A third perspective, explored in chapters 9 through 12, is to extend visual communication theory by proposing that we think in terms of an ecology of the visual for 21st-century life. The ecology places visual reportage within the repertoire of human visual behavior and suggests a verbal and visual typology to facilitate discussion. The book concludes by outlining an appropriate, crucial role for photojournalism in the future development of humankind.

WHY PEOPLE SHOULD READ THIS BOOK

Why does the role of photojournalism in our culture matter? Why should anyone but news professionals be concerned? I am convinced that visual reportage is a unique and significant contributor in contemporary culture. Yet, universities and high schools continue to debate its appropriateness as an area of substantive study, closing photojournalism programs as technologies have shifted from silver gelatin to digital. Much of the important ground visual communication gained in 1970s and 1980s education is threatened by calls to return to a focus on verbal skills, with apparent disregard for the proliferation of the visual in contemporary media. Rather than attack the problem of illiteracy and declining verbal skills with up-to-date data about human perception, many educators have retreated to the pedagogy of the past, a pedagogy dominated by unidimensional linear thought. Students of journalism and communication are required to take multiple courses in word skills, yet few universities require them to study visual skills—if they do, one course is often considered sufficient. One look at contemporary media—whether magazines, newspapers, the Internet, television, film—offers ample evidence of the proliferation of the visual in our lives. Educators, in fact, bemoan the loss of young people's verbal abilities. Why not embrace the visual by turning the concept of "loss of the verbal" into a call for sophisticated use of the visual, thus enhancing human's abilities to communicate? Any educated, functional citizen of global culture must learn to understand and use visual communication appropriately. Where better to begin than with a clear comprehension of how the visual affects our sense of the real?

Toward that goal, *Visual Truth* offers students, educators, scholars, professionals, and the public a comprehensive analysis of visual reportage as a form of human visual behavior in contemporary culture. This book assesses the role of photojournalism in contemporary culture in terms of the complex, cross-disciplinary pool of literature and ideas required for comprehensive analysis. Few studies of "truth" media—the news and information media in their various forms—have focused on the role of reality imagery in legitimizing the news, attracting audiences, constructing reality, and affecting consciousness. Many studies focus on verbal reports as carriers of the most substantive news content, usually discussing news images in one chapter, on the periphery, or leaving them out entirely.

This volume is appropriate for use in a variety of undergraduate and graduate courses, including still photography and broadcast journalism; newspaper, magazine, and new media journalism; documentary; media law and ethics; mass communication theory; critical/cultural theory; popular culture; visual studies; U.S. civilization; media sociology; and art and photo history.

Journalism and mass communication professionals, including writers, reporters, photographers, videographers, editors, and publishers, concerned with improving media credibility and maintaining journalism in future culture—regardless of technological shifts in media—will find the book helps to fill a void in literature assessing the changing role of their chosen profession in contemporary culture.

Scholars in visual studies, media studies, journalism, nonverbal communication, art history, cultural history, and psychology will find this volume a valuable, comprehensive base for studying reality imaging and human visual behavior.

The book also will appeal to increasingly sophisticated members of the public who seek to understand the role of visual media in the formation of their views of the world and of their own identities.

THE GROUND BEFORE

Important to acknowledge are the many fine books and other works that have laid important groundwork for this book and that explore other aspects of the story of photojournalism. These include Kobre's (1996) *Photojournalism: The Professional Approach*, the most popular text; Lester's (1991) *Photojournalism: An Ethical Approach*, the first text devoted entirely to photojournalism ethics; Fulton's (1988) *The Eyes of Time: Photojournalism in America*, an excellent history; Goldberg's *The Power of Pictures*, a chronicle of influential photographs; Chapnick's *Truth Needs No Ally*, a seasoned picture editor's advice on pursuing photojournalism as a career; and Hagaman's (1996) *How I Learned Not to Be a Photojournalist*, a former photojournalist's view on how to do visual ethnography. Several other significant contemporary works address theoretical and ideological questions relevant to this volume. Critical to the initial study of the visual were Worth's "Margaret Mead and the shift from 'visual anthropology' to the 'anthropology of visual communication'" (1980) and *Studying Visual Communication* (1981). Other important works include Burgin's (1982) *Thinking Photography*, Sontag's (1973) *On Photography*, Hall's (1973) "The Determination of News Photographs," Benjamin's (1969) "The Work of Art in the Age of Mechanical Reproduction," and Messaris' (1994) *Visual Literacy: Image, Mind, and Reality*. Lutz and Collins' (1993) *Reading National Geographic*, Mitchell's (1994) *Picture Theory*, and Tagg's (1988) *The Burden of Representation* apply a critical studies approach. Books such as Beloff's (1985) *Camera Culture* and Freund's (1980) *Photography and Society* also examine issues of the impact of photography on human life within a critical/cultural context. Kozol's (1994) *Life's America: Family and Nation in Postwar Photojournalism* focuses attention on the power of one dominant publication of photojournalism to construct a nation's image of itself. Zelizer's *Covering the Body* (1992) and *Remembering to Forget* (1998) cogently address media influence on collective memory.

Each preceding work exploring the way we know via our eyes has moved us closer to drawing the theoretical map. My hope is that this book moves us another step along the road.

ACKNOWLEDGMENTS

- To all those whom I photographed. They were my best teachers.
- To all those students who helped me understand parts of the story.
- To the professional journalists across the United States and in Australia and Brazil who opened their doors, minds, and vision to me.
- To The University of Texas Research Institute, the College of Communication Jamail Grant Program, and the Department of Journalism for funds supporting this project.
- To the anonymous reviewers who read earlier versions of the material in this volume and offered invaluable feedback along the way.
- To my visual communication colleagues around the country, who struggle faithfully to enlighten our logocentric academic culture.
- To Max McCombs, Linda Bathgate, and Jennings Bryant for bringing this book to fruition.
- To J. B. Colson, who opened the door to my intellectual journey into vision and ethics.
- To my mentors and colleagues whose unfailing support carried me through the worst of times—especially Wayne Danielson, Bill Korbus, Max McCombs, and Jim Tankard.
- To my friends, whose love and affirmation sustained me: Ave Bonar, Steve Clark, Mary Lee Edwards, Sandra Eisert, Roy Flukinger, Nick Lasorsa, Marilyn Schultz, Rich Scroggins, Pam Shoemaker, Janet Staiger, Patsy Watkins, and Jeanne Young.
- To my dear mother, to Eva and Taylor, to Fred and Iris, who taught me the value of courage, perseverance, and fulfilling dreams.
- And to my wondrous children, Matt, Josh, Kate, and my beloved, steadfast soulmate and all-time very best friend and love, Rick.
- Thank you for believing in me and in this project throughout it all.

—J.N.

FROM HUMAN EYE TO DIGITAL CODE. Coveted passes to Lafayette Press Stand in Washington, DC give photographers prime positions but hours to wait for President Bill Clinton to review his second inaugural parade, January 20, 1997. The President and members of his entourage watched and waved from behind a bullet-proof shield in their own stand directly across the street from the press. As the parade continued into the evening darkness, lights kept the area around the President bright as day for the benefit of cameras. Visual reportage equipment ranged from the human eye to video to still film and digital cameras. (Photo by Julie Newton.)

Popular perception among those who study the media is that photo-journalism is in serious jeopardy—if not already dead—not only because of changing technologies, image saturation, and shifting media economics, but more importantly perhaps, because of a perceived concomitant decline of public belief in visual truth. Two groups of questions guide this book. One concerns the status of visual reportage: How is it practiced? How is it perceived by journalists and by viewers? What are the effects of technology, image proliferation, and media economics on the practice and perception of photojournalism? What is the substance of photojournalism imagery? The second guiding group of questions concerns the status of visual truth. Do people still believe reality images? Do photojournalists still believe they can capture and reveal truth? How have critical attacks on objective reality and the ocularcentrism of the 20th century affected our understanding of visual truth? How do concepts of visual truth in first-world nations compare with those in third-world nations? What is the appropriate role for visual reportage in our future global culture?

This book addresses one of the most critical concerns facing global citizenry as we begin the 21st century: the status of visual truth. And the status of visual truth is inextricably linked with visual reportage. Technology has made possible the seamless alteration of images and the realistic creation of any photographic illustration or image one can envision. The line between fact and fiction, science and art, news and entertainment, information and advertising has become increasingly blurred. Yet, somehow we must continue to disseminate the visual and verbal information necessary to inform the public about matters within and beyond their local universes. Successful and reasonably truthful communication through visual images is possible—but we must frame the production and use of reality images as "mediated communication," rather than as "objective truth." The "seeing-is-believing" phenomenon is being tempered with visual literacy. The future of visual truth depends on the integrity of the photojournalist and everyone else—subjects, editors, viewers—involved in the process of making and consuming visual reportage.

It has become a truism backed by survey data that media rank low in public credibility ("Americans' view … ," 2000). As the media move toward even more varied and easily manipulated forms of representation and creation, the issue of truth and how we come to know anything about our world becomes increasingly critical. If the media are to continue the time-honored and necessary tradition of informing the public, media professionals and users alike must be committed to carrying the standard for visual truth. The burden is twofold: first, to recognize the ability of visual

CHAPTER 1

Introduction

*The camera eye and the mind's eye share a vision that has imposed
itself on this century. Photographs now confirm all that is visible,
and photographs will affirm what is one day remembered. Human
affairs have not quite been the same since the first images formed
on plates of copper, but after a century and a half we are still
uncertain if it is for better, for worse, or neither.*

—Wright Morris (1978)

O nly 100 years ago, people believed that what they saw in photographs
was true. As we embark on a new century, a Virtual Age even, we know
that many visual representations that seem to be true are not. In fact, an
increasingly common response to an unusual photograph is, "They did that
in the computer!" Where does this leave a medium whose mission is to
deliver instant, realistic, "eyewitness" accounts of people and events
throughout the world? Advances in digital-imaging technology, the proliferation of alternative and violent shock media, and growing visual sophisti-
cation of viewers and readers have left media scholars and professional
journalists wondering if we are now witness to the demise of a way of
knowing characteristic of modernism and 20th-century life: the assumed
veracity of the photographic image. This volume explores the status of
visual truth in this era of appropriate skepticism by positioning photojournalism as a requisite form of human visual behavior responding to, contributing to, and mediating the understanding of contemporary culture.
Whether visual reportage will continue to play this central role in the
global culture to come may well determine the degree to which any form
of visual truth survives as well.

CHAPTER 1

Introduction

Photojournalism, perhaps better identified as visual journalism in 21st-century media, may be the only credible source of reasonably true images about world culture in decades to come. Two sets of questions guide discussion of this critical concern: What is the status of visual reportage as humankind begins the 21st century? What is the status of visual truth? This chapter first defines photojournalism, visual truth, and a critically related concept—objectivity—and then introduces the theoretical and practical issues that inform and convolute attempts to answer those questions.

image makers to mediate reality in positive and negative ways, and, second, to acknowledge that reasonably true images not only are possible but also are essential to contemporary society. This book takes a hard look at how images are being made and used during this volatile period of merging technologies, questionable ideologies, and sophisticated understanding of knowledge construction. The burden falls heaviest on photojournalism because its core function is to record and convey events truthfully and visually.

DEFINING PHOTOJOURNALISM AND VISUAL TRUTH

For the purposes of this book, *photojournalism* is defined generally as a descriptive term for reporting visual information via various media. When people discuss photojournalism, they often are referring to still photographs in print media, such as newspapers and magazines. Increasingly, however, the photojournalism profession also encompasses television news, which relies primarily on video but often uses still photographs in broadcasts, and Internet news, which uses both still and moving images. The term *photojournalism* typically applies to a genre of images with a range of subgenres published or broadcast with accompanying words and usually as part of a package that may include other visual elements, such as headlines, charts, or multiple images. Subgenres include spot news, subject matter that is immediate and significant; general news, information on a wide range of topics and individuals; features, which highlight individuals or activities via a variety of styles; illustration, viewed as conceptual imagery that can be completely made up; and sports news, which encompasses all four categories but focuses on athletics.

An important term in the definition of photojournalism is *reporting*, the traditional underlying rationale for journalism itself. To report is to gather information and to convey that information. The gathering can involve observing an activity or directed research, such as interviewing or scanning data. The conveying can be simply telling, or it can involve elaborate verbal and/or visual presentations. In photojournalism, reporting has too often been considered synonymous with recording. And therein lies the crux of any discussion of visual truth. Photography's inherent capacity for gathering visual information by recording points of light reflecting off physical entities and for conveying that information in a form that looks so much like the world we perceive with our own eyes fostered an early and prevailing assumption about the authenticity of photographic representation.

Photographers were deemed *recorders*, rather than *reporters*, as if their points of view were as neutral as those of a machine. Even scholars took a good part of the 20th century to discern that, as the anthropologist Margaret Mead observed, even a video camera set on a tripod to record automatically has to be pointed in a particular direction at a particular time that includes and excludes certain information (Mead & Bateson, 1977). However, once we determined that our projection of objective truth onto photography was naive, we responded as if we had been betrayed by an intimate friend, rejecting visual reportage as nothing more than subjective constructionism. In giving up the idealistic belief in the possibility of an absolute visual truth, we gave up hope of coming to understand even a reasonable truth. Underscoring this idea was our newfound ability to alter undiscernably the information in a photographic image after the moment of recording light.

It is important here to distinguish between the material, chemically based processes traditionally making "photography" possible and the electronic, computer-coded processes known as digital imaging. *Photography*, which traditionally is defined as "writing with light," is dependent on an analogic recording of light-based information on a reactive surface. The relation between the information out there and the information recorded on the light-sensitive surface (be it film, coated glass, or metal plate) is direct and correspondent. A point of light reflecting off the surface of a tree trunk physically passes through space and lens to change silver halide crystals embedded in film emulsion. To alter the information recorded by the crystals requires another physical process—adding more light, changing their response via chemistry, cutting them out, or painting over them. In digital imaging, the information out there is still gathered via the physical reflection of a particle of light from a surface. But there the similarity ends. The point of light is translated into a digital code that can be read by a computer. Not only can that digital code be altered easily, but its alteration also can be done in such a way as to be undetectable. Issues of subjective vision are the same in each medium: The photographer and subject can directly and indirectly influence what information is recorded. But in digital imaging, a new point of light is no longer required to alter the physical information represented. Note that definitions are therefore critical here: Photography means recording light; digital imaging means converting light. And in the simple use of the words *record* and *convert* lies the heart of our original trust in photography and our relatively new distrust of digital imaging. Is there really any difference? Photography uses reflected light to initiate a chemical reaction. Digital imaging converts light into binary codes that are then converted back into light for us to see. Both media save visual information for perception by the human eye. Both media are only as trustworthy as those who made them.

The issue at stake is larger than a physical process, although common wisdom has tried to reduce it to a physical process because it is so much easier to comprehend, dissect, criticize, and contain. But the issue will never be about a physical process, which changes through time with technological advances. The issue is how people know, believe, understand, represent, communicate, persuade, lie … and, perhaps most importantly, remember. Memory after all, is the internal human analog to external, technological forms of recording visual information.

So, is visual truth a matter of the level of correspondence between *out there* and the recording of *out there*? Or is it about something larger and more profoundly philosophical and psychological residing deep within the human knowledge system and deep within human communication?

When trying to consider familiar terms, such as *visual* and *truth*, turning to basic dictionary definitions is quite helpful. Beginning with established scholarly definitions not only can convolute the core meaning we are trying to discern, but also can taint our efforts to examine a term with a fresh approach. Although we can never hope to step completely out of any ideological or cultural boxes within which our minds have matured, there is value in the effort to do so. As we move more deeply into theoretical levels of our discussion, the next section adds opinions of individuals who have grappled with these issues.

Visual Truth

Defining *visual truth* is difficult and much debated; moving closer to understanding the concept is a goal of this book. Turning to the dictionary definitions of *visual* and *truth* we obtain *verifiable, indisputable optical fact* (*Random House Webster's*, 1995, pp. 950, 1432, 1490)—a worthy target but not so simple to achieve. Consider the *Webster's* 1979 definition of verisimilitude: "the quality of … representation that causes one to accept it as true to life or to human experience." This is more helpful than "optical fact," but employing the term *representation* is problematic and deserves its own discussion (see chap. 9–11). Note that by 1995, the definition of verisimilitude was "the appearance or semblance of truth; likelihood, possibility … something having merely the appearance of truth" (*Random House Webster's*, 1995,

p. 1480), placing more emphasis on the appearance of truth. Consider this: *Visual truth is authentic knowledge derived from seeing.* Authentic is defined in *Random House Webster's* (1995) as "not false or copied; genuine; real ... having an origin supported by unquestionable evidence ... reliable; trustworthy ... authoritative" (p. 92). Although including the term *unquestionable* can be challenged, we have a point from which to begin.

The Problem of Objectivity

A key concept in any discussion of truth is *objectivity*, which *Random House Webster's* (1995) defines as the state or quality of "being not influenced by personal feelings or prejudice" (p. 933).

The subject of an enormous body of literature in media criticism and postmodernism, objectivity is closely linked to the eye witness role in photojournalism and the idea that a "camera never lies." Discussions about the media, at least until the 1960s and the advent of the New Journalism, which invited subjectivity (Weber, 1974), emphasized the standard of objective reporting by word journalists, and textbooks taught ways to obtain and convey supposedly unbiased information. Since the 1960s, research in the social sciences has increasingly supported the idea that objectivity is an unobtainable value, a myth, a societal ritual, an organizational routine, or a fall-back ideology to protect the hurried journalist in everyday practice (Goffman, 1974; Shoemaker & Reese, 1996; Tuchman, 1978). Social and natural scientists alike have come to question everything from the scientific method to our ways of understanding the world and ourselves (Berger & Luckmann, 1967; Capra, 1996).

Somewhat ironically, little attention was given in the early part of this century to the need for objective visual reporting. One explanation is that words were considered the primary conduit of news, but pictures were considered illustrations supplementing the words and breaking up monotonous, gray columns of type. Another, somewhat contradictory explanation is the mechanistically driven assumption that photographs were valid, reliable, "exactly repeatable pictorial statements" made by a neutral camera (Ivins, 1953/1978). Despite the fact that photographs have been overtly manipulated since the invention of photography, little attention was paid to overt manipulation by visual journalists—much less to covert manipulation—until the development of literature in photojournalism ethics in the 1980s and 1990s. Codes of ethics for photojournalists now insist that no news photograph should be staged, posed, set up, or recreated. But the codes are upheld differently by editors in different media. Reaves (1995a,

1995b) documented that magazine editors, for example, are more likely than newspaper editor to allow manipulation of images. Although the constructionist frame—the idea that we make or construct truth in various forms—may be generally accepted in contemporary theoretical literature, little is known about the effect of this relatively newfound understanding of subjective reality on the production and use of news imaging.

Theoretical Bases

Building this discussion on a solid theoretical base is fundamental. Applying relevant theory to photojournalism rests on examining visual reportage within the context of two symbiotic and dialectical concerns: its role in human life, and its relation to reality. Because these larger issues are the focus of chapter 2, only a cursory note is offered here.

As with any human activity, photojournalism has origins in a complex array of human needs and characteristics that can be traced to survival and expressive behaviors of early humans. I locate visual reportage within the organic origins of vision and aesthetics through surveillance and visual perception theories. Other especially useful theories include social responsibility theory, critical/cultural theory, frame analysis, constructionism, and symbolic interactionism.

Practical Bases

This discussion also is built on a solid base of practical knowledge. This book draws heavily from my own experience as a word journalist, editor, photographer, and social scientist since the late 1960s. Recent observation and practice strongly suggest that visual reportage not only is alive and well, but, contrary to perception in postmodern literature, thriving. Furthermore, the data suggest that the meaning of visual truth has matured beyond the idea of objective evidence recorded by a transparent medium to a concept of accurate and honest reporting. But, of course, there are complications.

According to one photographer I interviewed, "Ten years from now we will still be doing newspapers ... the use of images will increase ... our appetite for them is expanding."[1] Yet another photographer said, "We're

---

[1]This and ensuing quotations in this chapter are from personal communications (Newton, 1994–1999), in the Burden of Visual Truth Research Project. Sources were promised anonymity. The content quoted is typical of the interviews, rather than isolated comments.

headlong going [toward glitz and loss of content] and nobody wants to talk about it." One editor said decisions he had made recently for his newspaper regarding technology were "made with one key idea in mind: that newsprint will be one of several forms of the newspaper." In some cases, online publications are using more still photography than print versions and are welcome outlets for photojournalists. On the other hand, many photojournalists believe online publication is not as respected as print media, and they express concern about its lack of permanence. In spite of predictions that still photojournalism will become lost in video journalism, the consensus is that there will always be a need for still photographs. Some point to the perception that we remember in still-image form. Others note that CNN often uses multiple stills in newscasts, rather than video. Others maintain that the still photograph communicates more quickly, succinctly, and powerfully than a moving image. Whether wishful thinking or future fact, many visual journalists believe the profession will survive.

Through the course of my own professional work and through my research, I have observed scores of photographers, writers, and editors who are passionately committed to the social responsibilities of their profession. They especially relish telling stories of how their photographs or stories helped someone or called attention to a problem: "That's what's in it for me … making a difference in people's lives." As one photojournalist said:

> I want to close the gaps between people. A photograph can cause you to stop and look at another person's life. It's the only way we'll get closer to each other. Those superficial pictures really scare me. One is not evil, two is not evil, 10 or 100 … but 100,000 is evil. It's a crime. It keeps us from under-standing each other. Even a portrait in some circumstances can be something that helps us understand how people feel. You feel some kind of connection to a person. You realize there are things you didn't know. A light bulb has turned on in your heart.

The visual journalists with whom I spoke also sustained a passionate commitment to the idea of visual truth. As one said, "I try very, very very hard to be fair."

Additionally, my research indicates that, despite journalists' low rank in credibility polls, readers still may intuitively believe images they see in newspapers. This intuitive belief system may be the result of a real level of trust in newspapers, of the perceptual tendency to trust what we see, or of a naive or anomic refusal to accept personal responsibility for questioning what we see and investigating reality ourselves. One reader said, "The paper wouldn't lie to us, so, yes, I believe the pictures." One photo editor said, "Newspapers are the last good bit of truth people can get from the media. ... The truth is 'no lies.'" He added: "Television and popular magazines, including news magazines, have left the impression on most readers that we fake it all anyway. ... There are enough checks and balances in the news room ... the ethics of journalism are alive in newsrooms." Another picture editor had a similar point of view:

> Newspapers really are the last bastion of truth in media. Television manipulates; magazine's the same way. I want to believe my paper because what's in it is true. The public doesn't believe it—they think of media as television and magazines; critics of the media have used the word generically—if the media distort truth, then they all distort truth. ... My belief is that newspapers are the most truthful of all. I worry that we are being brought down into the swamp of the rest.

Another high-ranking editor said the practice of setting up photos continues, but is not acceptable. Another saw the biggest threat to truth as economics, not digital technology. "What I see over and over again is that we need to get so many pictures done a day by so many people. ... We know we can get a picture in an hour and half—why should we break for truth?" For one photojournalist, the key to maintaining a sense of visual truth rests in the newsroom: "He or she with power in the newsroom is going to direct what we see." And still another said visual truth could not be defined because "nothing is true." He added, "It's all about point of view and opinion ... having to focus on a subject literally and figuratively." The critical point, he said, is that "we're trying to educate people about their world, to wake them out of their coma. We're telling people one thing ... a piece of the truth," he said. "I want to engage and enrage and annoy and enlighten ... I want them to not be able to not notice."

Critical to note is that although I have made a concerted effort to look fairly at the issues surrounding visual reportage, in the end, this book represents my own subjective analysis of a wide variety of situations and information. This book is my best interpretation of what I have seen, heard, and felt over years of critical, deliberate study and practice as a reporter, editor, documentarian, scholar, social scientist, and educator. I am convinced that a core of photojournalists and editors dedicated to producing the most truthful images possible—and that means the least manipulated, most accurate, fairest images they can make and publish—with awareness of their potential to mislead and misinform readers and viewers through the manipulation of those images, are the standard bearers for visual truth. Photojournalism practice does seem to have proceeded through postmodern skepticism of objective reality as if we still can know or objectify some things. In fact, one ideological contribution of photojournalism may be that we can indeed know some things: We know Bob Dole fell off a speaker's stand during his campaign—and quickly got up; we know Robert Kennedy lay dying; we know bodies were stockpiled in Rwanda. Paradoxically, another ideological contribution of photography is that it so fervently reminds us of the subjective nature of perception of the world (Newton, 1984).

At stake is a primary way of knowing—gathering information with our eyes. Visual reportage manifests that way of knowing in public discourse as a form of reality production—at once mediated and true. The paradox is that in this unreal, constructed, perceived world of ours, we sometimes see sparks of something we can call *reasonably true* because of the skill and integrity of those who mediated the sparks. Far from being the demise of photojournalism, new technologies are clarifying our standards and ethical codes. As we proceed into what some are calling the Virtual Age, we live in an era when one of the few things we can trust as reasonably true is good visual reportage.

A MATTER OF SURVIVAL. Threat of destruction of historic Schofields Airfield near Sydney, Australia, led to a photo session between *Sydney Morning-Herald* photographer Brendan Esposito and World War II veteran Jim White. The image of the photo shoot manifests a few of the complex human behaviors of photojournalism, which evolved in part from basic human survival instincts. Note the levels of seeing: You, the viewer, are looking at the image via a book-publishing process, which was supervised by editors, who obtained the photo from me, after I had witnessed and selected this moment to photograph a photographer recording the image of a man who was posing to look as if he were naturally surveying the surrounding area. (Photo by Julie Newton.)

CHAPTER 2

The Vision Instinct

The challenge to understanding the viability of visual truth—and, therefore, photo-journalism—is twofold: (a) to examine its role in human life, and (b) to examine its relation—if any—to the real. As with many contemporary human activities, we can easily conceive of possible origins of photojournalism in a complex array of human needs and characteristics that can be traced to survival and expressive behaviors of early humans. Articulating why photographs have evidentiary power in today's multimedia world is more difficult. This chapter highlights issues that confound attempts to comprehend the seemingly unique authority of a photographic image. The discussion draws on surveillance and visual perception theories to locate visual reportage within a larger realm of human visual behavior.

CHAPTER 2

The Vision Instinct

The story of photojournalism begins at different points in history, depending on which book of history is read. A 1950 book published by the National Press Photographers Association goes back 25,000 years to artists who "painted pictures on cave walls—and thereby told men of today something about the prehistoric world" (p. 8). In the same book, *The Complete Book of Press Photography*, Soule described other early works of "pictures that tell stories," including a four-picture sequence of bas-reliefs carved in 3000 BC (p. 8). Kobre (1994) opened the history chapter of his classic text, *Photojournalism, The Professional Approach*, with a vivid account of a 19th-century news photographer who shot what was then an unusual amount of imagery—12 exposures—of a fire, despite technical and physical difficulty of working with a 5×7 view camera. The photographer then developed his pictures, made contact prints, and handed them to an artist. The artist used the pictures to make drawings (often "improving" the picture with variations)—which in turn would be used to make zinc engravings so the *New York Graphic News* could run visuals on its April 16, 1887, front page.

Historian Michael Carlebach (1992) traced U.S. photojournalism to a time shortly after Louis-Jacques-Mandé Daguerre announced his process in 1839. One editor wrote in 1846 that daguerreotypists were already on to news photography:

> A man cannot make a proposal or a lady decline one—a steam boiler cannot explode, or an ambitious river overflow its banks—a gardener cannot elope with an heiress, or a reverend bishop commit an indiscretion, but straightway, an officious daguerreotype will proclaim the whole affair to the world. ("Picture Pausings," cited in Carlebach, p. 2)

Some attribute the development of visual reportage to technology, some to developments in art, some to the economics of capitalism, some to ideology, some to the half-tone process or the hand-held camera, and some to the origins of human behavior.

Although each factor has contributed to the development of media, I favor the argument that the cultural practice of photojournalism grew out of the human tendencies to survey the environment visually as a matter of survival and curiosity, to better understand the environment, to facilitate memory, and to observe others as a means of social control.

The roots of photojournalism tap deeply into the multifaceted psyche of human beings and the cultures and societies they create in the process of living. From the standpoint of early humans, visual reportage was part of an intuitive and rational surveillance system that determined who would live and who would die. From the standpoint of Aristotle, watching a solar eclipse through tiny holes in a leaf was part of a rational system of discovery, insight, and supposition about the nature of optics and representation. From the standpoint of Foucault (1973, 1977), analyzing the panoptic structure of contemporary society was part of a passionate challenge to the oppressiveness of dominant institutions. From the standpoint of a subject of photojournalism, being photographed can be an invasive experience—or an opportunity to communicate with the world.

Photojournalism is pegged as a paparazzi-like profession of voyeurs—or as an essential part of the Fourth Estate's checks and balances on government and industry. Photojournalism can be viewed as guardian of the real—or as a set of codes and practices prescribed by culture. Some theorists argue that photojournalism is part of the dominant group's way of controlling the masses and of commodifiying life. Word journalists often dismiss photojournalism as illustration, as something to break up the gray space of their words. Yet many visual journalists consider their profession a calling to witness and to record what the world cannot as one way of moving toward a more just global community. And viewers see it either as truth or lies—or they refuse to "see" pictures they do not want to see. How did this contradictory mass of perspectives about visual reportage emerge? How did photojournalism come to be? How did pictures of war victims, of starving and ill children, of political protests and the catch of the day became part of the everyday visual environment?

HUMAN VISUAL BEHAVIOR

When we think about how the contemporary practice of photojournalism came about, we have to broaden our understanding of photojournalism within the context of larger issues of human behavior, particularly human visual behavior. Human visual behavior refers to all the ways human beings use seeing and images in everyday life. For sighted persons, that includes the navigational seeing that enables them to move their bodies safely and purposefully through the physical world, or using the "mind's eye" to imagine what a house might look like when it's finished, or even the process of dreaming while asleep. For nonsighted persons, it may mean using the mind's eye to construct a system of forms and patterns that enable them to navigate the world without physical sight.

Gesture expert Jürgen Streeck (personal communication, 1994) suggested the term *human visual behavior* to replace *nonverbal behavior*, arguing that the former shifts attention to action that can be observed rather than to action in negative relation to words. As a major component of human communication, visual behavior constitutes the core focus of visual journalism and social science and of a great deal of human interaction. Here, we should distinguish between the terms *behavior* and *communication*. *Behavior* typically refers to observable evidence of activity, whereas communication refers to shared meaning. I argue, however, that they are one and the same. *Visual behavior*, as I use the term here, refers to nonverbal activity. That activity can be external or internal, meaning that people can observe something outside of themselves, such as someone else or a photograph, as well as engage in interior visual activity, such as imagining or dreaming, that is not observable to others. Visual behavior includes how people act in front of cameras, as well as behind them. It includes seeing of every kind: looking at photographs, watching a sunset, noting the way a cat slowly stalks a bird, absorbing the beauty of a sleeping child, scanning the galaxy for changes through a telescope. It includes witnessing the enactment of countless deaths in *Die Hard II*, watching in mesmerized numbness the real-time bombing of a city via a medium that is more often about make believe, consumerism, and entertainment than about attempts to convey truth. It includes police mug shots, family albums, roadside billboards, and Internet zines. It includes all the ways people use these various visual artifacts, both consciously and subconsciously. It includes the ways people pose, mask their intimate personalities, project false personae, take on roles in order to manipulate opinion, model clothing, and unconsciously reveal that they are lying. It includes an editor's decision to use one photograph over another, a judge's decision to forbid cameras in the courtroom, a school board's decision to use video cameras on school buses, the military's decision to use a satellite to spy on another country. It includes an artist's decision to use bright red and yellow acrylic paints, a teenager's decision to sport purple hair, or an aging person's decision not to color graying hair.

And what do all of these seemingly disparate actions have to do with photojournalism? On one side of the continuum, they affect the content of photojournalistic imagery as visual forms of human behavior. On the other side, photojournalism affects those same actions; its content becomes part of the visual dialectic of human life.

Does this mean that human beings have a vision instinct, similar to the sucking instinct of newborns? Consider dictionary definitions, which I have found to be remarkably lucid starting points for discussions of concepts on which tomes have been written. *Vision* means sensing with the eyes, sight; foresight; "something seen in or as if in a dream or trance ... or the experience of such a perception"; "a vivid, imaginative scene conception," an object of sight;" a scene, person of extraordinary beauty (*Random House Webster's*, 1995, pp. 1489–1490). So *vision* can be both "seer" and "seen." Instinct is "an inborn pattern of activity or ... action common to a given biological species," "a natural or innate impulse, inclination or tendency," "a natural aptitude or gift," "natural intuitive power" (p. 698). And intuition? Intuition means "direct perception of truth, fact, etc., independent of any reasoning process; immediate apprehension," a "keen and quick insight" (p. 709).

The primary application to the discussion of photojournalism is that recording or transcribing what one sees is a longstanding behavior for human beings. We have moved from cave drawings to hieroglyphs to woodcuts to paintings to photography, and, interestingly, our sense of portraying the "real world" has shifted as we have learned to use different media. Galassi (1981) suggested that photography was invented because of our desire to represent things outside of ourselves realistically. The problem is that what appears to us as visually realistic changes through time and culture (Gombrich, 1961; Gombrich, Hochberg, & Black, 1972). Consider Giotto's invention of perspective in the early 14th century (Shlain, 1991, p. 48). Perspective is a technique painters can use to make objects they paint appear to recede in the distance, thereby creating the illusion of a third dimension in a two-dimensional space. Photography has been the most significant means of recording in the 20th century, and photographers learn to control perspective in order to avoid the uncomfortable, apparent distortions that occur when light reflected from different points is passed through a lens to be recorded on a light-sensitive surface. Yet, since the invention of photography, we have also invented movies, three-dimensional images, and virtual reality. Does any one form communicate better than the others, or does each simply communicate in its own ways?

The critical point for photojournalism may be Bazin's (1967) observation that a photograph is a trace of what was. And by holding that trace, a photograph appears to hold a close relation to the real. This correspondence between subject and image led to our placing great faith in the truth-telling capacity of photographs, being the closest things we had yet invented to a non-mind's-eye-created picture. We now know that photographs, too, result from conventions of seeing, framing, point of view, memory, and so forth, and further, that reading them, interpreting their content appropriately, can be just as culture specific as viewing a painting. So why do photojournalism?

SURVIVAL AND EXPRESSION

The larger questions driving this discussion can best be understood by beginning with *surveillance* and *visual perception* theories as rationales behind the development of visual reportage and its relation to our interpretation of the world around us. Recent developments in surveillance and visual perception theory offer significant clues regarding the development of photojournalism. Both tie visual reportage to survival and to the visual processing tendencies and abilities of the human brain (i.e., curiosity, voyeurism, imagination, memory, dreams, visualizing). Surveillance and visual perception theories have extended the understanding of how human beings operate beyond abstract concepts of mind by looking deeply within the psychological and physiological makeup of the human creature. Both surveillance and visual perception theory take us back to the early history of humankind, focusing attention on biological determinants of the importance of vision in human survival.

Both theories continue to mature as science and art move closer to uniting in their contest to understand how people relate to the world. Recent developments, such as explorations of the link between visual perception and consciousness (Crick, 1994), between biological determinism and news (Shoemaker, 1996), between brain processes and knowledge (Bechara, Damasio, Tranel, & Damasio, 1997), urge a redefinition of what it means *to see*. In addition, such mid-20th century theories as social constructionism and symbolic interactionism, together with late-20th-century postmodern theory, both challenge and inform earlier notions of reality. I draw on a few of these other ideas throughout this book.

The following section traces the larger issues underlying the development of visual reportage as it is known today. Note that each theoretical area summarized here is far more complex than space allows for a detailed discussion. However, the core tenets underlying each theoretical strain profoundly inform our analysis of photojournalism.

Surveillance Theory

A few years ago, my husband, a friend, and I hiked up a small site near Albuquerque, intent on viewing Anasazi rock drawings. The site was well traveled, hardly a wilderness discovery. Yet it retained a sense of those who had walked there centuries before, their presence preserved and communicated through their drawings. As we climbed the proverbial beaten path of tourists, guided by occasional 20th-century signs put there by the U.S. Park Service, I could not help but take my mind's eye back through time, into the space in which the drawings were made. It occurred to me that we were walking through an old-world form of reportage. The symbols and figures clearly communicated something to those who spoke the vernacular of the time—informing, leading, guiding, warning, protecting, stimulating (Schramm, 1988).

Schele and Friedel (1990) wrote of feeling similarly in their book, *The Forest of Kings*, in which they unraveled the culture of the Maya via what is left of their art and architecture:

> The connections the Maya put into their public history between things spiritual and things human, between things ancestral and things current, between things of the king and things of the community, were not a matter of accident or personal taste. The Maya put them in the public forum of life because they were the things they saw as important. The inscriptions and imagery we have are the propaganda the kings thought their people would

believe. They represent the strategies everyone thought gave them a chance to live beyond dying (p. 63)

Following Lasswell's (1948) theory of the surveillance function of communication, Shoemaker (1996) argued that human beings are hard-wired for news. It is in our physical interest to stay informed. And it is easy to envision ancient humans keenly scanning areas around them for predators or human enemies, and perhaps leaving a visual sign to mark a spot or to warn others. Although interpretations of the purposes and meanings of ancient symbols left on the earth continue to change as cultural theories and historical information change, one thing remains unchanged: People have been making visual records and expressing themselves visually for a very long time. These ancient records may seem far removed from contemporary photojournalism. But think ahead for a moment, to the year 5000. How will people living in the 51st century interpret the signs and symbols we have left behind? Chances are we will be viewed as primitive humans moving through early stages of a technological revolution. Our newspapers and magazines, if any semblance of them survives 3,000 years, will be treasured two-dimensional artifacts of earlier, primitive times on earth. Our rituals, our survival stories, our images of clothing and commodities, will be viewed holistically as parts of culture, not as separated images of news and advertising. Still photography may be collapsed in historical time lines with painting and drawing by hand (whether on rocks or canvas). Photojournalism may be viewed as a primary surveillance tool of 20th-century life, a time when humans actually sent other humans into war zones and hurricanes, into private living spaces and public arenas to make visual records for the rest of the world to see. Photojournalists may no longer be needed; instead, society will rely on a panoptic array of mechanical eyes capable of seeing and recording every movement in our galaxy. Farfetched? Perhaps. But remember: Only 200 years ago humans could not make an exact copy of anything or anyone in the world. Photography had not been invented; nor had journalism. At the very least, surviving images of reportage will provide a map of the 20th century—as Schele and Friedel wrote about the Maya, "These texts and images are a map of the ancient Maya mind and history, of the world as they understood it" (p. 63).

Human abilities to observe and make images have come a long way since ancient times. Consider, for example, a recent newspaper article about computer vision research that may lead to the "ultimate security system" ("UT Engineer," 1998, p. B1). In the article, engineer Jake Aggarwal described his vision of an airport equipped with a computer-video system that can track every person's move to the point of knowing when "something is amiss" (p. 1). As Lyon (1994) clearly articulated in his book *The Electronic Eye*, late-20th-century technological developments can be interpreted positively and negatively. Although surveillance systems can invade and control, they also can protect and illuminate. When examining contemporary photo-journalism, we must consider both ends of the continuum as well. Photo-journalism can invade the privacy of individuals and control social behavior via stereotyping and carrying out the hegemonic impulses of such institutions as government, corporations, and cultural practices—and it can protect by exposing social problems and errant behaviors.

Tagg (1988) suggested that still photography's role in social control was clear from the beginning. Consider his chapter on 19th-century photographic records of such criminals as the child who was arrested and beaten for stealing a piece of bread. It seems that we are now only one step removed from that time. Rather than gather in the town square to stare at someone being publicly flogged, we now watch a symbolic flogging carried out by our emissaries, the press. Recall coverage of the teenage parents who killed their newborn and dumped him in a trash can rather than be found out. The ritual of public persecution via the media is less brutal than 19th-century humiliations only in terms of physical pain. The main differences are the extent of public knowledge of their actions and the extent of public memory about their actions.

Now consider the issue from another perspective. Jean-Marc Bouju and his Associated Press colleagues won a Pulitzer Prize for their coverage of the Rwandan massacres. Without their passionate determination to visually record the horrors of genocide in practice, the rest of the world might never have known of, much less seen, the events. Because we know, we are reminded of humankind's abilities to commit atrocious acts on other humans. We may try to improve the world as a result of seeing visual evidence. Is such an approach nothing more than neo-romantic idealism? Or do the photos harden us further?

In *The Power of Photography*, Goldberg (1991) presented 279 pages of evidence that photographs "have been altering people's minds and rearranging their lives for a long time" (p. 7). Among the examples Goldberg cited are photographs of emaciated Union prisoners held in Confederate camps. Publication of reproductions of the images "taken from life" sparked public furor and an 1865 congressional effort to legislate retaliation. Labeled propaganda by the South, four of the photographs were used as evidence leading to the hanging of the commander of one prison camp.

Jumping into the 20th century, Goldberg noted that when written reports from eyewitnesses of atrocities in Nazi concentration campus first were published, readers were skeptical. "It wasn't until the newspapers published pictures of the camps, usually on the inside pages, that these images forced people to accept the enormity of the Nazi war crimes" (p. 33).

Goldberg concluded her book with a 1989 photograph of a man standing in front of a tank during student demonstrations in Beijing, "risking his life to stop the advance of all that armor." In the West, the image meant "individual courage standing firm before the armed might of the state." In Chinese exhibitions, the picture shows "the restraint of the troops, who chose not to run over a lone man blocking the march of an entire line of tanks." Goldberg maintained that in each case, the photograph told its story "faithfully and honestly ... for photographs do not give us truth—we give truth to them" (pp. 250–251).

Therein lies the issue: Is there such an entity as "visual truth" beyond what we want to see and believe? A good place to begin answering that question is *visual perception theory*.

Visual Perception Theory

Perception is the psychological and physiological response of a person to a stimulus (Denton, 1994). Visual perception is a person's response via visual means. For purposes here, a *visual stimulus* is a phenomenon with observable characteristics. A chair, for example, is a visual stimulus in the sense that when one sees a chair, it triggers a mental pattern associated with sitting down. If the chair is a particular kind of chair—say, a velvet, overstuffed recliner—seeing it might trigger mental pictures of a close family member lying back for long periods of time in such a chair. Any psychological response we have—say, nostalgic feelings of home—to the chair might then be related to how we feel about the color blue or about the family member. Our physiological response might also relate to the color blue—does it make us calm down—or to the idea of sitting down—relief to be off our feet—or to the family member—do we recall dad asleep after dinner and feel a rush of warmth about snuggling up with dad in the big chair when we were children? As one can quickly tell, psychology and physiology are so intricately linked that it is difficult, if not impossible, to separate them.

We do not have space in this book to delineate the intricacies of visual perceptual theory, if indeed they can be outlined. Nobel laureate Francis Crick (1994) used an entire book to explain his theory that what we know as the human soul is actually linked to visual perception in that we are nothing more than neurons firing in response to various stimuli. However, we can outline a few principles of visual perception theory that inform our understanding of how photojournalism came about. According to current research, visual perception:

- Depends on biology and culture.
    Some universals:
        Sexual response.
        Self-protection.
        Aggression.
        Friendliness.
    Many culture-and time-bound responses:
        Purple in U.S. versus purple in another country.
        Red as passion—in love or war.
        Picture of starving child:
            In past—moving.
            Now—cliché.
        Landscape:
            Forest—closed in or safe.
            Plains—free or vulnerable.
- Affects our attention and arousal.
    Communicates quickly and powerfully.
    Engenders a range of responses.
- Appears to be closely linked with memory.
    Involves both brain hemispheres.
    Right-brain hemisphere is more often associated with visual.
    Visual stimulus can shortcut memory.
    Visual is more closely linked with memory than words:
        Storage.
        Retrieval.
- Affects the way we understand ourselves, others, and the world.
    Getting to know ourselves via external images of ourselves is one way to improve self-concept.
    If the images we see are stereotypical, we are more likely to see a stereotyped world.
- Affects the way we act.
    If the images we see are violent, we are more likely to become violent.
    If the images we see are persuasive, we are more likely to act as the image creators intended.
    If the images we see are one-sided, we are more likely to see and to remember that side.

Visual perception theory underscores the idea that even when we know cognitively that something we see cannot be true, or have been told that it is not true, we still tend to believe what we see (Gregory, 1970). Research in visual information processing indicates neurophysiological bases for the "seeing-is-believing" phenomenon. As Gregory noted, "Though visual perception involves problem-solving, evidently it does not follow that when we know the solution intellectually we will necessarily see it correctly" (p. 56). One recent study of reader credibility in news photographs supports applying this idea to news work. Kelly and Nace (1994) found that although readers rated *The New York Times* more believable than the *National Enquirer*, they rated "the photos in the *National Enquirer* as more believable than was the newspaper in general" (p. 18).

Compounding the problem is the ease with which we read visual information. Potter, Bolls, and Dent (1997) cited new empirical evidence, as well as previous studies, that "visual encoding is relatively automatic and cognitively cost-free" to the point that they suggest television producers "rely more on visual information [than text] to deliver their themes" (p. 12). It is reasonable to apply such evidence to still photography by theorizing that such "relatively automatic" visual encoding of published photographs occurs daily in the hurried review of news. For example, we may perceive a page-one photograph of President Clinton saluting troops in Bosnia as true in spirit as well as letter—even though, if we stopped to analyze the photo for a few moments, we might wonder if the situation were more one of a carefully constructed photo opportunity than an occurrence that would have taken place had cameras not been present.

The problem also may be in part cultural. Barry (1997a) maintained that because "we have become accustomed to believing that photographs don't lie," we still have a "'seeing is believing' attitude." She suggested that "advances in technology have given commercial and political interests the ability to manipulate the way we see and comprehend our world before our understanding of visual technology and the psychology of the visual image has fully matured" (p. 22).

Social scientists use frame analysis to study how humans organize our experiences and subjective involvement in social events (Goffman, 1974). A "frame" refers to basic elements that organize an experience (pp. 11–13). Photojournalists, for example, typically work in an "eyewitness" role: Their job is to observe, to record what they observe and to report it to those who were not at the scene, to serve as "eyewitnesses" for the world. Traditionally in photojournalism, this frame has been based on at least two assumptions: that the photojournalist "sees" accurately, fairly, and objectively, and that the photographer has both the right and the responsibility to do what is necessary to get the picture for the world to see. As a result, photojournalists often say they do not manipulate reality, that they just "take what's out there in front of the lens." For example, a photojournalist covering a fire is not allowed to direct a firefighter to splash water over his or her head, even though the firefighter might have done so on his or her own eventually. Ideally, if something did not happen in front of the camera without the photographer's intervention, it is not considered visually "true."

SUMMARY

By integrating theoretical approaches, we can better understand how the neurophysiological tendency to believe what we see, combined with such cultural frames as the eyewitness and objectivity imperatives of the 20th century, have led us to draw heavily on media imagery, particulary news imagery. Furthermore, our biological surveillance system insists that we constantly scan our environments, searching for threats to life and livelihood. During the 20th century, we created a practice, photojournalism, to do the scanning that was no longer possible for us to do individually due to the ever-growing expanse and density of the area that had to be watched. And for a while we thought we could believe the images produced by that practice as transparent, authentic records for us to witness vicariously. Twentieth-century technological development slowly taught us how limited even the camera eye is, leading us to question realistic-appearing images. We began to question not only the nature of reality but also the means by which we come to know. It is no wonder postmodern humans have suffered from feelings of disintegration. The primary tool we have used for millennia, our eyes—extended now by the camera—can no longer be trusted to give us reliable information. Our need to survey the environment for our own survival conflicts with our relatively new cognition that things are not always what they seem.

Is it possible that photojournalism can do what it purports to do: visually report the happenings of the world with some level of truth? Yes and no. The fact that all knowledge has limitations can be true, and good photojournalism also can be reasonably true. As with any human endeavor, photojournalism is both behavior and cultural practice constructed over time as a result of a variety of human tendencies and needs.

The roots of photojournalism can be traced to the beginning of humankind—to that time when seeing clearly could literally mean the difference between life and death. It is hardly curious that we have grown into a society of voyeurs ... with so many eyes on us and available to us, our internal organisms must feel in constant danger, and even go numb with the overwhelming number of only-too-real-appearing dangers we see daily via the media. But what is the alternative—not to look? Given that we appear to be hard-wired to look, perhaps we should learn to look with increased understanding of the significance of photojournalism as a form of visual behavior in our lives. Perhaps we can learn to use the vision instinct in conscious ways to help us advance as a species.

A 20TH-CENTURY ROUTINE. Nancy Lee, right, picture editor for *The New York Times*, and staff photographer Chester Higgins, Jr., review a few of the more than 200 rolls of film that came through the *Times'* picture desk the day of the presidential election, November 5, 1996. The light table was a fixture in 20th-century picture editing, which was dominated by 35-mm transparent film—whether in black-and-white or color negative, or positive slides. Training the eye to read negatives and slides using an $8\times$ Lupe magnifier was an important part of photojournalism practice and was how most images were selected for publication. (Photo by Julie Newton.)

CHAPTER 3

From Instinct to Practice

Understanding why people want and need to know about the world in which they live is fairly easy. Understanding the role of contemporary visual reportage in that process is more difficult. One way to begin is to study those who do photojournalism. This chapter discusses the translation of human visual instincts and needs into visual reportage by outlining key issues in the practice of contemporary photojournalism and defining such terms as *image, observer,* and *observed.*

CHAPTER 3

From Instinct to Practice

hapter 1 defined the genre of *photojournalism* as reporting visual information via various media. The term typically applies to images published
or broadcast with accompanying words as news, features, and illustrations
reporting any aspect of human life.

Chapter 2 addressed this question: "Why did humans invent photojournalism?" Chapter 3 addresses two questions that underlie core issues in
visual reportage:

■ How do we practice photojournalism?
■ What do the products of that practice—the images—mean?

BACKGROUND

A number of theorists have explored these questions as part of a growing
field known as *photojournalism ethics*. Since the late 1960s, *News Photographer*,
the monthly magazine of the National Press Photographers Association, has

carried a small but steady stream of articles by photojournalists, editors, and media critics voicing concerns about photographic ethics. Media critics such as Sontag (1973) and Freund (1980) have questioned the aggressive nature of photography in contemporary society and its impact on our lives. Books on journalism and media ethics now regularly carry sections on photojournalism ethics. For example, Christians, Fackler, and Rotzoll (1995) discussed invading the lives of private individuals cast into the news spotlight.

Empirical evidence concerning photojournalism ethics has slowly increased since the late 1970s. Hartley's (1981) groundbreaking survey suggested that photographers, editors, and the public think about photographs differently and have differing expectations. For example, although a photographer might think it reasonable to stand at a distance, use a long lens, and discretely document the pain of a grieving mother at her child's funeral, a viewer or reader might view the resulting photograph a gross invasion of privacy. Another empirical study specifically asked how people felt when they were photographed, indicating that factors as wide-ranging as photographer control and subject personality traits interact to affect subject response (Newton, 1994). A growing body of qualitative analyses addresses such subject concerns as invasion of privacy and emotional distress during the photographic act (Sherer, 1985, 1990), explicit or implicit consent (Henderson, 1988), and various photographers' ways of approaching and interacting with subjects (Brown, 1995; Nottingham, 1978). One recent study offers convincing evidence that the images published with a news story significantly influence the way readers and viewers will remember the content of the text (Sargent & Zillman, 1999).

Lester (1990), a photographer and ethicist, has consistently examined photojournalism ethics in comprehensive terms. His first book, *Photojournalism: The Ethical Approach* (1991), was written as a guide for preparing visual journalists to conduct their work in the spirit of humanism. A more recent book, *Images That Injure, Pictorial Stereotypes in the Media* (Lester, 1996), focused attention on the individuals who are harmed via stereotypical imaging and on the ways in which media facilitate such injuries.

A broader but related area of study is the more general field of *photographic ethics*. Social scientists, led by visual anthropologists and visual sociologists, have been among the most vocal of those concerned about photographic ethics, focusing on issues of representing human beings (Bellman & Jules-Rosette, 1977; Beloff, 1983, 1985; Carpenter, 1975; Collier, 1967; Harper, 1979, 1982, 1993; Mead, 1956; Mead & Bateson, 1977; Newton, 1984; Ruby, 1982, 1987; Worth & Adair, 1972). Among the issues discussed are the need to give those "observed" the camera so their points of view will be more authentically and appropriately represented (Bellman & Jules-Rosette, 1977; Ruby, 1992, 1987; Worth & Adair, 1972). Another concern is the effect a photographer or researcher has on the people he or she is observing—and on the content of the images made (Carpenter, 1975; Mead & Bateson, 1977).

A closely related area of study is *photographic behavior*, a term coined by social psychologist Stanley Milgram (Desfor, 1979) to label how people act in front of and in regard to the camera. The current discussion broadens the term *photographic behavior* to include how people act behind the camera and how people use images produced with a camera.

We have learned a good deal about photographic behavior in the 160 years of photography's use. For example, in the 1850s, psychiatrist Hugh Diamond (1856, cited in Gilman, 1976) used the facial and body language revealed in photographic portraiture as an aid to diagnosing and treating the mentally ill.

Contemporary research in social psychology indicates, however, that people often behave differently in the presence of cameras. After conducting a series of experiments, Milgram (cited in Desfor, 1979) concluded that "all people modify their behavior to some degree" when they are aware a camera is pointed at them (p. 103). Milgram called the altered actions *photographic behavior*, maintaining that the making of a photograph creates events by creating "a new plane of reality to which people respond" (p. 103).

Milgram (1977a) suggested that a subject and a photographer enter into an interpersonal relationship during a picture-making event—an event that is, by its very nature, its own event: "Even the most mundane occasion for taking a snapshot involves us in a relationship, and moreover, it is a relationship that others perceive and in some degrees respect" (p. 54). Milgram noted that the activity involves social rules that are widely shared but may vary by culture, and that the personalities of the individuals involved and the desired outcome of the photographic event also affect the interaction.

One way to interpret this behavior as an interpersonal relationship is to view it in terms of people exchanging information—or even power and control (Roloff & Miller, 1987). Applying this interpretation to photographic behavior, one might say a photographer and a subject interact by exchanging information—permission, instructions, smiles, a revealing pose, a flattering camera angle, an image to keep. Extrapolating further, the process of one person observing another can involve a range of exchanging, or transferring such other resources as control, power, authority, friendship, intimacy, fame. May (1980) referred to such exchange—when handled ethically—as a covenantal ethic.

Photographic behavior can work in other ways, too, whereby a photographer takes something from a subject (such as a candid pose) or a subject hides discomfort behind a mask (such as a silly face).

Milgram (1977b) also studied how people outside the photographer–subject relationship respond to the "separate plane of reality" created by the photographic event (p. 349). For example, people walking down a sidewalk will walk around a scene in which a photographer is taking a picture of someone. Furthermore, people are more likely to walk around a photographer who appears to be in a position of authority (e.g., looks like a photojournalist with several cameras) than they are a tourist.

Aesthetic, critical, and cultural theorists have contributed significantly to the kinds of questions asked about photojournalism ethics by focusing on the subjective nature of human perception and on the tendency to consider anyone but oneself the "other." A growing body of studies specifically analyzes photographic representation of human beings ranging from negatively stereotypical images of women in the media to hegemonic images of sexual orientation (Bolton, 1989; Dates & Barlow, 1990; Dyer, 1993; Gross, Katz, & Ruby, 1988; Lester, 1995; Lutz & Collins, 1993; Squiers, 1990; Tagg, 1988). In addition to addressing representational concerns, such literature interrogates the complexities of abstracting self and others via various media. Most of these approaches focus on the negative effects of selectivity and subjectivity, particularly in regard to those observed. Additionally, major themes of postmodern theory include the impossibility of imaging reality, as well as effective critiques of traditional notions of subject, observer, and observed (Baudrillard, 1994; Debord, 1967; Derrida, 1993).

CORE ISSUES

As suggested when we began this chapter, one way to address these questions is to divide concerns into two categories: *methodological* (the study of process, or how the image is made) and *epistemological* (the study of meaning, or what and how we know from an image; Newton, 1983, 1984). Although epistemological issues are always at stake during and after the process of making an image, the discussion must begin with issues of process: How do observer and observed deal with one another? How should a photographer approach a human subject, for example? Should a photographer approach that human subject? How should—or does—a human subject behave? How does a person being observed feel? Is the observer the one being manipulated, rather than the one manipulating? Then, in turn: How do the feelings and behaviors of observer and observed affect the content of any image they make during the process—and, ultimately, the perception of that content? How does the end-observer, the viewer, feel about him- or herself and about the person in the image?

DEFINITIONS

At this point, clarification of key terms is in order.

Image

The word *image* is at once the final product of a process, such as photography, film, or hand art, and the continually changing form in which people conceive themselves and others: something as concrete as a self-portrait or as ephemeral as a vision in one's mind. On one level, an image can be the physical likeness of an observed person, meaning the material qualities of a human face and body that reflect light onto a recording substance, such as silver-based film or a digital receiver. Examples include a school yearbook portrait, a newspaper mug shot, or a social scientist's descriptive photographs of a ritual. An image also can refer to the psychological likeness of the observed, to the usually unseen interior of a human being, what is sometimes described as the "real self," the "unmasked self," "a side rarely seen by others," or a mood or state of mind that communicates a psychological attribute of an individual through an externally recorded form. Examples of psychological likeness include images of photojournalism depicting someone in emotional trauma, or the stylistic photographs of a great portraitist, such as Richard Avedon or Annie Liebovitz. An image also can refer to the level of self that transcends ordinary reflection to a plane of uncommon meaning (Stott, 1973). An example of a transcendent likeness might be an Irving Penn portrait of a New Guinean looking into the camera—and therefore into the eyes of anyone viewing the photograph—as if he is communicating into eternity.

Observer

An *observer* is defined as a person who looks at another. The observer can have different personality characteristics, ranging from passive to controlling; different interpersonal skills, ranging from agreeable to antisocial; different roles, ranging from photographic artist to visual anthropologist to editor to casual reader. The observer can use bare vision, meaning using his or her unaided eyes, or an external device, such as a camera, that can record what is viewed. Image-recording equipment can range from automatic 35-mm still cameras to large-format view cameras to video cameras—any device with a means for gathering light rays reflected from someone and recording them on light-sensitive material, which ranges from silver-based to digital forms. An observer also can look at a person via a visual equivalent, such as a photograph. Note the purposeful avoidance of the terms *gaze* or *glance* in order to focus on the interactive nature of the visual behavior.

Observed

Beloff (1985) wrote that the portrait photographer "Arnold Newman works hard to enable people to lose their self-consciousness and 'become what they are.' But, of course, they decide what they are" (p. 211). Beloff also noted Henri Cartier-Bresson's idea that a "photographer is searching for the identity of his sitter, and also trying to fulfil [*sic*] an expression of himself" (cited in Beloff, 1985, p. 173). Such is the difficulty in defining the concept of the *observed*. In photography, the most commonly used term for the observed is *subject*. In everyday use, *subject* most commonly refers to something or someone who is the object of study or the focus of attention for a photographer, artist, or researcher. *Webster's* (1979) definitions included: "one that is placed under authority or control," "substance ... or agent of whatever sort that sustains or assumes the form of thought or consciousness," "one that is acted upon ... an individual whose reactions or responses are studied ... a dead body for anatomical study and dissection," something represented or indicated in a work of art." JEB (1981) suggested the term *muse* to avoid the idea of subject. The term *observed* is effective for the current discussion because it allows the observed and observer to shift visual point of view within their interaction. *Observed* means a person who is the focus of study or view, whose image may or may not be recorded. The definition uses the words *person* and *focus* in order to concentrate on the idea of human beings who have potential for active or passive participation in the observation process. The definition also includes persons observed as well as persons photographed to acknowledge different ways one can become the object of observation. Additionally, *observed* refers to the photographer, who can be the focus of a subject's and/or an onlooker's attention.

CONCERNS ABOUT OBSERVER–OBSERVED INTERACTION

One way to examine these issues is to consider extreme conditions circumscribing visual behavior. One extreme is the exploited victim of observation, whose image is taken and manipulated by the photographer. The other is the manipulated or exploited observer, who sees a behavior and records an image controlled by the observed, believing he or she (the photographer) has witnessed and captured an authentic occurrence.

Observed and Observer as Co-Image-Makers. The process of making an image—whether externally or internally manifested—is interactive, involving both observer and observed, a premise with considerable support (Beloff, 1983, 1985; JEB, 1981; Milgram, 1977a, 1977b; Newton, 1983, 1984, 1991, 1994, 1994–1999; Nottingham, 1978). In the practice of visual journalism and social science, the interactive process typically involves one or more human subjects and a photographer or participant observer. As noted earlier, Milgram (1977a) suggested that the subject and photographer enter into an interpersonal relationship during the picture-making event, which is its own event within and apart from any other event (such as a birthday party or a political rally) that may be taking place.

Philosopher Edward Martin (1990) also noted that the photographic process can be an interpersonal relationship involving consequences similar to those incurred through speaking.

Recall that an *interpersonal relationship* can be defined as "a means by which individuals control their environment by obtaining resources through direct exchanges within interactions or by negotiating future exchanges" (Roloff & Miller, 1987, p. 7). In a photographic relationship, photographer and subject exchange and negotiate resources ranging from smiles a to power.

Figure 3.1 presents a general model of a photographic event, which occurs between observed and observer, and a viewing event, which occurs among subject, photographer, and viewer via the photograph. Note that context, which includes time, place, culture, and medium, is critical at all levels. (See chap. 10 for a more extensive explanation of Fig. 3.1.)

Observed as Victim. In *Let Us Now Praise Famous Men* (Agee & Evans, 1940/1960), Agee addressed methods used by observers with somewhat differing motivations—journalists and ethnographers:

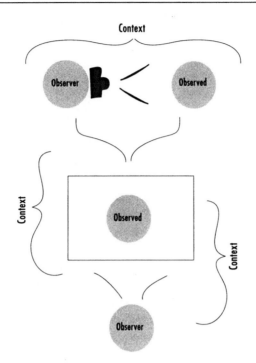

FIGURE 3.1 The interactive process of photography.

It seems to me curious, not to say obscene and thoroughly terrifying, that it could occur to an association of human beings drawn together through need and chance and for profit into a company, an organ of journalism, to pry intimately into the lives of an undefended and appallingly damaged group of human beings, an ignorant and helpless rural family, for the purpose of parading the nakedness, disadvantage and humiliation of these lives before another group of human beings, in the name of science, of "honest journalism" (whatever that paradox may mean), of humanity, of social fearlessness, for money, and for a reputation for crusading and for unbias which, when skillfully enough qualified, is exchangeable at any bank for money. (pp. 7–8)

Agee went on to ask: "Who are you who will read these words and study these photographs?" (pp. 8–9). For Agee, the meaning of an actual person is "much huger" than what can be conveyed in words or pictures: "It is that he exists, in actual being, as you do and as I do, and as no character of the imagination can possibly exist. His great weight, mystery, and dignity are in this fact" (p. 11). The irony, of course, is that some of Evans and Agee's subjects later revealed that they felt exploited by the "journalist/ ethnographers" (Maharidge & Williamson, 1989).

Harper (1982), a visual sociologist, expressed similar concerns, arguing that the social scientist must earn the "ethical right" to photograph by spending enough time with subjects to become sensitive to situations that should not be photographed. Ruby (1987), an anthropologist, noted his concern about using human beings to produce realistic images of people in art, science, news, or entertainment. He was particularly concerned about the transformation of human beings into aesthetic, economic, political or symbolic objects "without their knowledge and sometimes against their will" (p. 10).

In photojournalism, typical concerns about subjects include invasion of privacy or adding unnecessary emotional distress to victims of tragic events. Literature in the field recognizes the use of subject emotion to make images that "burn themselves into people's souls" (Bryant, 1990, p. 20) and often justifies publication of such images if the public can learn something from seeing them (Sherer, 1990). Some photojournalists stress that they must protect their rights to photograph people under all circumstances (Sherer, 1985), whereas others note their personal difficulty in taking pictures of distressed people (Bryant, 1990; Hartley, 1990). "When you take somebody's picture, you take two things from them ... their images ... [and] their anonymity," wrote one photojournalist (Sherer, 1990, p. 12). In another article in *News Photographer*, media critic Ellen Goodman (cited in Sherer, 1990) wrote, "Where do we get the right to bring other people home in a canister?" (p. 12). Yet one photojournalism ethicist went so far as to note that photographic subjects have no copyrights to a photograph, asserting that "the subject is not a co-creator of the photograph and does not enjoy a legal property right to it" (Martin, 1990, p. 32).

Sherer (1985), a specialist on photojournalism law and ethics, discussed how the tort of emotional distress has been applied to photography and subject privacy. He noted that the courts have supported distressed subjects only in cases in which the photographer's conduct exceeds "all possible bounds of decency, ... and [is] utterly intolerable in a civilized community" (p. 3). An example of such intolerable behavior was Ron Galela's infamous, incessant pursuit of Jacqueline Kennedy Onassis. Sherer pointed out that although some distressed photo subjects have filed suits and won, most court decisions favor the photographers. Sherer defended the public's right to know over "the need to protect individuals from conduct by the press which does not exceed the bounds of extremely outrageous conduct" (p. 9).

Warwick (1977), a social scientist, explored ethical concerns regarding social science methods by listing types of harm that might come to those observed in the name of research: death, physical abuse or injury, psychological abuse or injury, damage to interpersonal relations, career damage or economic harm, and invasions of privacy. Warwick's degrees of harm can be expanded to include degrees of benefits for those observed: life protection, physical protection, psychological improvement, improved interpersonal relationships, improved career or economic benefits, and extension of self (Newton, 1984). In many respects—goals, methods, uses—social science research is an extended form of good journalism. Individuals conducting either form can exercise great power over their sources—or subjects.

Observed as Powerful Image-Maker. On the other side of the victim–abuser continuum is the idea that the person being observed can assume power in the process. The complexity of this side of the issue is illustrated in *The Presentation of Self in Everyday Life* (Goffman, 1959/1973), in which the author reported his theory that "when an individual appears before others he will have many motives for trying to control the impression they receive of the situation" (p. 15). That need to control impressions can be so strong that the observed becomes a performer and the observer becomes the audience. Goffman (1967, 1969) maintained that human beings are so concerned about controlling the impressions others have of them that they become performers rather than mere participants.

Much of this behavior is unconscious, part of the learned responses of human beings in interaction with others. Increasingly, however, the behavior is conscious and carefully performed for a camera—and hence an observing public. Newspaper pages offer regular examples of this kind of control by those observed: Politicians, for example, regularly create and manipulate their public personae to match what they perceive to be desirable public images. Less public individuals also have learned the value of using images to gain press—and therefore public—focus for themselves or a political cause. In one study, a photojournalism subject who was promoting a quilting exhibition in a small community repeatedly assumed the identical smiling, stiff pose next to a prized quilt each time the camera was pointed in her direction (Newton, 1994). Another group of individuals in the same study artfully orchestrated a photo op to promote a neighborhood cause (Newton, 1994–1999). Excruciatingly horrible examples of behavior intentionally performed for the public eye include the Buddhist priest who burned himself to death in Vietnam (Goldberg, 1991, p. 212) and the public official who shot himself at a press conference (Kobre, 1996, p. 307).

Another example of the power of the observed comes, ironically, from the faces of women who were forced to be photographed against their will (Naggar, 1990). In 1960, Marc Garanger was ordered by his French army major to photograph civilian prisoners for identification cards. Garanger recalled that 2,000 Berger and Muslim women were forced to be photographed unveiled: "They had no choice in the matter. Their only way of protesting was through their look ... I held up for the world a mirror, which reflected this lightning look that the women cast at me" (cited in Naggar, 1990, pp. 2–3). In analyzing the images, Naggar noted that the women were doubly raped: To be seen without their veils by strangers was a violation, and in Islam, representation is forbidden and shameful. Yet their control over the images of themselves remained strong. Although the subjects were victims, the intensity in their eyes as recorded in the resulting photographs indicated defiant refusal. "Saying no," Naggar wrote, "the women seem to add: 'Even if you have photographed us, we remain uncontrollable'" (p. 8). An aggressive act of subsumation was met with an assertive—and lasting—response.

Even less clear are issues of candid versus posed photographs. The issue of whether a candid photograph is more valid than a posed one has received some attention in the literature. In the early days of photography, when exposures took minutes rather than fractions of seconds, subjects had time to assume a pose, which could be anywhere from a pose of their own choosing to one carefully directed by a photographer. The limitations of 19th-century technology required long exposures and subject cooperation. When cameras became smaller, however, candid photography became the vogue and subjects' consenting participation in creating an image no longer was required. Those writing about photography during the turn of the century noted the public's dismay with "ubiquitous" and intrusive photographers (Jay, 1984). The assumption was, and to a large extent still is, that the candid shot was the "most honest" view of someone. This assumption ignores the fact that the candid shot can be more the photographer's view than the subject's and therefore is just as vulnerable to manipulation as a shot of someone who is aware of the camera. In his seminal work on the documentary genre, Stott (1973) asserted that the posed photograph is perhaps more revealing than the candid shot. In analyzing Evans' photographs for *Let Us Now Praise Famous Men*, Stott (1973) wrote that Evans did not expose reality but "lets it reveal itself. ... In short, he records people when they are most themselves, most in command, as they impose their will on their environment" (p. 268).

One paradox found in the conventions of photographic practice is that photographers are taught to "capture the real person," which usually means trying to get beneath so-called personal masks and roles to essential character within a human being. Photojournalists are taught to make revealing portraits by constantly watching their subjects and shooting many frames of people in their natural environments in order to catch the one moment of supreme revealment. Such thinking has led to photographic activity that is like a hunt or grand safari in which the goal is to catch the big cat, stalking the creature until, finally, through the bushes, the living being is seen, targeted through the scope and "shot." Portrait photographers, on the other hand, are often taught to place a person in a neutral setting with a backdrop of white paper or painted canvas—in other words, to isolate the human creature *until she* reveals her essence through a long session with the image maker. Anthropologists worry that their presence alters the nature of people's behavior to the extent that they must live for long periods of time with those they study in order to know what their subjects are "really like." Yet a photojournalist is often expected to record an authentic image in very short periods of time.

All these techniques seek the "real subject," whatever that may be, as if there were a real subject to be seen and recorded. Furthermore, we assume one can learn about this real subject through manipulation or candid observation. Although we have come to understand that our very presence as observers alters what we see and that, at least to some extent, we construct ourselves, others, and our worlds, we continue to probe and stare and study as if a "real reality" or a "real person" can be viewed.

SUMMARY

These concerns highlight a few of the problems of observing and representing human beings—and of being observed or using photographic information. As observers and agents of representation, visual journalists fall somewhere between the so-called real world of first-hand seeing and the systematically observed, dissected, and analyzed world of the social scientist. As the observed or represented, subjects of visual journalism exhibit behaviors ranging from submission to manipulation—as do the observers—and can be powerful or helpless. The visual equivalent resulting from observer–observed interaction (the photographic image) then assumes its place in reality formation, based at least in part by yet other hearts and minds—those of anyone looking at the image. Editors and readers or viewers continue the cycle by selecting images to publish or not attending to a photograph.

Photojournalism, a contemporary cultural practice, grew out of human beings' tendencies to survey their environment visually as a matter of survival and curiosity, to better understand their environment, to help them record and remember events in their lives, and as a less violent means of controlling people than corporeal methods. As a practice, visual reportage has evolved from the activities of early humans, who left their traces through drawings, paintings, and sculptures for those who came after them, to the hieroglyphs that we now have discovered told important stories, to detailed and increasingly realistic hand art, to the invention of photography, film, television, satellites, and the Internet. Humans have grown from accepting realistic-appearing imagery as a form of self-evident fact to levels of understanding the ways we encode and manipulate all forms of expression and representation. Even X-rays and other methods of visually investigating the body can mislead through angles of view and individual interpretation. We have come to understand that photographic behavior can range from making an authentic visual record to complete visual deception.

Where does this leave the ideas of visual reportage and visual truth in the 21st century? One way to answer this question—and the questions with which this chapter began—is to examine photojournalism as a mediating cultural entity. Shoemaker and Reese (1991, 1996) delineated five levels of influence on media content: individual, media routines, organizational, extramedial, and ideological. Adapting these levels to the analysis of photojournalism, I next examine photographers, subjects, viewers, gatekeepers, society and culture, and the ideologies driving photojournalism practice.

The next five chapters examine human visual behavior by focusing on various levels and components of the process of photojournalism. Important to remember throughout the volume, however, is that, when it comes to human visual behavior, at any given moment each person is both observer and observed.

FRIENDS AND COMPETITORS. *The New York Times* photographer Andrea Mohin, seated, and an international press colleague end a day of covering President Bill Clinton's second inaugural parade, January 20, 1997, in Washington, DC. About 20% of photojournalists are female—which means that 80% of all news images are taken from men's perspectives. Mohin arrived at the Lafayette Press Stand hours in advance to ensure her digital equipment would work properly. She set up a telephone line, computer with modem, and digital camera to transmit her photos immediately from the parade site to the picture desk in New York. Note that she also had to rig a light shield for her laptop computer screen to help her see images outdoors. (Photo by Julie Newton.)

CHAPTER 4

The Heart of the Seer

The key to effective visual reportage is the person doing the seeing. Although the *seer* can be anyone involved in making, using or reading a photograph — photographer, editor, reader, society at large, even the subject — this chapter focuses on photojournalists: the front-line individuals whose profession requires them to make pictures of real people in real life and in real time. What drives these people to pursue photographing others as a life's work? What kinds of people become photojournalists? What are their values? What makes one ethical and another unethical? This chapter addresses the motivations, roles, and responsibilities of those who undertake visual reportage.

CHAPTER 4

The Heart of the Seer

Press Photographer ...
One who reports the news
to the general public through
the medium of photography
in newspapers, magazines,
newsreels and television.

—NPPA (1950)

The greatest thing a human soul ever does in this world is to see
something, and tell what it saw in a plain way. ... To see clearly is
poetry, prophecy, and religion, all in one.

—Ruskin (1904)

Lesson one is if you're an eyewitness to history, be clearheaded and
impartial. ... In looking back on my 20 years with the AP, I realized that
it was frequently impossible to avoid becoming involved in the
story. ... Not only were we eyewitnesses to history, by our presence we
influenced it.

—Arnett (1998)

A century ago, before the term *photojournalist* even existed, a news pho-tographer's mandate appeared relatively simple: Get the picture. What he (and it almost always was a he) brought back was unquestioned, assumed to be visually recorded fact. In the year 2000, the photojournalist's mandate is more apt to be a self-imposed, personal goal to document events in the world than it is a news organization's motto. The photojournalist of the 1950s was challenged to produce technically perfect photographs; the pho-tojournalist of the 21st century more often is expected to bring back sig-nificant content—the shot published may even be a technically poor grab frame from video. More important is a photojournalist's interpretative role:

Photographers today do more than just record the news. They have become visual interpreters of the scene by using their cameras and lenses, sensitivity to light, and keen observational skills, to bring readers a feeling of what the event was really like. (Kobre, 1996, p. 322)

The role of the photojournalist in contemporary culture resonates in the psychiatrist's story about sanity: The mentally healthy person is one who has one foot in the circle of the rational and one foot in the circle of the irrational. A fine photojournalist plants one foot firmly within the visual pursuit of objective reality as we now know it—the most accurate recording of life events a human being can make. This person is keenly aware of a role as a professional eyewitness, working as proxy for the world at large. But a great photojournalist also plants the other foot firmly within subjective experience, with its passion, dedication, artistry, and drive to document people at their best and worst—and often with a clear point of view and at great sacrifice.

The photojournalist assumes the role of a covert artist with an acute social conscience, intent on naming the nameless, revealing the contradictions of life, and exposing the emotions people often would rather ignore or suppress beneath our supposedly rational culture. The photojournalist's tools and style apply a method that relies on conventions of seeing and believing derived from the positivist tradition. The work of the photojournalist abounds with an apparent realism that refuses to be subverted by conventions visible only to the educated elite. The result is an everyday, seemingly transparent, aesthetic realism dropping into our homes in a steady drip of blood, smiles, tears, triumph, and sorrow. The point of visual reportage is realism, not art. Yet, often, art is created in the process (Weber, 1974) and is what makes an image of photojournalism compelling. And although one can pick apart claims to realism in terms of perceptual subjectivity, this aesthetic realism of photojournalism may be the closest a person can get to recording the real. In fact, the lens of aesthetic realism can help see with vivid clarity what would be lost without its unique filters. The photojournalist watches for moments of "deeper purpose" (Mayo, 1989, p. 170, Note 2) latent in the everyday life of the world.

The heart of a good photojournalist also is like the mind of a critical theorist who constantly searches to expose the inadequacies of the status quo. Is this a romanticized view? Perhaps. For certainly many photojournalists are consumed by the consumer giant themselves, falling prey to the economic mandates and allure of capitalism, wrapped in the cloak of good income, mass media journalism, Pulitzer Prizes, and fame. But for others, the ideal of showing the world to itself, of exposing the corrupt, revealing the pain and joy of everyman, ferreting out the best and worst of life remains their raison d'être. Like many good journalists, they consider themselves the front lines of humanity's quest for a reasonably good life of fairness, justice, abundant food and care, and general equality.

This chapter examines those conflicting forces guiding the hearts and minds of today's photojournalists. Several themes emerge: the human being versus dispassionate observer, the watchdog versus voyeur, the reporter versus artist, the storyteller versus social scientist.

HUMAN BEING OR DISPASSIONATE OBSERVER?

A 1996 issue of *News Photographer*, the primary publication for professional photojournalists, addressed a core dilemma of the photojournalist: Are they human beings first, or professional observers first? One article tells the story of presidential candidate Bob Dole's fall while campaigning—and of the photographer who helped him. Many photojournalists following the campaign ran to take pictures of Dole sprawled on the ground. The best resulting photograph of a grimacing Dole ran several columns on the front page of *The Washington Post* the next day. Not long afterward, news analysts Sam Donalson, David Brinkley, George Will, and Cokie Robertson noted that the picture's use as front-page news was probably unfair to Dole, who, reportedly, grimaced only briefly before quickly getting up, regaining his composure, and joking about the incident (FOX, 1996). The fair view, they argued, was to show two photographs, one of the unique moment of the fall and a second of the recovered candidate. The analysts argued that to show the first without the latter would confirm voter fears about Dole's age, when, in fact, the real story was that Dole was in such good health that he was able to get up from the fall immediately. *The Washington Post*, in fact, did run both pictures, although the recovery photograph ran only 1.5 columns wide.

Agence France-Presse photographer David Ake is credited with saving Dole from serious injury by preventing his head from hitting the ground. Ake later declined other photographers' accolades that he had "'shown that we're caring people'": "I think any one of us would have done the same thing. It really wasn't extraordinary. The man simply fell on me." Reuters photographer Rick T. Wilking, who, according to *News Photographer*, "was clear of the falling candidate and in no position to break Dole's fall, instinctively shot eight frames: "I took pictures that I didn't know I had until I looked at them later," Wilking said (Hale & Church, 1996, p. 23). Both photojournalists indicated they had responded instinctively—one in aid and one as witness. And emotion made the moment that "has become a powerful image" of the 1996 campaign (Hale & Church, 1996, p. 23). And Dole? Although the article noted that Dole thanked photographers for helping him, no mention was made of his response, either to the incident or to the photographs. Most significant, however, is that no matter what the context of the incident, what remains in public memory is the image of Dole grimacing in pain and lying on his back.

A related article, "Helping Hands of News Photographers," recounted 17 stories of photojournalists who helped people or saved people's lives—they could have been taking "great" pictures (Hale & Church, 1996, pp. 24–25). The story addressed the recurring criticism that photojournalists are more interested in getting their pictures than in the people they photograph.

WATCHDOG OR VOYEUR?

The same issue of *News Photographer* (1996) contained yet another relevant item, an inside-cover ad for Fuji film:

> When you're the eyes of the world, your film had better share your vision. Photojournalism demands that you capture life with absolute, unfailing accuracy. Without distortions. And without losing the drama. The question is, how do you do it? The answer, for thousands of photojournalists, is Fuji film. In countless situations, Fujicolor Super G. Plus is the perfect film. ... No one can say what each day will bring. But there is one thing you can count on. With Fuji film in your camera, you'll be bringing back the truth. Fujifilm. A new way of seeing things.

So, on one hand is the expectation that photojournalists be "the eyes of the world," to show the world what it cannot be present to see. Yet if photojournalists work to fulfill that expectation, they risk moving beyond what the public generally agrees is acceptable practice—into the role of the paparazzi stalking stars, the ambulance chasers at an accident scene, the merciless pack of competitors staking out homes of private citizens cast into public view through tragedy, the surreptitious intruders of backyards and funerals. What a photojournalist might believe is something the world has to see—for example, the screaming face of a child who has just seen his brother's body pulled out of a treacherous lake—the "world" may believe should not be photographed, much less published in a newspaper. And the question remains: Does the world really need to see the agonizing photo, perhaps to make a public impact on a repeatedly dangerous situation, or are the photographer and editor really just a voyeur and a sensationalist going for a prize and more readership?

REPORTER OR ARTIST?

The artist is forced by the nature of art to render the fluid, evolving world of his experience in static, fixed forms; to do this, he must find common terms in the contradictions of the world which presents itself to him, so that its disparate and contradictory elements can be represented in a single, unified whole. Any discovery of unity in contradictions is necessarily the realization of their human, historical purpose of "Tendenz" (tenor, tendency), since even the simplest acts of perception, such as the recognition of a face in a jumble of lines, require that we impose or discover the human significance in what is otherwise only a confusion of data. And the "timelessness" which we commonly recognize as a quality of great works of art is nothing other than such a discovery of the deeper purpose [emphasis added] latent in the historical moment itself to which the work points and out of which it arises. (Mayo, 1989, p. 170, Note 2)

Photojournalism has suffered from much the same debate as photography in general regarding its aesthetic and epistemological value to society. And as with photography, in some circles, the debate regarding its value as art versus its value as information is intertwined with debates about the nature of reality and how best to represent or express reality. The solution, however, is to avoid a dichotomous characterization. Even as great art can simultaneously inform, inspire, and repell, so can the great images of photojournalism.

Consider the work of the preeminent documentarian Eugene Smith. His "Walk Through Paradise Garden" was a spontaneous document of his children walking from darkness toward the light. Yet viewing the moment through Smith's photograph has inspired viewers beyond its real-world representation, to look via visual metaphor into the struggles of everyday life. Similarly, images of everyday newspaper photojournalism move and inform readers. I would even go so far as to say that every image of photojournalism is "a metaphor for a part of life" (Newton, 1990), at once addressing the specific and the general.

STORYTELLER OR SOCIAL SCIENTIST?

The core of photo-documentary work is seeing and knowing, and then telling. Although the telling cannot possibly represent what was seen and known completely, the telling can communicate—if not "the story," then "a story" (Coles, 1997, p. 250). In fact, another way to examine the role of the photojournalist in society is to think of the journalist as an ethnographer, a researcher who often has less time to produce a report than most researchers. The journalist is charged with gathering information and reporting that information in a quick, accessible fashion.

Photojournalism is visual anthropology. Photojournalists study humankind through their reportage; they are professional observers. Anthropologists may bristle at this assertion, arguing that journalists are not social scientists. But the best journalists are indeed social scientists. They observe, they participate and observe, they record, they analyze, they immerse themselves in the culture of the observed, they report what they find, they reflect on the meaning of what they have seen. They have mass audiences and many more opportunities to influence how members of those audiences see and remember than most anthropologists. Differences in techniques rest primarily in the traditionally systematic nature of social science, which typically requires methodical, long-term investigation. However, using methods other than quantitative procedures or scientific protocols does not invalidate data (Blumer, 1969): "It is a tough job requiring a high order of careful and honest probing, creative yet disciplined imagination, resourcefulness and flexibility in study, pondering over what one is finding, and a constant readiness to test and recast one's view and images of the area" (p. 40).

Well-done photojournalism requires years of training, practice, and knowledge of a subject area. Consider the great war photographer David Douglas Duncan, who was trained as a Marine, served as a Marine, and spent most of his life studying men in battle. His books are rich, carefully considered, first-hand reports of the culture of war in the 20th century (1951, 1970). Similarly, his studies of the 1968 Republican and Democratic national conventions (1969) and of Picasso's life and work (1958, 1961, 1974) exemplify visual ethnography.

The dilemma of the journalist is that he or she often is expected to "bring back the truth" for publication in the next morning's newspaper or on the 10 o'clock news. If we could redefine journalism, whether verbal or visual, in a manner that openly acknowledged the relativity of individual perspective and presented information as the best available information, not as a conclusion or as "the truth," journalism would benefit tremendously. The benefit would be the integrity that accompanies doing what we say we do and knowing our limitations, as well as the potential engendering of public trust in what we say.

In *The Politics of Social Research*, Hammersley (1995) pointed to the Enlightenment paradigm as a primary influence on the perceived relationship between research and social and political practice. The paradigm "sees research as providing a theoretical basis for social interventions which will transform social life in a rational manner that is in everyone's interests … . It involves excessive expectations about the practical payoff of research" (pp. 141–144). Hammersley added that the "knowledge produced by research is always fallible." He stressed that, "what research offers is not a God's eye view but rather perspectives from particular angles, whose appropriateness can always be challenged" (pp. 141–144).

In many ways the photojournalist suffers from the same false sense of omniscience that guided a great deal of 20th-century research. But what a photojournalist does is to show "perspectives from particular angles." We just need to say, that is what we do. Further, Hammersley (1995) noted, "We should value knowledge about matters relevant to human life above ignorance about such matters. And such knowledge has value in terms of its relevance to our lives, irrespective of whether it can be shown to have a direct and powerful influence on our practical activities" (pp. 141–144). For the photojournalist, this can be interpreted to mean that the passion to make a visual record rather than to let something go unseen in a public fashion should take precedence as a form of knowledge production that may be relevant to people's lives. Not taking the picture, then, could be considered shirking the journalist's responsibility to society. Jarecke (1992), a Contact Press photographer who covered the Gulf War, took just such a stand. When challenged about the appropriateness of photographing the charred body of an Iraqi soldier, Jarecke (1992) asked, "How could I *not* take the picture?" To Jarecke, photographing the gruesome scene was imperative in order to show the world what occurred during the war, despite military censoring. Although Harold Evans (1992), then editor of *The London Times*, decided to publish the photograph, setting off a round of discussion about the war, the photograph was not published in the United States until months after the end of the war. When a westerner first looks at the photo, the tendency is to assume it documents the remains of an American or European soldier. Only by reading the caption does one learn that the victim was Iraqi.

Hammersley (1995) offered one other opinion that sheds light on photojournalistic practice: "We need to recognize that research is itself a form of practice, in the sense that it is an activity pursued by human beings which takes place in the world, is directed towards a particular set of goals and uses social resources" (p. 141). Photojournalism, like research, is a form of practice, part of human visual behavior in contemporary society. Photojournalism practice can be seen as extending the eyes of the world into situations no one but those immediately involved would see were it not for the photojournalist. Yet, as a practice, visual reportage is directed toward "a particular set of goals."

As both a social scientist and a documentarian, Coles took the reader on an inspiringly honest, self-disclosing journey examining the photodocumentary tradition in journalism, film, and social science research. Coles' (1997) *Doing Documentary Work* explored these concerns in terms of documentary photography, which can be considered a form of visual reportage. He drew on his own experiences, the experiences of people who have been "studied," and the experiences of such wide-ranging luminaries as James Agee, Dorothea Lange, Orson Wells, Erik Erikson, and Oscar Lewis. Much of Coles' reflection has been written before: questions regarding editing, cropping, point of view, exploitation of subjects. But his revisit to old issues is strengthened by careful attention to those who have been the target of documentary, expressed through verbatim commentary.

The secret, Coles maintained, is that documentary is more about the doing than about the work. The purpose of the "doing," Coles courageously and unabashedly maintained, is humankind's desire "to know, then tell," to confirm our own humanity by "connecting with others during the brief stay we are permitted here" (p. 145). As evidence of this "documentary impulse," Coles pointed to young children. "This eagerness to catch hold of, to catch sight of, to survey and inspect, to learn and then convey to others what the eyes and ears have taken in," Coles wrote, is "an expression of our creaturely interest in exploration, narration." As in good psychotherapy, Coles maintained, good documentary is "jointly conducted." He cited Nietzche: "It takes two to make a truth." Yet Coles also considered documentary work "a narrative constructed by the observer ... meant not only to represent 'reality' but inevitably to interpret it," fulfilling "the reflective side" of service to others (pp. 249–252).

Coles addressed what he considered the dilemma of documentary, "the gulf that separates the reality of the subject from the point of view of the observer," by stressing the personal connections people make while "doing documentary." Citing Oscar Lewis' assertion that "maybe, sometimes, I hear a voice that says this is the way to go, here, not there," Coles affirmed his faith "in a writer's, a researcher's, a documentarian's subjectivity as it takes hold of objectivity, the muse our nearest approximation of God" (p. 248).

In his chapter on "Fact and Fiction," Coles compared "real" documentary content with the "imaginary life" of novels:

> Participating in, observing, reporting such "enveloping truth" is the "doing" of a continually developing "'record' ... made in so many ways, with different voices and visions, intents and concerns ... ."

> What emerges, if it is done successfully, is a kind of truth, sometimes (as in Tolstoy, George Eliot, Dickens; we each make our choices from among these storytellers) an enveloping and unforgettable wisdom that strikes the reader as realer than real, a truth that penetrates deep within one, that leaps beyond verisimilitude or incisive portrayal, appealing and recognizable characterization, and lands on a terrain where the cognitive, the emotional, the reflective, and the moral live side-by-side. (p. 189)

Coles' words and style, reminiscent of Agee's, may turn off the skeptical critic of documentary who believes that subjective perception and "otherization" preclude any benefits of trying to do reality photography. But, again, one must ask: What is the alternative? Is it to allow the fear of connecting poorly with someone, of telling someone's story inappropriately, keep us from connecting with them at all, just because the process is complicated?

Those who "do documentary," Coles concluded, give us "the heartfelt tenderness that informs an attention to what is, what happens—documentary work as a kind of love that becomes expressed in those words, those pictures, a kind of love that is handed over, thereby to others" (p. 268). Although great reportage can express anger and fear as well as passionate concern, it is "a kind of truth ... a terrain where the cognitive, the emotional, the reflective, and the moral live side-by-side."

A MATTER OF ETHICS

In the end, the fine lines between human being and professional observer, watchdog and voyeur, artist and reporter, storyteller and social scientist are drawn within the heart of each seer. Why does someone "do photo-journalism"? How does he or she go about it? Another way to look at the issue is this: What is the most important moral problem faced by professional observers when they study the lives of actual people (William Stott, personal communication, 1990)? How does professional observation compare with everyday visual information gathering? Do we need to look at all? Is staring a problem? Are there appropriate and inappropriate ways to do it? Is appropriate staring a matter of good manners, a moral issue, or both? And the most basic of all: Why do we stare?

As others have noted before me, photographic observation is not dissimilar to hunting with a gun: A person is caught and frozen in the frame, much as other kinds of creatures are shot and stuffed for display—or consumed. However, a significant and obvious distinction between the two is that in the former, the organism is killed; in the latter the organism's reflectance during a given moment is captured. Does the way we do this really matter? Is there something inherently wrong about doing this at all? Or are such concerns once again sublimating those observed as passive victims of our vision, admonishing them to the status of victims who are incapable of resisting or presenting themselves with self-possessed agency? Have we simply created a supposedly more civilized form of subsumation?

The watchdog, the reporter, the social scientist, the artist, the human being, the storyteller, the dispassionate observer, or the voyeur—all those who stare in order to know—have the opportunity to stare with little regard for the person on the other side of the stare, or with little regard for the unethical process they facilitate. Or they have the option to proceed with the understanding that the best way to understand another human creature may be to enter an existential dialectic, keeping a careful eye on oneself and inviting the other human's participation in the visual dialectic. Then the observed has the authentic opportunity to become the observer, to "frankly, interminably" (Stott, 1973) stare at the world.

Well-considered observation examines how and why we look at others and what we look for. Good observation is an interactive, reciprocal venture in which the reality framed in the image is the result of a collaborative process. Good observation considers the looking process as important as the "reality" mediated via a photograph. It considers the rights and responsibilities of both the observer and the observed to participate actively and consciously and to be as honest as possible, as well as the need for and reality of sharing locations of power in the process. It considers the relationship between the observer and the observed to be reciprocal, equal, and the reality that is recorded to be one that is mediated through interaction.

Well-considered observation acknowledges that every observer is privileged—someone who has set him- or herself apart—not just to watch, but to stare and to record what is seen. However, good observation also acknowledges that all agents in the process are active and that all agents are observers. This dialectic does not negate the photographer's awesome responsibility, whatever his or her professional frame: to remain conscious of the knowledge that the vision that gets recorded, the vision that is remembered, that enters the continuum of images over time, contributing to our individual and collective understanding of life.

As professional observers, we can take an important cue from the world of good manners: It's impolite to stare. Whether the "impoliteness" is ingrained as a matter of custom or as an atavistic tendency is a subject for another book. I can argue here that unconsidered professional staring has an element of immorality to it, that it is unethical—not only in terms of the kind of visual information we think we obtain and convey, but also in terms of human behavior and interaction. But, again, I ask: What is the alternative? Not to look at all? I think not. There are times to look and times to avert one's eyes, times to remember we are all human creatures, rather than professional and other. Good observation is like good conversation: It advances communication to the best of the ability of those conversing through a continual process of mediating knowledge. It listens and it speaks. Further, good observation invites, entreats, beckons everyone involved to enter the perpetual dialectic of visual conversation as a way of knowing, and of becoming known. If we can mature into a global culture that recognizes the photojournalist as a professional seer practicing a research method, as well as following the heart, we will go a long way toward releasing the photojournalist from the impossible expectation of absolute objectivity and toward an appropriate understanding of the profound wisdom to be found in the best images.

ELOINA AND THE ANGEL. Although Eloina may not believe the process of being photographed steals her soul, she does take the moment seriously. She prepared herself by grooming carefully, choosing to sit beneath the image of a guardian angel, and summoning personal power as she looked into the camera. In turn, I chose the moment to press the shutter, and I chose to include the angel picture and Eloina's ephemeral extension—her shadow—in the frame. As subject and photographer, Eloina and I co-created the photograph, to which you, the viewer, now contribute your own perceptions. (Photo by Julie Newton.)

CHAPTER 5

Stealing the Soul

This chapter focuses on concerns for and of a human subject, ranging from how people feel about being photographed for publication to neo-colonial issues of social power. The central idea of the chapter is that society can no longer assume that taking pictures of people, or being the subject of visual representation, is a harmless activity. Visual reportage impacts people's lives, positively and negatively, and has taken its place among the rituals of culture.

CHAPTER 5

Stealing the Soul

Anthropologists tell us there are still humans in our world who believe someone is stealing their souls when they are photographed. We've all heard such stories, and most of us have labeled them mythological, charming beliefs of unsophisticated cultures.

I wonder. Perhaps, on one hand, these highly sensitive humans understand something we have forgotten, something about the nature of the human life force and personal image. Perhaps we are the misguided ones.

LET'S THINK ABOUT THIS FOR A MOMENT

What if capturing the light energy reflected from the face of a human being onto film or leaving some other kind of imprint or image of oneself does indeed involve a transmission of life energy? What if the taking of that energy is unwanted? Is this akin to having some of one's life force stolen? As Belloff (1985) wrote, it is not uncommon to fear that "the self may leak out" (p. 178) when being photographed. We need not prove that physical transference or leaking of energy takes place to consider the profound metaphorical insights these questions pose in this Age of the Virtual. At the very least, we can consider how contemporary imaging has taught us to *steel* our souls.

One way to begin this analysis is to define the idea of "life force" or inner self, often called the soul. The *Dictionary of Anthropology* (Winick, 1956) defined *soul* as the

> essence or animating substance of individual life, especially human. ... Souls may be multiple and may be in the body, in shadow, or in reflections. An early notion saw the soul as a kind of human shadow that caused life, possessed an independent personal volition and consciousness, and could affect man's existence and appear in his fantasies. ... Everyone has life, which leads to consciousness and is extinguished at death, as well as an image which appears in dreams. These can disconnect themselves from the body. Inasmuch as they both belong to the body, they belong to each other, and are part of the general or ghost soul. (pp. 495–496)

The idea of soul crosses ethnic boundaries, cultural boundaries, cognitive and affective boundaries, philosophical and musical boundaries. In recent years, popular culture has focused on *soul*, which traditionally falls under the purview of religious culture. Literature ranges from Moore's *Care of the Soul* (1992), a psychologist's thoughts on affirming the authentic self, to Crick's *The Astonishing Hypothesis: The Scientific Search for The Soul* (1994), a Nobel Laureate's discussion of visual perception and neurophysiology as the key to consciousness.

For this volume, *soul* refers to what people usually think of as the unique, authentic core of an individual human being. Whether the soul is immortal or a pile of all-too-mortal neurons firing in patterns humans consider meaningful is not the issue. The issue is the impact of visual reportage on those who are both its sources and its subjects. For this discussion, soul refers to something larger than self-concept in that it encompasses what makes a human being a living, thinking, feeling and behaving creature, a unique and authentic individual who can be affected by the way others view him.

■■■

Try to imagine a time when having one's picture taken was impossible. The elites of the world were wealthy enough to commission painted portraits, which were highly stylized and largely controllable in terms of content and personal presentation. Only in the last 160 years have we come to expect picture-taking to be part of everything—birthdays and weddings, press conferences and automobile accidents, war and everyday life. What have we lost and gained by this transformation of the way we record the visual image of a person?

In "The Tribal Terror of Self Awareness," anthropologist Edmund Carpenter (1975) described his experiences with people who had never seen their images reflected in mirrors nor recorded by still photographs or film. When shown Polaroids of themselves, most individuals reacted with fear and went somewhere to be alone and study the image. Carpenter suggested that for industrialized humans, image-making technology has made the process of being "hoisted ... out of both ... environment and ... body ... so casual, so environmental, we make that trip with the numbness of commuters, our eyes unseeing, the mystery of self-confrontation, self-discovery, gone" (p. 461). Carpenter also reported, however, that the New Guineans quickly became accustomed to the process.

A key term in our discussion, as noted earlier, is *image*, as a representation of another object, often invested with special properties by early humans. In anthropology, one way *imagery* is defined is as

> any symbolic representation the purpose of which is to ward off demons or evil influences. Quite frequently it takes the form of staring eyes (related to hypnotism). Apotrophic imagery exists in most primitive cultures and is based on the assumption that any likeness has the power of what it represents. (p. 277)

Beloff (1985) wrote of this in late-20th-century terminology:

> A photograph is a kind of clone. Although we hold ourselves open to all kinds of inspection, both on our own territory and when we enter a public space, a photograph of us is different. It is a visual clone that is permanent, portable, reproducible, public and saleable. (p. 216)

Among the so-called modern humans who have offered further analysis of the concept of representation is Alfred Stieglitz, the great turn-of-the-century photographer and aestheticist. Stieglitz explained the translation of the physical world into metaphysical concepts through his Theory of Equivalents. Stieglitz maintained that form, rather than subject matter, conveys emotional and psychological meaning (Newhall, 1964). Stieglitz made hundreds of photographs of the sky and clouds and called them "equivalents," explaining that they were "equivalents to his thoughts, to his hopes and aspirations, to his despairs and fears" (Rosenblum, 1984, p. 335). Newhall (1964) wrote:

> Viewed objectively, many of these rich prints with deep blacks and shimmering grays and incandescent whites delight us for their sheer beauty of form. They are photographic abstractions, for in them form is abstracted from its illustrative significance. Yet paradoxically the spectator is not for an instant left unaware of what has been photographed. With the shock of recognition he realizes almost at once that the form which delights his eye is significant, and he marvels that such beauty can be discovered in what is commonplace. For this is the power of the camera: it can seize upon the familiar and endow it with new meanings, with special significance, with the imprint of a personality. (p. 113)

Applying Stieglitz's theory to imaging human beings, we can argue that a photograph of someone translates or abstracts some part or instant of them into an equivalent, not only imaging the person via shapes and forms in a two-dimensional space, but also "endowing" the equivalent with new meaning or "special significance." The photograph may also be an equivalent for the photographer's feelings, or the subject's feelings, or the microcosm of time and interactions surrounding the moment the image was made. Stieglitz's Theory of Equivalents helps explain the tension many people feel when being photographed: The image being made may be endowed with meaning, taking on a significance beyond the moment of its creation. One image can stand for both the formal representation of the person and the "imprint" of the person. Is it so far to reach to consider that an image equivalent might eventually become confused with a functional equivalent in our minds?

Now, let's look at the issue from another perspective. Think about the ways we use pictures as equivalents of people or of moments, events, places—weddings, new babies, beloved people who are no longer with us for some reason. A photograph of a grandparent, a painting of an ancestor, a portrait of the two newlyweds who eventually became our parents become treasures—at least to some of us—because they hold something of what can never be again and they inform us with otherwise unobtainable vision. Why do we insist that yearbook portraits be taken of school children year after year if they do not mean something? Why do we take pictures on vacation? Why do we care what we look like in a photograph? Why do we photograph 50th wedding anniversaries ... and, depending on one's culture, photograph a funeral, or the last remains of the dead? Because the resulting image means something to us—either inherently through its literal and symbolic content, or through the content we project into it.

One reason we take or view these pictures is to prolong the experience of something or someone no longer physically present. What the equivalent means to us arises both from our past experiences and memories and from our present experience of viewing the image. Thus, the equivalent meaning of a picture is dynamic, in that it integrates memory with present experience to create meaning. Even if we are viewing an image for the first time and it is of something we have never seen or experienced, the image stimulates conscious and unconscious memories through its inherent symbols and integrates those memories with our present experience to impart a personal meaning to the image.

Thus, this integration of intrapersonal memory with a new, interpersonal viewing experience creates new levels of equivalents that influence our perceptions and guide our behavior in the physical world. This process, in turn, empowers the imagery of human violation or idealization to influence behavior with actual human beings. The effects of the process apply to images taken of us or by us, as well as to images taken by others for us to view.

VISUAL REPORTAGE AND EMOTION

Visual reportage depends on the people it serves—the human beings whose life stories are photographed and published. Yet we know little about how a photographer's behavior affects those he or she photographs for the mass media, nor do we understand how people feel when they are photographed in different ways.

The richest body of literature informing this issue is found in visual social science: social psychology, visual anthropology, and visual sociology. As noted in chapter 3, Milgram, a social psychologist, studied what he called human "photographic behavior" (1977b). Through a series of experiments, Milgram and his associates discovered that people are more likely to act prosocially when a camera is present (1977b). For example, people give more money to charity and are more likely to honor stop signs when they can see a camera pointed at them. When another human being, a photographer, is added to the equation, subject and photographer enter into an interpersonal relationship, even for snapshots (Milgram, 1977a). In a street experiment, Milgram found that passersby considered the space between a subject and photographer to be privileged. People altered their behaviors according to the perceived context of the photographic activity. Photographers and subjects also tended to follow social norms during a photographic event. Such social rules may vary according to culture, personalities of the individuals involved, context, desired outcome of the event, and authority of the photographer.

Milgram is better known for another study, which also directly relates to this one. In his controversial experiments on obedience and authority, Milgram (1974) found:

> With numbing regularity good people were seen to knuckle under the demands of authority and perform actions that were callous and severe. Men who are in everyday life responsible and decent were seduced by the trappings of authority, by the control of their perceptions, and by the uncritical acceptance of the experimenter's definition of the situation, into performing harsh acts. (p. 121)

Milgram's observations of people issuing electrical shocks (bogus, but that was unknown to them) to screaming "victims" when they were so instructed support the idea that photographic subjects may alter their behaviors to do as a photographer instructs because they perceive a photojournalist to have authority. Photojournalists, on the other hand, may numb themselves to the feelings of those they photograph under the authoritative role they perceive they play as "eyewitnesses" for humankind.

STUDYING EMOTION

The issue at hand is about more than authority and obedience, however. It also relates to how people feel when interacting with photojournalists. How do we study people's feelings? By definition, emotion arises from within a person "as temporally embodied, situated self-feelings that arise from emotional and cognitive social acts that people direct to self or have directed toward them by others," according to psychologist Denzin (1984, p. 49). Emotions are best studied then, "as social acts involving interactions with self and interactions with others" (p. 61). Interestingly, Denzin suggested that the "cardinal significance of emotionality and its study" is that it "lifts ordinary people into and out of themselves in ways that they cannot ordinarily achieve" (pp. 278–279). And that, of course, is also the core of much reportage—reporting on ordinary human beings caught in extraordinary circumstances, and sometimes making the ordinary special.

One aspect of these "social acts" is the tendency for people to play certain roles, especially while interacting "with self and others" in a public setting. Goffman (1973) called this tendency to try to control the impression one makes on others the "presentational self." Research on a related topic, self-consciousness, suggests that people have varying degrees of emotional response when something happens to them in public. Psychologist Arnold Buss (1980) theorized that people's public responses differ according to an individual's level of self-consciousness. Buss focused on the social anxieties—"discomfort in the presence of others"—that develop when an individual is in a state of "acute public self-awareness": embarrassment, shame, audience anxiety, shyness, all of which are states individuals might experience when being photographed. Buss (1980) further suggested that human beings possess selves with covert and overt behavioral components:

> We are aware of thoughts, feelings, images, memories, and ambitions that no one else knows about. We are also aware that we laugh, cry, converse, and aggress—all of which can be observed by others. And we are keenly aware of the distinction between these two classes of events: between inner and outer, between private feelings and public behavior, like knowing that you had a terrible dinner and thanking the hostess for a delicious meal. (p. 3)

In other words, a person can feel one way, but behave in another way, further complicating the study of emotion.

When one person takes a picture of another person, a number of factors contribute to the subject's feelings about the encounter. In many cases of photojournalism practice, the photographer's direction is completely absent. For example, a photojournalist may record a scene from a riot without those being photographed even knowing they are being photographed. In such a scenario, actions are usually beyond a photographer's control. In other cases, the photographer's direction may be subtle. As in the Hawthorne effect common to social science observational practice, subjects who are aware they are being photographed may alter their behavior in response to the mere presence of the photographer. Sometimes, the photographer's direction may be elaborate. The photographer may ask the subject to perform a complex behavior or multiple behaviors. For example, one well-known photojournalist asked family members to repeat their celebratory embrace of a newly awarded Olympic champion. The resulting photograph carried more visual impact than the nonstaged photograph that another photographer recorded. In years past, such re-created photos were standard. Now they are forbidden—though some photojournalist continue the practice in order to obtain more appealing images (personal communication, in Newton, 1994–1999).

One study examined how people felt about and responded to being photographed under relatively ordinary circumstances—having one's picture taken for publication (Newton, 1991, 1994). If, indeed, people change their behavior in front of a camera and photographer (and, in fact, are conditioned by experience to do so), and feel self-conscious—and therefore somewhat uncomfortable—in a relatively nonthreatening photographic setting, we could argue that people might feel even more uncomfortable being photographed in a real-life situation, where they are not supposed to alter their behavior, may be even more self-conscious because of the nature of the event, may be quite vulnerable due to the circumstances of the event, and know their photograph might be published internationally via the mass media. In the event that a photojournalist records activities of an individual who has not been conditioned in photographic behavior, as in a nonmedia culture, the subject's naiveté may pose even greater ethical questions regarding potential effects of a photographic event.

In the study, a scientifically conducted experiment, people took significantly longer to respond to more directive instructions and to unconventional instructions (Newton, 1991, 1994). Subjects also reported feeling significantly less positive about unconventional instructions and about more directive instructions.

Photojournalists may question the applicability of this study by maintaining that they do not direct their subjects—that they just report "what's out there." Staging photographs or directing subjects, common in the past, have indeed become verboten in contemporary news photography. Few would argue that a photojournalist directed the assassination of Robert Kennedy in order to get a better picture. But most photography published in the daily press is of a far more subtle nature, in which subject and photographer often interact. Extensive observation of photojournalists in practice indicates that they do indeed direct their subjects in many situations, even in some spot news events (Newton, field notes and photographs, 1994–1999). We can easily characterize a photographer's request for a subject to stand nearer a window for better light as direction. Just as influential, however, may be the aggressive movement of a photojournalist toward his or her subject to get a closer picture, or a photographer's request to "Just do that one more time." Also frequent are implied "nondirections" from a photographer. For example, while photographing someone for a feature story, the photographer might say something such as, "Just forget I'm here; I want to be a fly on the wall." But his or her presence, nonverbal behavior, and equipment choices alter the situation. Anthropologists Mead and Bateson (1977) noted this phenomenon in their fieldwork, maintaining that even arranging a camera to fire automatically without human interface requires pointing the camera in a particular direction and framing the scene in a particular way. And, as Milgram (1977b) noted, people change their behavior in the presence of a camera, a phenomenon that has led to such contemporary practices as affixing cameras at busy intersections to discourage drivers from running red lights.

SUMMARY

Photographers face many obstacles to authentic visual reportage: uncouth and image-controlling politicians who direct *them* (rather than the other way around), terrors of war and weather, traumas of the street and intimate spaces of the world, and even battles with editors and word reporters over what is the best picture to publish. So why be concerned about people's feelings when the world's citizens face physical perils that must be reported? A First-Amendment truism applies here: Even though we believe, at least in theory, that everyone has the right to say what he or she thinks, we usually use discretion in what we say and write. Surely the feelings of photographic subjects fall into an analogous truism: Even though photojournalists have the legal right to document the human condition in all its despair and glory, they should use discretion in photographing people. Few good photojournalists would dispute using such discretion, and professional codes of ethics stand as guidelines for not harming subjects (American Society of Media Photographers, 1998; National Press Photographers Association, 1998). What is missing is research that informs those standards of professional behavior among press photographers. Also missing is public education to increase understanding of these concerns among subjects and viewers.

Although all photojournalistic interactions cannot be comfortable because reporting the news frequently and necessarily focuses on people in distress, we can at least acknowledge and seek to understand the inherent significance of the feelings and responses of those whose stories we chronicle. How people feel about and respond to being photographed as part of an act of reportage is a matter for ethical inquiry as a humanistic issue in and of itself. Rejecting the criticism that concerns of this nature are "high-level worrying," ethicist Christians (1996) called for theory that places "the radically human at its epicenter" (p. 241).

ELECTION DAY, 1996. During a mid-day production meeting on November 5, 1996, *The New York Times* editors discuss which photos to publish in the next day's newspaper. Nancy Lee, then picture editor, holds up the photo desk's picks. Tom Bodkin (front right), AME Graphics, has just discarded a set-up shot of a photographer's hands on a voting-machine lever. Clockwise from Lee are Lonnie Schlein, photo editor; Jim Quinlan, art director; Margot Slade, special projects editor; Margaret O'Connor, later the picture editor; and Corinne Myller, art director. (Photo by Julie Newton.)

CHAPTER 6

Tending the Gate

Those who tend the gates of reportage tend power. They are the ones who decide what the public "needs to know," what is "appropriate," what is "news," what the public will "see," and, to some extent, even who the "public" is, by the ways they direct content and marketing. They decide whether to lead on page 1 with a controversial story or to bury it in an inconspicuous place on an inside page, whether sources are considered reliable, whether to publish a story even if it angers advertisers and readers or viewers, whether to spend more air time on features and soft news than on hard news, whether to target a little-represented community or mainstream areas of a city. The gatekeepers must answer the question: "Will publishing a picture of the body of a drowning victim prevent others from drowning at the same spot, or will it only exploit a tragic situation to sell newspapers?" This chapter examines the process through which an image or video clip passes on its way to publication or broadcast.

CHAPTER 6

Tending the Gate

*Photographers meet more real people than anyone at the newspaper—
but they don't decide what runs.*

—Eisert (1998)

I have no agenda. What happens out there is my agenda.

—Stapleton (1998)

*A lot of people trust us and read us and consider what
we put on page 1 is important.*

—Ralph Langer (1997, *The Dallas Morning News*)

*Current AP President Louis D. Boccardi says his primary goal
is to keep the trust of the news industry. When news breaks,
Boccardi says, for generations newsrooms and news desks
have asked, "Well, what does the AP say?" It's a signal of
our importance in the news flow and their trust in us.*

—Arnett (1998)

An important idea in mass communication theory is that the real power of a news operation resides with the *gatekeepers*: those who control the flow of information by deciding what to assign and what to run, when and where to run it, and how the story will be framed. Typically, we think of editors as the primary gatekeepers. Yet many media crities argue that editors in late-20th-century news media lost power as conglomerates who owned the news media became the real gatekeepers, subtly drowning the standards of good journalism in the interest of the bottom line and corporate values (Herman & Chomsky, 1998; Herman & McChesney, 1997; McChesney, 1997, 1999; Miller, 1996; Schiller, 1996). Further complicating the discussion of gatekeeping is the seemingly infinite number of variables affecting the production, content, and use of a message (Shoemaker & Reese, 1996).

This chapter examines six levels of gatekeepers typical in a large newspaper—reporters, word editors, picture editors, designers, marketing directors, and publishers. *Word editors* are usually the news, city, or section editors, and senior staff of a publication. *Picture editors* usually are in charge of the visual aspects of news reporting. They assign photographers to cover events, review the images shot, decide which images are be published, and set policy for handling and archiving original images. *Designers* are often liaisons between photo and wordside, bringing visual and verbal elements together into a cohesive package. At each level, a gate is opened or closed to publication content. The job for those at higher levels is to oversee the publication as a whole, blending words and pictures to report the news, and targeting issues for visual and word reporters to investigate. Yet even the lowliest copy editor has power—the power to frame a story with a headline, to crop a picture or perhaps even whether to use it, to ensure accuracy and fairness in the news report. These are the more traditional categories discussed under the theory of gatekeeping.

Increasingly, however, journalists have come to realize the power of *marketing* over publication content. In times past, advertising and editorial departments were physically separated at a newspaper plant, symbolizing an idealized separation between advertising and journalism. Now, advertising and editorial staffs find themselves talking to each other, considering ways each affects the other in terms of circulation, profit, and survival in the marketplace. Finally, there are the *publishers*, who range from heads of families to chains to international conglomerates, such as America Online, Disney, Westinghouse and General Electric, in which the journalistic enterprise is relatively minor compared with other interests (Miller, 1996).

Thus, the influences on content are many and varied, and must be considered important determinants of the group of images composing a day's "visual truth." So, what factors determine how someone tends his or her gate? They include good coverage of public events, news values, publication policies, readership or circulation issues, survival of the publication—including legal and ethical issues—and the bottom line.

Let us begin beyond the picture-taking event: the role of the picture editor in tending the gate. The "tending" can begin long before the event itself, with an idea in an editor's mind, picture assignment specifications, and the selection of the photographer for the shoot.

Consider the following scenario: At a large national newspaper, plans for covering a major election begin weeks or even months in advance. How many photographers will be assigned to cover events in which locations? Stringers, nonstaff freelance photographers, are lined up to supplement regular staffers, and equipment is prepared. On election day itself, everyone goes into operation, shooting film or digital cameras for their assigned stories—and keeping an eye out for the unpredictable. If film is the medium, photographers working near the newspaper or its bureau bring the film to the paper to be processed. Two hundred rolls would not be uncommon for a few hours of shooting by a dozen photographers. The film comes out of the processor, and photographers (if they are still around) and editors hunch over big light tables selecting the best frames from long strips of negatives. Discussions take place:

"Oh, that's great! Look at that expression."

"Man, you got him just at the right moment."

"Is that your hand in the picture? We can't run that."

"That's a great shot, but the metro editor will never run it. It's too artsy."

"Should we use this one of the cowboy voting in Texas?"

"If you want to reinforce a stereotype."

"But it's fun!"

"Do you realize what I had to do to get that photo?"

"Yes, I know. We'll run it inside, but we need a photo of the snow on the front."

"This one tells the story ... look at that."

"Yeah, but it won't grab people's attention."

And so the discussion goes. Soon selected frames are digitally scanned, and the discussion moves up the gatekeeping ladder. If the photographer used a digital camera, he or she could have transmitted images from the scene to the editors via a modem. In that situation, the photographer may have edited images at the scene or may have run them through an intermediary edit at a nearby bureau before transmitting to the newsroom.

The role of the picture editor, then, includes assigning photographers, setting policy, selecting photographs for publication, answering to higher ups, and looking at the big picture. At a small publication, the picture editor does some of everything. In a large operation, the picture editor's role is narrowly defined unless he or she is near the top of the management chain. Increasingly, the picture people are moving up the editorial ladder into positions of authority over more than pictures. And when the word people and the picture people communicate well, the probability that good journalism will occur improves.

Although the bottom line calls the shots in many newsrooms, editors often are a fiercely independent lot who have great influence on what becomes known news. One theoretical frame influencing how they tend the gates of visual news is social responsibility of the press. The history of the press is part of the history of media—some would say the press began the mass media, with books, newsletters, newspapers, and magazines developing to include broadcast media and film, and finally the Internet (Media History Project, 1996). But the most important idea for the discussion is that people originally viewed the newspaper as a tool for political liberation and social and economic progress, a legitimate means of opposition to established orders of power—hence the protection for the press in the original Bill of Rights amending the U.S. Constitution in 1791—along with freedom of speech, petition, assembly, and religion.

TWO CONTEMPORARY EDITORS

Sandra Eisert, then senior graphics editor for Microsoft and a long-time picture editor, explained how the "leg bone's connected to the hip bone" (personal communication, 1998):

> Photographers meet more real people than anyone at the newspaper, but they don't decide what runs. Photographers' agenda are set by what wins POY [Photographer of the year] awards. Picture editors' agenda are set by what they think news editors will publish. The news editors' agenda are set by what we learned in journalism school about news values—what's news is what's new and unexpected—and by what they think the public is interested in. We've got to have some happy news out there—not just death, destruction, mayhem.

Another point of view comes from Sally Stapleton, then vice president of photography, international division, The Associated Press:

> I have no agenda. What happens out there is my agenda. We have it easy— we're the conduit. We let the members make the decision to run or not based on their policies and readership. ... During the Gulf War, we made a decision not to run a picture of an incinerated Iraqi soldier—our competition did—in hindsight I think we decided we had made a mistake. Eight years ago, we were squeamish about what we sent out. Now we're not squeamish at all ... a blood-soaked body is very common.

If it happens, even if it's horrible, people need to know about it. Pictures can influence public opinion—we learned that in Somalia with the picture of the soldier's body being dragged through the streets: People in this country saw it and wanted us to get out of there. In Europe it's not like that—if they see a picture of one of their soldiers, they don't react like we do. In our country, a picture like that sets off all kinds of responses about our involvement and concern for our soldiers.

One thing that's interesting is what happens when the press decides a story is big. If everybody's there, it's big, whereas if we have someone out there somewhere, and they send in a good story, it may not move because it's not a big story.

People talk about how editors have agendas, but we don't have one.

THE BOTTOM LINE

The potential for profit in a capitalist society can override the best of editors' intentions to honor sociopolitical ideals that originally led to the concept of freedom of the press. News publications now are part of the maelstrom of mass communication—large-scale social interaction through technologically mediated messages. And the reality of mass communication is that content is influenced by personal, political, social, economic, and ownership forces (McQuail, 1994; Shoemaker & Reese, 1996), even though we would like to believe in journalism for journalism's sake. The gap between the ideals of free press/free society and the reality of contemporary mass media is further widened by the media's hegemonic role in society, the tendency to maintain the ideas of dominant groups (Severin & Tankard, 1997). Far below the conscious intentions of many conscientious gatekeepers are their subconscious tendencies to maintain the status quo.

THE FEATURE ILLUSTRATION. *Seattle Times* photojournalist Betty Unisden works with women for a photograph to accompany a feature story on pantyhose. Posing subjects for feature photographs and to illustrate a story remains within the boundaries of ethical photojournalism. Editors reason that viewers can read visual codes indicating an image is set up when the codes are obvious. In this instance, for example, the women are looking directly into the camera. (Photo by Julie Newton.)

CHAPTER 7

Is Seeing Still Believing?

The bridge between seeing with one's mind and seeing with one's heart is often so short that it is not there. This chapter addresses physiological, psychological, and cultural aspects of seeing, particularly in regard to viewer and reader perception of reality-type imagery. The analysis is located theoretically within the context of critical concerns about 20th-century ocularcentrism and work on visual perception.

CHAPTER 7

Is Seeing Still Believing?

The eyes They see and They see further and longer.

—*New York Times* t-shirt

Marshall McLuhan wrote that life is like looking into a rearview mirror. We never fully understand where we've been until we are beyond where we were and can contemplate what happened, as if we're driving down a road looking into a rearview mirror (McLuhan & Powers, 1989, p. ix). He believed, for example, that the 19th century, not the 20th century, was the Visual Age. The 20th century is better labeled the Acoustic Age, said McLuhan, for during the last 100 years we have advanced from the two-dimensional communication of words and pictures requiring physical proximity between viewer or reader and a print medium into multidimensional communication media in film, video, and digital forms that carry sound and depth instantly through time and space.

Yet a significant characteristic of 20th-century culture is its attention to the visual. Theorists have noted a "pictorial turn" occurring (Mitchell, 1994) through which we began to realize image-dominant media had overtaken word-dominant media. Postmodern theorists are quite critical of this turn, denouncing the development as spectacle (Debord, 1967), simulacrum (Baudrillard, 1994), and panopticon (Foucault, 1977). It is interesting to note that postmodern criticism of the visual, which typically is grounded in a philosophical approach, followed a physiologically based movement that produced now-classic work: Arnheim's *Visual Thinking* (1969) and *Art and Visual Perception* (1974), Gombrich's (1961) *Art and Illusion,* Dondis' (1973) *Visual Literacy,* and Ivins' (1953/1978) *Prints and Visual Communication.* Combining backgrounds in art history and psychology with new under-standings of the hardware of visual perception, these thinkers epitomized the growing awareness that visual communication circumscribes a unique and overwhelmingly complex interplay of factors within the human creature. Furthermore, image-dominant media in print, film, video, and digital forms—whether art, information, or persuasion—began to crowd our visual environment with a confusing density. In the 1990s, a third wave of 20th-century literature on visual communication began to examine the visual from more encompassing viewpoints. Lester's (1995) *Visual Commu-nication: Images with Messages,* for example, describes six perspectives for studying visual messages: personal, historical, technical, ethical, cultural, and critical. Messaris' *Visual Literacy: Image Mind and Reality* (1994) and *Visual Persuasion,* (1997) Williams' (1999) "Beyond Visual Literacy," and Barry's (1997b) *Visual Intelligence* made major leaps toward synthesizing the array of parts that constitute the whole of visual communication.

Also significant to note is that photojournalism came into its own, stok-ing the fires of visual credibility, even as we began to understand the sub-jectivity of visual perception. And, for the first time in its history, new technological developments appeared to threaten the fundamental premise on which photojournalism was based—the search for visual truth—more than they facilitated its practice. All of these factors—developments in visual perception theory, postmodern criticism of the visual, recent synthe-ses of visual concerns—can strengthen our search for visual truth if they are clearly understood and appropriately, rather than fearfully, applied.

The central issue is our understanding of "visual truth." As Ivins (1953/1978) wrote, "The nineteenth century began by believing that what was reasonable was true and it wound up believing that what it saw a pho-tograph of was true—from the finish of a horse race to the nebulae in the sky" (p. 195). The apparent transparency of photographic representation of the real world led to the idea that one could indeed establish that some things were true. Muybridge's (1887) use of photography to establish the truth about how horses run is a classic example of the validity we attached to the content of photographs.

If we extend Ivins' idea about 100-year shifts in our understanding of truth, we could say: The 20th century began by believing that what it saw a photograph of was true and wound up by knowing, at least on a cognitive level, that many things that seemed to be visually true were not. We now know that we can make horses run upside down if we want to—in the world of representation. We can also make human beings actually walk on ceilings in antigravity simulators. These abilities, coupled with our relatively new comprehension of the subjectivity of perception, have resulted in a confusion about "visual truth" that has exploded into book after book from across disciplines examining the relationship of the imaged to the real, of the representational to the represented, of ways of observing to the effects of being observed. Some assert that all truths are constructions, that perception can never be objective, that even the photographs we have assumed to be truthful, such as Nick Ut's photo of Kim Phuc running from napalm, can be called into question. When *National Geographic* editors moved the Great Pyramids closer together for the sake of a cover aesthetic, they also shifted belief in photographic truth as used in news media.

It is only normal, then, that people would respond with feelings of betrayal and cynicism to the revelation that visual news media overtly manipulate their views of reality. U.S. civics classes teach the ideological expectation that the press is the Fourth Estate, a fundamental part of the system of checks and balances established via the U.S. Constitution. But the founding fathers could not foresee a major obstacle to the pursuit of an informed public: that the ingenuity of capitalist mass media would subvert visual freedom by using increased understanding of visual perception to manipulate a visually naive public (Williams, 1999). The ultimate irony is that this same naive public has come to believe that the media—not corporate capitalism—have too much freedom of expression and should be more heavily regulated by government (First Amendment Center, 1999).

Further complicating the issue are the news media's own disagreements about visual manipulation. CBS's decision to use new digital technology to replace an NBC advertisement in Times Square with the CBS logo during coverage of New Year's Eve festivities elicited industry criticism. Other networks decided against using the new technology, which was developed by the Princeton Video Image firm. Although CBS news anchor Dan Rather termed the digital alteration a mistake, the president of CBS news, Andrew Heyward, disagreed: "On New Year's Eve with confetti in Dan's hair, I saw this as an extension of our graphics, a change in this very festive, in effect, set" (Carter, 2000, pp. C1, C2).

So, where do we stand in regard to the nature of seeing, perceiving, believing, particularly in regard to visual news? What do we know about the process of seeing and about visual knowledge that can help us pull our concept of "visual truth" out of the quicksand—or must we leave it there? The remainder of this chapter will review what people *think* they know about seeing and its relationship to what people *think* they can count on when perceiving visually. I suggest that, rather than give up on the idea of visual truth, the news industry move quickly toward an interpretative theory of news images that combines the "reasonable" with the "photographicable" to search for the "reasonably true"—the best truth a person can perceive and convey at any given moment. In some ways, we never could believe our eyes; only now are we coming to comprehend the slippery nature of visual reality.

WHAT IS SEEING?

Seeing is such an integral part of the human system that it appears to be impossible to separate from our other senses. We can, however, discuss aspects of seeing as if they are separate—if we keep in mind that they are not. For example, if someone does not physically see light, that person nevertheless sees things in the mind's eye. An individual who sees physically also sees things in the mind's eye. And all are keyed to the way we know, feel, understand, and remember.

In the past we have tended either to romanticize or to demonize vision, in part because we knew so little about how it works. As we naively expected ourselves to be infallible, so we expected our powers of observation—and any manifestation of those powers—to be infallible. When they were not, it meant they were corrupted. And the fact that our eyes are part of our brains, rather than the windows to the soul, is difficult to conceive. Further, the idea that visual stimuli also affect our physiological systems in other ways, in terms of physical response, for example, adds to the mystery and the fear that there is something uncontrollable and beyond understanding about seeing. And perhaps there is.

For the present discussion, the construct "seeing is believing" is best approached in two ways: *perceptual/psychological/physiological*, which includes psychology and cognition (knowing and memory, response to stimuli), and *aesthetic/semiotic/cultural*, which includes society (institutions such as media, government, and corporations) and the practices of living we create. Each offers a means to understanding the role of the visual in individual and collective identity formation. The next section introduces the two approaches to studying the visual. They are explored further in chapter 9.

Perceptual/Psychological/Physiological: Seeing as Knowing, Feeling, and Remembering

When we talk about *seeing*, we usually mean that we are physically seeing something, or that we are perceiving or understanding something, as in "Now, I see!" Part of the problem of understanding what happens when we see is the ambiguity of the process—do we mean responding physically to visual stimuli, such as closing our eyes in extremely bright light after being in a dark room? Or do we mean responding cognitively to information, such as becoming enlightened about an idea after someone describes it to us in a new way? Or do we mean responding psychologically, as we might when we see the color red and become aroused? As we learn more about the workings of the human body, we are coming to understand that various forms of "seeing" can occur in tandem, affecting one another in a ricochet of responses to stimuli.

When we talk about *knowing*, the water is just as murky. Are we discussing fact, information that can be proven to be true, or are we discussing a kind of "perceiving" similar to that associated with seeing—a nonverbal, often intuitive flash of insight or understanding?

Then we have such variables as differences among individuals and how each responds to stimuli, as differences among groups of people and how cultural influences lead us to interpret stimuli in different ways, as situational differences that shift and shade the way something is viewed or known, depending on context and purpose. Consider John Berger's classic photographic examples in which diverse individuals were asked to look at photographs and explain how they interpreted each photograph. A picture of a little girl with her mouth wide open and holding a doll was read by one person as a picture of a child who was quite upset and crying about something and by another person as a picture of a child who was about to eat her doll (Berger & Mohr, 1982, pp. 54–55).

Such is the difficulty of understanding how and what we know when we see. The ambiguity of the image has been well established by audience reception studies indicating that viewers actively participate in constructing meaning from what they see (Staiger, 1992). In another example, Berger and Mohr (1982) offered a set of photographs of a woodcutter. On one level is what the photographer saw and decided we should see. On another level, we see what the woodcutter wanted the photographer—and therefore, us—to see. And on still another level, we come to know what the woodcutter's wife wanted to see. All are different, pieces of the whole, the Gestalt of multiple stimuli we seek to comprehend. Photographs add and subtract from that whole, in some ways muddling things further, in other ways clarifying. Often we can see much more through external means than we could ever hope to see with our own so-called "naked eyes." So what are we to make of it?

And what happens when we look at something "real" versus something "virtual" that appears real? Do we ever really distinguish the two in terms of how we know?

Perhaps more important than understanding any differences in the ways we view real versus virtual content is evidence that images are fundamental to memory. Consider the idea of flashbacks, those fleeting glimpses from the past—a mother's face, a mountain view. It's hard to imagine remembering anything without a visual component to the memory. Now consider the role photojournalism plays in that process. Photojournalism supplies the flashbacks and shows them to us repeatedly, both implanting a form of reality and framing that reality for long-term memory.

Think of images from Vietnam ... think of your own family scrapbook, pictures of yourself as a child that frame the way you remember yourself as a child and the things that happened to you. I can think of one example in particular from my own childhood—a view of a rainbow from atop a mountain cliff. I am looking down on the rainbow from above, and right at my feet are the iridescent, azure wings of butterflies blown to the ground by the mountain gales. The problem is, I am not sure if I remember seeing that rainbow firsthand or if what I am remembering is a slide my mother often showed when talking about our experiences in the Andes. I cannot distinguish them.

Research also has determined that we remember better what we see than what we hear (Graber, 1990; Schultz, 1993). We see printed words, as in the combinations of letters or characters on paper or on a video screen— they are as visual as anything else we see. One can even argue they are just one form of visual communication. Following the theories of Innis (1951) and Mchuhan (1964), Logan (1986) argued that the very nature of the linear progression of letterforms—a visual concept—affects the way Westerners think and interpret reality. T. C. Mcluhan (1994) maintained that even land shapes affect consciousness.

These links are important to our discussion of the role of visual reportage in mediating our sense of reality (Berger & Luckmann, 1996/ 1967) in that the dominant medium of visual reportage is, of course, pictures, whether still or moving. Usually the pictures are supplemented, guided through the gates of meaning creation, if you will, by words ... visually in print and video, and in the mind's eye in radio, and orally in radio, video, and, increasingly, the Internet.

Aesthetic/Semiotic/Cultural: Seeing as Culture and Society

From the early years of photography, the connection between personal identity and images of the self has been explored (see chap. 5). The relation between media images and self-identity also has received increased attention. Durham (1999), for example, explored media influences on girls' sexual identity.

But what is the relation between visual *reportage* and identity? The effects can be as profound as stereotyping. For example, studies have shown that newspaper photographs of minorities typically portray minorities either in negative situations, such as crime-related stories, or in celebrity situations, such as sports and the music industry. One can argue that repeated publishing of photographs of African Americans being arrested without publishing photographs of African Americans in pro-social roles contributes to a negative, stereotyping view of African Americans—among African Americans themselves as well as other racial groups. One might even go so far as to say that reality-type images of visual reportage are more harmful than other types of imagery precisely because they are so seemingly transparent in their relationship to the real. The context of their presentation, a newspaper or television broadcast, is a context of veracity, whereas a fictional portrayal is more easily removed from association with the real. Yet we also are learning more about the extent to which even fictional stereotyping harms (Lester, 1996).

Visual reportage legitimates ways of looking at other people and ways of looking at ourselves. It enters the public consciousness under the guise of authority of the press: This is true. This is what happened. This is what the situation looked like. This is what people looked like. The context has been one of *assumed truth*.

Further complicating this enmeshment of truth and fiction is the fact that interspersed among these legitimated images are images of persuasion and overt manipulation … the images of advertising. Now, if we see something extraordinary that looks real—such as Tiger Woods artfully bouncing a golf ball with his club—the reaction is one of disbelief: "No one could do that—they just did that in the computer." Consider another example from the pages of *The Austin-American Statesman*. Page 1 presents the editors' choices for the most important news of the previous day. Turn the page, and we see more news, but we also see an Estée Lauder ad and a women's underwear ad. Do the eyes perceive that some of what they see is meant to be true and that some is meant to be manipulative? Some would argue that they do, that the codes of the different kinds of imagery have taught us to navigate the streams of news and advertising with the agility of mental gazelles. Others say the distinction between the two has become so blurred (Nichols, 1994) that we do not discern it unless we consciously stop to "unpack" what we're seeing. The result is a delegitimization of reportage and an increased legitimization of advertising. And the ultimate result is general distrust of images. Yet people still believe X-rays and final photos of a "photo-finish" race.

Another concern is the association of imagery per se with the nonrational and therefore the noncredible. The visual has been debased as ambiguous, equivocal, easily manipulated, and nonsubstantive to the point that it has lost credibility. We have moved so far from our early-20th-century assumption that we could believe what we saw in a photograph, that now we feel we can no longer even believe our eyes (Goldberg, 1992). Lack of faith in our ability to know via the visual has compounded our lack of faith in ourselves and our institutions.

PHOTOJOURNALISM'S ROLE IN THIS PROCESS

So, is seeing believing? To some extent, yes. Our physiological hardwiring triggers a system of knowing based on our senses, and sight is, of course, one of those senses. Further, we have been acculturated through time to rely on our vision to determine the veracity of something. If a family member dies in an accident, often we cannot believe the death has occurred until we see the body with our own eyes. Furthermore, research evidence does point to the idea that people remember what they see better than they recall information obtained in other ways (Graber, 1990; Schultz, 1993) and that, even if we have had information to the contrary, we remember the information that dominated the content of the images, rather than verbally corrected information. One other way to think about "seeing is believing" is to consider that we tend to see only what we look for. In other words, we believe what we see because we have chosen to see something in a certain way.

On the other hand, the answer to "Is seeing believing?" also is "No." As a species, we have moved beyond dependence on initial physiological responses to stimuli, such that the powers of reason and intuition enable us to challenge things that appear to be true. Additionally, in a culture dominated by media imagery, we cannot possibly believe everything we see—in fact, people cannot even consciously see everything that passes by their eyes. The same creative, manipulative image culture also teaches people that they cannot believe all that they see.

Resolving this problem requires understanding the perceptual shift we have made during the last century from "seeing with our own eyes" to learning about the world via images that look like the world. In many instances today, the images *are* the world we see. Although seeing with our own eyes carries problems of selective perception and illusion, such problems multiply when we see through the eyes of others, who carry yet other perceptual lenses. For the professional "seer," this means a commitment of enormous weight. In terms of physical sight, a person who is sighted can lead someone who is not sighted off a literal cliff, or lead the nonsighted person to a secure place. The visual reporter has similar powers and responsibilities in terms of leading viewers to the best "visual truth" he or she can find and convey. Then each viewer must decide whether to jump off the proverbial cliff and "believe" what he or she "sees."

A CIRCLE OF VISION. Six-year-old Matt Newton (top frame) steps out from among the press photographers lining a red carpet laid for Texas Gov. Mark White. Spotting Matt, White asked, "Son, do you know how to use that camera?" Matt's response: "Click" (bottom frame). (Top photo by Julie Newton. Bottom photo by Matt Newton.)

CHAPTER 8

Whose Truth?

A common frame for publishing and exhibiting images of reportage is the "need-to-know" frame. An assumption underlying the First Amendment is that if people see what's going on in the world, they will be better informed and work to improve their lives and society at large. Research indicates that both readership and memory are closely tied to photographs, and new work in visual perception indicates images have long-lasting effects on behavior. If images are that important, "whose truth" is The Truth becomes an issue. What is the role of visual reportage in a socially responsible culture? As we noted in a previous chapter, "who" determines "what" truth the "world" will "see" is often a function of those who tend the gates of the news and information media. Gatekeepers include subjects or sources, photographers, editors, designers, publishers, institutions such as government and education, and economic entities such as corporations. We also know that viewers tend their own gates to some extent. The decision regarding "whose truth" is The Truth occurs at every step in the perceptual process, as well as in the collecting and disseminating processes. Furthermore, even if viewers perceive an image of photojournalism as "true," it is not clear that "seeing" changes their long-term perceptions or moves them to action. This chapter discusses the practice of photojournalism in relation to broad societal and culture issues.

CHAPTER 8

Whose Truth?

*Truth ... is something we make in the encounter with
the world that is making us.*

—McLuhan (1989)

*During my lifetime in photojournalism, photography has had a pro-
found effect on people's understanding of the world in which they live
and on their perceptions of important social and political issues.*

—Chapnick (1994)

Previous chapters have explored components of our contemporary system
for reality imaging from the standpoint of various levels of message production, dissemination, and perception: the subject, photographer, editor,
and reader or viewer. This chapter shifts the focus to a broader view—that of
society at large. In whose image are photographs made and used? Whose
truth do they convey? At stake is knowledge itself, a major source of power
(Eldridge, 1993). Toffler (1990) argued in his book *Power Shift* that those
who control information will hold the most power. This chapter uses the
term *power* to mean control of resources; this control is negotiated at each
level of the image-making and using system. The system is at once hierarchical and nonhierarchical, issue specific and part of a larger whole, interpersonal and global. Each negotiation contributes to the next, resonating
throughout subsequent negotiations. At societal levels, the image potentially

carries exponential power, the kind of power that can significantly influence a nation's citizenry to turn against a military intervention (as with the photograph of a U.S. soldier's body being dragged through the streets of Mogadishu; Buell, 1999, p. 223), or characterize the way an event will be remembered (as with the photograph of the fireman carrying a child's limp body after the Oklahoma City bombing in 1996 Buell, 1999, p. 233). Each level also can dissolve into the proliferation of *powerlessness* through desensitization, disbelief, and anomie.

This chapter considers the power of an image of reportage from four societal perspectives: public, government, press, and economic interests. Each group exerts and cultivates its power through visual codes developed over centuries of human interaction at personal and mass levels. Over the course of the last century, each group learned to construct sophisticated visual messages to carry the truths the group believes in—or prefers. Each group uses a variety of image forms, including visual reportage, with a variety of overt and covert motivations. So, the question becomes: Can any image be anything but a construction, a catalyst for someone's truth, and never *the* truth? Social construction of reality theory addresses that question.

SOCIAL CONSTRUCTION OF REALITY THEORY

Social construction of reality theory maintains that we produce our own universes—and they in turn produce us—in a perpetual dialectic of experience and knowing (Berger & Luckmann, 1966/1967). As McLuhan said succinctly, "Truth ... is something we make in the encounter with the world that is making us" (McLuhan & Powers, 1989, p. xi). Applying the theory to photojournalism, we might argue, for example, that the way a president is photographed, and the way the photographs are edited and published, construct a view of the president. A case in point was a public discussion of how to portray Franklin D. Roosevelt in a 1997 memorial. Because the public's memory-view of the late president did not include his wheelchair, the memorial designers did not include his wheelchair—until citizens in wheelchairs complained that image control excluded a significant part of Roosevelt's life. At stake was what would go down in popular culture as the best image of the president. Would "truth" be a construction from Roosevelt's time, when the press consciously avoided showing the president in his wheelchair, supposedly to protect his powerful image? Or would "truth" be a revised, inclusive construction that affirmed the power of differently abled individuals through the role model of a differently abled president? Each truth connotes a form of power on behalf of different interests.

POWER

The concept of "the power of the image" has become a cliché of contemporary society, used variously to chastise and glorify the visual. In the early years of the 20th century, media theorists ascribed awesome power to media in general, whether predominantly visual or verbal. As mass communication theory developed, however, researchers learned that media power is not exercised as the proverbial "magic bullet," shot into the consciousness of a passively awaiting audience. Research indicated that different media carry different messages in different forms with different effects on different people in different situations (Lasswell, 1948). Media theory moved into a period of "limited effects," in which the power of the audience with its varying needs and desires became a focus of study. Over the last 25 years, media theorists have reconsidered the idea of a powerful media, while at the same time recognizing that audiences are active (McQuail, 1994; Severin & Tankard, 1997).

A primary concern of this book is the power of visual reportage to influence perceptions of truth. One problem with trying to understand the influence of photojournalism, however, is that images of reportage enter the morass of images swirling in the public sphere. Some of those images are intended to present a truth accurately. Some are designed to manipulate and mislead. Additionally, power is afforded to different groups in different ways. For example, in U.S. society, it is generally assumed that the public has a right to know, the press has the right to freely express, government has responsibilities to the public, and individuals have rights to personal and economic independence. One argument in critical theory maintains that all such groups and manifestations of power are only abstract concepts that have been created through time. Furthermore, the groups are inseparably connected: Individuals make up the public, who supposedly create and are served by government, which is watched by and manipulates the press, which in turn is supposed to serve the public by watching everyone. Corporations and other economic structures arise from and have levels of interconnected control over each of those groups. These various, evolving bases of culture further confuse identification of the truth because it can be difficult, if not impossible, to distinguish a truth from those who disseminate it and those who ally with it.

The Public

So who is this public? Think of the public in terms of the levels of analysis we already have outlined. Members of the public are individual seers, those who view, read, and make images. Members of the public are subjects and sources whose various life scenarios compose the content of images of photojournalism and who vary according to the infinite factors that make up the human species. Members of the public are editors who select, ignore, or draw attention to specific images. The public includes societal institutions—education, religious groups, government, medicine—that compose the structures that create the cultures in which we live. The public are small-town citizens who expect their newspapers to publish photographs of Maria's birthday party, big-city citizens who expect Internet news to explain the day's stock-market drop, Brazilian *flavela* residents who are looking for shelter, or ingenious South Africans who run televisions with generators.

We also can examine the concept of "the public" in terms of mass audiences, those who partake of the mass media in its various forms. Especially relevant to our present discussion is the concept of "public opinion," or what large groups of people think about issues and events that occur in the world.

A common concern for those who practice visual reportage is the "public-needs-to-know" frame. As noted previously, a key rationale supporting the idea of a "free press" is that if people know what's going on in the world, they will be better informed and work to improve society. Traditionally, journalists have used words and statistics to report what people think about important issues. Often they rely on scientifically valid poll information for evidence. Yet research indicates that readers and viewers not only are drawn to pictures more than words, but also remember pictures better. If that is true, then "whose truth" is conveyed or evoked via those pictures is significant. Who or what determines the content of those images? Does photojournalism report public opinion or shape it or both? So, the "public's truth" is both consequential and as varied as its constituents.

The Press

Harry Chapnick, the late president of Black Star Photo Agency, had clear views about photojournalism's relationship to public opinion. "Photography, as witness to history, gives testimony in the court of public opinion," Chapnick (1994) wrote in his book, *Truth Needs No Ally: Inside Photojournalism* (p. 13). In answer to the question "Can Photography Change the World?" Chapnick noted:

> Those who say that photographs cannot make a difference have not thought the matter through. More to the point are the specific questions of whether

photographs can change public perceptions on social issues, stimulate people to be more active in support of their causes, affect the ways in which people live and governments conduct business. During my lifetime in photojournalism, photography has had a profound effect on people's understanding of the world in which they live and on their perceptions of important social and political issues. (pp. 11–12)

He continued:

Photojournalists are not always aware that the pictures taken today are the history of tomorrow, or that pictures taken for specific editorial purposes may resonate beyond their original boundaries, having a far-reaching impact on the public's consciousness, or indeed that the world is made better by their being taken. (p. 13)

Lippmann (1922) wrote that people act based on pictures in their heads. It makes sense to explore possible connections between photojournalism and those "pictures in our heads." Do images of photojournalism affect those pictures in our heads, and if so, how? Applying agenda-setting theory, one can argue that, at the very least, images of reportage can lead us to think about certain things—and to think about things in certain ways (McCombs & Shaw, 1972, 1993). Examined from another direction, if photojournalism is indeed visual reportage, does it report public opinion or does it merely offer anecdotal evidence of happenings related to public issues?

Many of those who practice journalism consider themselves neither disseminators of propaganda nor Aultschull's (1984) agents of power. For the working press, the overt rationale for newswork is grounded in social responsibility—the press as guardian and conduit for information that is important to society. As McQuail (1994) noted, a newspaper can be viewed as a tool for political liberation and social/economic progress, or as a legitimate means of opposition to established orders of power. And, as with any human enterprise, some newsworkers take their responsibilities more seriously than others. For some, newswork is a job. But consider the Associated Press:

At a time when the death of even one American soldier can lead to national anguish, where does the AP find the courage to ask people to risk their lives in the pursuit of news? Six AP men and women have died these past four years.

On reflection, I would say that only a news organization that is very, very sure of its mission can ask its employees to routinely do this. To me, that separates the AP from the rest of the news industry. (Arnett, 1998)

Clearly, the Associated Press believes the truth its eyewitnesses find is significant. Those eyewitnesses—visual and verbal reporters—send their collected evidence to central offices around the world, which then select and disseminate images to member news organizations, who then tend the gate as they see fit. Member newspapers and television stations also serve as eyewitnesses for the AP, sending their own best evidence to the central offices for mass distribution.

Other centralized organizations for collecting visual reportage include Reuters and Agence France Presse (AFP), and such picture agencies as Magnum and Contact Press. Each has a mission and policy, which affect the collecting and distribution of visual data throughout the world. For example, Sally Stapleton, international photo editor for the AP, noted significant changes in the kinds of pictures the AP will "move," or send to members, over the last few years. The New York bureau will distribute more explicit photographs of violence victims today, as well as more explicit pictures accompanying a story on radical mastectomies (personal communication, 1998).

The Government

According to a public opinion poll released by the First Amendment Center at Vanderbilt University on July 4, 1999, people in the United States believe the press has too much freedom. The First Amendment to the U.S. Constitution states, "Congress shall make no law respecting an establishment of religion, or prohibiting the free exercise thereof; or abridging the freedom of speech, or of the press; or the right of the people peaceably to assemble, and to petition the government for a redress of grievances." Yet the Federal Communications Commission (FCC) regulates broadcasting and advertising, attendance at movie theaters is regulated according to suitability for age, and high school principals can prevent young journalists from publishing stories about drugs. Such controls are said to be in the public's interest. But who decides what is in the public's interest? The complexities of these issues are illustrated by an example from military control of press activities during the Gulf War. Visual journalists were prohibited from photographing coffins containing bodies of U.S. servicemen being loaded off air-cargo planes. Photographers also were carefully monitored on the battlefield in an effort to prevent images of bodies or the wounded from reaching the public. The concern was that seeing such pictures might dissuade Americans from supporting the war. The attack on Iraq was said to be in the public's interest. Who was controlling what truth would reach whom and was in whose interest?

Politicians win campaigns based on their staffs' abilities to manipulate the press, and thereby to manipulate public opinion. A well-planned photo opportunity or one visible slipup can make or break a candidate's chances for success. When elected, those same politicians continue to manipulate public imagery to gain support for legislation—for better or worse.

Consider also that government entities regularly rely on visual evidence in the courts, in space exploration, in satellite surveillance. Photographs were significant in the O. J. Simpson criminal and civil trials, the National Aeronautics and Space Administration relies on photographic evidence secured by the Hubble Telescope, and the U.S. military maintains a global satellite surveillance system. All are forms of visual evidence, although in each case, the interpretation and use of the evidence—in other words, what becomes known as "visual truth"—must pass through a set of gates, some as extensive as the locks of the Panama Canal. "Government's truth," even in a so-called free society, is then a primary source of public manipulation.

Economic Interests

One strain of the history of the press as a socially responsible entity points to the penny press of the mid-1800s. The U.S. public of that time apparently believed print publications carried the propaganda of elite, wealthy capitalists who could afford the six-cent newspaper. Alternative newspapers costing only a penny sprang up to carry the truth as voiced by the common man. We can draw rough parallels between the climate of public opinion that supported the growth of the penny press and the contemporary public opinion that spawned rapid growth of the Internet, zines, and culture jamming as ways to counter what people perceive to be a press dominated by corporate interests (Schneider, 1999). Aultschull (1984) maintained that contemporary media are "agents" for those who hold economic, political, and social power. Although the press may base its operations on a concept of social responsibility, in practice, the press often operates differently, producing content that reflects the economic interests of those in power. So, "economic interests'" truth is information that best results in profits.

Summary

Literature relevant to these issues is complex and broad, expressed according to particular theoretical viewpoints—in its own way a matter of "whose truth?" I have suggested that we think about the issue of visual truth by examining visual reportage as a form of human visual behavior within society and culture. In this manner, images of reportage are both agents and artifacts. They are agents in the sense that they are part of the cultural dialectic of formation, change, response, and so forth. They are artifacts in the sense that they tell us something about individuals, moments in time, and places for which we may no longer have other evidence.

When viewed in this manner, photojournalism becomes its own meaningful form of human visual behavior:

- People act and are photographed.
- Photographers look and photograph.
- Editors select.
- Societal institutions seek to control content of images.
- Audiences view, absorb, act, reject, and ignore.
- The conversation continues.

As an example, consider visual coverage of the moment when O.J. Simpson learned his criminal jury had determined him not guilty. Millions watched the moment live via television, even pausing while eating lunch or conversing in order to witness the event. Photographers throughout the country documented public responses. At White gatherings, the response was often one of negative disbelief. At Black gatherings, the response was often one of surprised joy. To report public opinion fairly, newspapers had to run both responses, and a number of newspapers did so. Yet how often do newspapers run a photograph showing only one side of a story because the photograph is particularly strong in aesthetic values? And how often do those newspapers point out that the photograph shows only one side? How often does a videoclip showing only seconds of a complex event dominate newscasts? How often do newscasts repeatedly show the same clip, thus compounding its potential effects?

These concerns are matters of ethics:

- How we report.
- What we say we are reporting (Newton, 1983).

How anyone addresses those issues—be they subject, photographer, or viewer—is an issue of ethics involving the use of power. McQuail (1994) called for new social theory of the media that focuses on the interests of society as a whole. Any new social theory must encompass a strong and specific component regarding the nature of visual truth. The next chapter proposes one approach.

VISUAL REPORTAGE

In conclusion, one must consider a few hard questions regarding the role of visual reportage in society:

- How does photojournalism report, affect, construct, or cater to various truths?
- Does photojournalism overstimulate the vision instinct to the point that it no longer serves its function?
- Is photojournalism an idealistic myth? Are the images really about good reportage, or are they about selling newspapers or air time and contributing to the profits of owners of news organizations?
- Some photojournalists are willing to die for the sake of visual truth. Does that not mean something?

SOCIOBIOLOGY AND CRITICAL/CULTURAL THEORY

When we view a photograph of an emaciated victim of war or natural disaster, we participate in a form of human visual behavior. The image becomes, as Lutz and Collins (1993) termed it, an "intersection of gazes." Extend that concept beyond a critical/cultural approach into a sociobiological framework that includes critical/cultural concerns. What this means is that when someone views a photograph, he or she views in many roles: the voyeur interested in what a person looks like after going through a life trauma, an organism searching for information that might help it survive, a human being drawn through empathy to connect with another human via a visual equivalent, a consumer of the commodification of human suffering, a reader or viewer whom the publication wants to attract to increase advertising revenues, a member of one class or race or gender looking to confirm stereotypes of another, a pawn of politicians manipulating public attraction to the visual, or simply a member of the human species, witnessing something happening to another human being. Visual reportage in its ideal form records and presents information about the world in authentic ways. In everyday practice, it can be used as an instrument of power to convey and evoke other truths—or to suppress and manipulate truth. The issue of "whose truth" then become a matter for conscious reflection by everyone involved in the process of determining The Truth.

A LIVING VISUAL SYSTEM. High above the streets of Rockefeller Plaza in New York City, picture editors at the headquarters of the Associated Press gather, edit, and transmit photographs from and to their member news organizations around the world. Visual elements documented in the scene include the human body in female and male forms, newspaper type and imagery, books, clothing, logo designs, computer monitors, maps, television screens, furniture, physical space, and seven clocks keeping global time. (Photo by Julie Newton.)

CHAPTER 9

Toward an Ecology
of the Visual

Human visual behavior in the form of reportage, gesture, expression, art, theater, media, and virtual reality increasingly dominates human life. Recent scholarly literature in the humanities and social sciences tended to dismiss the visual as less significant than the verbal, the rational, or the physically experienceable. This chapter proposes an ecology of the visual in which human visual behavior is framed as its own form of human experience, with primal and symbolic components that affect and shape our lives in profound but often imperceptible ways. Visual reportage plays a key role in this human system.

CHAPTER 9

Toward an Ecology
of the Visual

New evidence in both the physical and social sciences indicates that the process of seeing and understanding is far more complex and far more critical to the shaping of consciousness and behavior than previously thought. As discussed in earlier chapters, what we perceive to be visually true is affected by many factors: who is doing the seeing—and whether anyone sees, how and why the seer looks, whom or what is seen, the context in which the seeing occurs, those who decide what will be used in what form, and the truth filters of individuals, media, commerce, and social institutions. Visual reportage is practiced both within what can be called the mainstream press and outside of it. Some independent photojournalists go about their work on their own terms—and using their own points of view.

How, then, can we grasp the complexity of the visual environment, which we create, in which we live and perceive, and on which we depend? One way to begin is simply to ask, how best to study the visual, in hopes of ultimately learning what *the visual* is.

Framing the principal question of study in such a manner helps to remove the more standard epistemological verbal veil, which attempts to translate the visual into or via the verbal. Additionally, asking how best to study the visual allows us to begin with the visual as a system in and of itself, rather than as a system that is less sophisticated than, supplementary to, dependent on, or equal to the verbal. The idea is to put the visual in front as a target of comprehension in and of itself, rather than as something to be examined in relation to the verbal. In so doing, we may find more fertile opportunities to discover a valid, reliable base for studying the visual. The goal is not to isolate the visual as scholars have tended to do with the verbal, but rather to bring the visual into the foreground while keeping an eye on how visual elements interact with other elements of communication.

Visual scholars, whose numbers in disciplines other than art have increased over the last decade, have for some time searched for a way to reframe the visual within a paradigm that is both inclusive and practical and that has the integrity of investigating the visual in visual ways. If we can hold aesthetic/semiotic/cultural concerns about the visual within a cultural frame, and perceptual/psychological/physiological concerns within a physiological frame, while remembering that none of these approaches can be completely isolated from the others, perhaps we can achieve some clarity about the role of the visual in human behavior. Then the task is to study how the cultural and physiological frames overlap and interact.

This call for synthesis in visual theory is consistent with recent analyses in other areas of communication theory. Consider, for example, Cooper's (1998) inventory of ethical issues in new technology effects, Rogers' (1998) "Anatomy of the Two Subdisciplines of Communication Study," and Craig's (1999) "Communication Theory as a Field." Craig called for a cohesive effort to address the disparate field of communication theory (he noted 249 theories) under a central rubric: "the social practice of communication" (p. 153). Similarly, visual theorists would do well to look beyond such disciplinary categories as art history, visual perception, or cognitive science, to relate their contributions to the broader scope of knowledge about the visual.

This chapter proposes to study human visual activity as an integrated cultural/physiological system—an ecology of the visual. As a highly public form of visual behavior, photojournalism plays a key role in that system. The ecology resonates from the central postulate that the visual is more primal—in the sense of being core to human behavior—than it is symbolic. The tendency of theorists to focus on the symbolic, while necessarily and fruitfully exploring visual codes, has occluded the study of physiological aspects of human visual behavior. Balancing our study of the symbolic with a focus on the primal brings into better perspective the role of human visual behavior within the interdependent system of living things. That, in turn, will help us position visual reportage within that system.

An ecology of the visual refers to a synergy that can help explain the relationships between human beings' visual behaviors and their visual environments. Thinking ecologically is thinking visually, a means for considering an amorphous, unmanageable entity as a complex whole. Visual ecology includes how images impact individuals and their realities and, in turn, how each impacts the whole. What if we thought of the visual as systemic, with waste, order and chaos, stasis and dynamism, predictability and unpredictability? We could, for example, term a great deal of advertising *visual waste* because of the way it uses mass communication to establish unrealistic and harmful values. How then do we dispose of it? Can it be recycled to nourish the human system in some way? One possible answer is the contemporary practice of "culture jamming," which uses bits of a commonly viewed or heard entity, such as an advertisement or popular song, to create an inverse statement (Schneider, 1999). An example is a billboard image of Joe Camel connected to an intravenous tube, which presumably is feeding him cancer-stopping chemicals. In subverting an icon of popular culture, culture jammers recycled Joe Camel the cigarette pusher into Joe Camel the victim of his own behavior.

Here is another example of examining an occurrence within the context of a visual ecology.

In the summer of 1995, I observed a phenomenon of human visual behavior. While reviewing my design students in the principles of visual perception, I recited figure–ground theory, illustrating the concept with a classic face–vase drawing.

Pointing to the projected image, I noted a familiar phenomenon: "You see, you cannot see the face and the vase at the same time. Human beings cannot simultaneously see figure and ground."

Fortunately, I looked away from the example long enough to notice puzzled looks on my students' faces.

"You can't see the face and the vase at the same time … can you?" I asked them.

The students believed they could, in fact, simultaneously discern the face and the vase. With a little practice I could, too—or at least I thought I could. On hearing this story, media psychologist Jennings Bryant (personal communication, 1999) suggested that our eyes were making the perceptual shifts between figure and ground so rapidly that we could not discern the shifts.

Is it possible, however, that my students and I had just become aware of a new stage in the evolution of visual perception? I could not help but recall a presentation by designer Nigel Holmes (1994), who pointed out the increasing tendency of younger designers to layer elements in what seemed to older designers an illegible fashion. My own teenagers had no difficulty reading such designs in *Wired* and *Ray Gun*. A reasonable guess is that new developments in three-dimensional imagery, the proliferation of visual media, and the development of virtual reality technology are evidence of some kind of shift in our visual perception abilities, evolving either cultur-ally or biologically or both. Yet these advances still are overshadowed by criticism of the visual as "the merely visual," as "simulation," as "merely sig-nification," and by concerns that we are regressing to a preliterate existence. In the 1994 book *Finitude's Score: Essays for the End of the Millennium*, Ronell succinctly articulated the critical position when she wrote of "the vanish-ing of the experienceability of the world" (p. ix).

It is time to conceptualize an alternative to the idea of the "loss of experienceability." What if the human organism has moved into new terri-tory, new forms of "experienceability"? What if McLuhan were right: We cannot yet comprehend how we as cultural and physiological organisms negotiate those realms? What if humans have possessed these visual capa-bilities all along, but our rational minds are only now developing to the point that we can consciously discern them?

This tendency to dismiss or to discount what we do not understand is, ironically, hardly characteristic of an enlightened time, but rather of an enfrightened time. It is as if we are scaring ourselves with our own abilities. One root of our problem has been trying to study the visual using verbal systems of analysis. This concern is not a new idea. Many of those working in visual studies have noted the difficulty (or even the apparent impossibil-ity!) of discussing or conceptualizing the visual using words. But we have attacked the problem from the wrong perspective. We have tried to translate "the visual" into "the verbal." The concept of *visual literacy* is a case in point, as others have noted. Additionally, the most influential literature in con-temporary visual theory focuses on deconstructing visual messages, cri-tiquing the visual as a subversive force, trying to analyze either the relationship of the visual to the verbal, or considering potential effects (usu-ally viewed negatively) of the visual on our species and our culture. Fur-thermore, most of this literature is expressed verbally, albeit with illustrations.

What if we reframe the visual within a paradigm that is both inclusive and practical, that draws on the most convincing literature available from a variety of disciplines, and that has the integrity to investigate the visual in valid ways? The goal is an interrelated, networked system of human visual behavior that we can then break down into small parts for study while maintaining a view of the whole. The goal is not to produce an oversimplified, reductive theory, but just the opposite—to produce a theory that calls attention to the complexity and interdependency of various aspects of human visual behavior within the broader view of living systems.

SUPPORTING THEORY

A number of related ideas support studying the visual within an ecological framework.

The core cultural/physiological frame underlying the ecology is supported by several strains of thought, most significantly living-systems theory (Capra, 1996), sociobiology (Ornstein, 1991; Shoemaker, 1996; Wilson, 1992, 1998), nonverbal communication (Knapp & Hall, 1997; J. Streeck, personal communication, 1996; Wilson, 1998), cognitive studies (Barry, 1997b; Bechara et al., 1997; LeDoux, 1986; Moriarty, 1996; Sperry, 1973; Williams, 1995, 1999), mass communication (McLuhan, 1951, 1964; McLuhan & Powers, 1989), social constructionism (Berger & Luckmann, 1967), symbolic interactionism (Blumer, 1969), and art history (Foster, 1998; Stafford, 1996, 1997),

Although each theoretical approach is complex and subtly nuanced, space allows only a cursory review of a few tenets from each. They resonate an *I see, therefore I am—I am, therefore, I see* (Williams, 1999) perspective when applied to visual theory. The most relevant themes are summarized next.

Living Systems

Systems thinking focuses on the complex, integrated network of life, whether that life be a single cell or a social community. *Ecology*, a concept central to living-systems theory, focuses on the interrelatedness of organisms and their environments in a cycling, nonhierarchical network of networks (Capra, 1996, p. 33). Capra, a physicist, described the deep-ecology paradigm as a holistic worldview that "recognizes the fundamental interdependence of all phenomena and the fact that, as individuals and societies, we are all embedded in (and ultimately dependent on) the cyclical process of nature" (p. 6). The basic principles of ecology include interdependence, recycling, partnership, flexibility, diversity, and sustainability (p. 304).

Sociobiology

Wilson (1998), the pioneer sociobiologist, wrote, "In order to grasp the human condition, both the genes and culture must be understood, not separately in the traditional manner of science and the humanities, but together, in recognition of the realities of human evolution" (p. 163). As noted in chapter 2, Shoemaker (1996) argued that humans' need to survey their environments evolved biologically and culturally into contemporary news media practice. Ornstein (1991), a psychologist, argued that humankind has advanced as far as it can via an unconscious evolutionary path. He suggested that humans can consciously influence their evolution toward ever more sophisticated ways of knowing.

Cognitive Studies

Moriarty (1996), a visual communication theorist, argued that visual communication is a primary system equal to the verbal system. Williams (1999), Barry (1997b), Ornstein (1997), and others agreed that knowledge is derived through two predominant processes, which are primarily directed by the right hemisphere (visual/spatial) and the left hemisphere (verbal/logical) of the brain (Jaynes, 1976/1990; Sperry, 1973). Bechara et al. (1997) and LeDoux (1986) found convincing evidence that visual cognition stimulates the unconscious mind to motivate or guide behavior before the rational mind is consciously engaged. Williams (1999) suggested that we think of the two processes as rational and intuitive, arguing that our inability to comprehend the synergy of the processes within the human organism has led to an overemphasis on the rational in contemporary society. Williams (1999) proposed *omniphasism*, a theory of cognitive balance. He wrote:

> The development of a holistic educational model that embraces a balanced curriculum, developing both Intuitive and Rational Intelligences as equivalent and complementary, has the potential to prepare a more balanced, fully educated, self-determining individual, less susceptible to manipulative media influences and better prepared to apply classroom experiences to life experiences in ways that generate balance within the individual and thus within the cultural systems subsequently developed. (p. 164)

His holistic theory encompassed dreams, visions, meditations, and internal imagery, as well as physical sight, and supported the idea that media-generated imagery operates on unconscious levels much as dreams and meditation do.

Barry (1997a, 1997b) maintained that humans possess *visual intelligence*, which uses visual mosaic logic to synthesize information and transcend rational thinking. Barry (1997b) wrote:

> The relationships that arrest our attention within the environment and the principles that govern the universe are not at odds. Rather they are reflections of the same profoundly deep rhythms of existence. These nonlinear relationships cannot be expressed in a straight line on a graph. A higher, multidimensional logic and wider perceptual view is necessary to begin to understand the world. This is the essence of visual intelligence. (p. 337)

Barry also based her theory on brain research that indicates visual information bypasses the neocortex, the site of conscious processing, and moves from the eye to the thalamus, and then straight to the amygdala, which promotes behavior before the neocortex is informed (LeDoux, 1986). Barry (1997a) made the provocative suggestion that most of what we consider rational thinking is our mind explaining and justifying to itself what our visual intelligence has already processed.

Nonverbal Behavior

Wilson (1998) wrote about "visual nonlinguistic communication," noting humans' predilection to processing audiovisual information (p. 152). Streeck (personal communication, 1996) stressed that calling visual behavior "nonverbal behavior" biases research to frame the visual in negative relation to the verbal. A specialist in gestures, Streeck suggested the term *visual behavior* instead. Knapp and Hall (1997) noted that the definition of nonverbal communication as "communication effected by means other than words" is useful but inadequate (p. 5). They stressed thinking of "behaviors as existing on a continuum with some behaviors overlapping two continua" (p. 32).

Media

McLuhan (1964) argued that humans extend themselves via technology and that the way content is delivered affects that content. A television, for example, can be considered a multimedia, global extension of human com-

munication. Furthermore, the way television records and transmits information influences the way humans perceive that information.

Social Construction of Reality

McLuhan (1951) articulated the theme of what would become known as
social constructionism in his early book *The Mechanical Bride*, which
explored the power of media to influence our thoughts and behaviors.
Berger and Luckmann formalized the theory in their 1966 classic explicat-
ing the sociology of knowledge. The core idea is that truth is something
people construct in the process of living in a world that is constructing
them (McLuhan & Powers, 1989).

Symbolic Interactionism

Blumer (1969) believed that humans act toward others and information in
meaningful ways. He conceived of this interaction as core to human behavior, warning that theorists' emphasis on the signification level of behavior
veiled what he called the translation of human activity from the physical to
the visual and from the internal to the external.

Art History

Stafford (1996, 1997), frustrated with attempts by linear thinkers to draft
theories of vision, argued that visual theory should be done by visual theorists. Reviewing the state of visual criticism, Stafford (1997) addressed the
"radical epistemological, pedagogical, political, and organizational consequences" of the "shift from linear text to overall pattern." Stafford suggested
that a cross-disciplinary approach to "an expertise in imaging" would not
only show "how vision matters," but prepare an indispensable multiskilled
individual who "would give the lie to the ubiquitous sophism that anything
pictorial does only negative work in our society" (pp. 214–216).

Foster (1988) pinpointed the dynamic nature of visual studies when he
argued that visual theorists must constantly seek "alternative visualities" and
"critique the critique."

A few definitions can move us further toward formulating an ecology of
the visual.

- Symbolic: Being used for or regarded as representing something else.
- Primal: First, original, primeval, of first importance.

- Ecology: Deals with the relations between organisms and their environments.
- Environment: Organisms' milieu (which includes the resulting interdependency between people and institutions).
- Ecological niche: The space, role, and function an organism occupies or fulfills in relation to other organisms.
- Behavior: The aggregate of observable responses and activities of organisms in their interrelationships.
- Cognition: The act or process of knowing; perception, knowledge.

Now, recall the main idea of chapter 2, that humans have a vision instinct. Considering vision as a type of instinctual behavior within a larger system of human perception, which in turn is within a larger system of activity, focuses attention on vision's first-order aspects rather than on its symbolic aspects. We might even go so far as to argue that the symbolic also is primal in that the symbolic also is part of the ecology of human behavior. In that sense, media are primal. As extensions of humans, as mechanisms through which we extend our behavior, the symbolic can be understood as experiential, as significant to human behavior as the beatings of our hearts. In this way, we can frame media as part of us, not things external to us that operate on us, but originating *out* of us, both in our creation of them and in our responses to them.

Focusing on the symbolic aspects of the visual detracts us from considering the core role vision plays in the lives of human organisms. Recall that Crick (1994), the DNA pioneer, looked to visual perception in his search for the key to consciousness. Is it possible that nothing we do is symbolic—that it just *is*? Our capacity to think and act in different ways has caused us to try to outthink our own system. But we cannot outthink our system because we are immersed within it. We think we live in a symbolic world—yet that thinking clouds our ability to feel the corporeality of human living. We are still so heavily influenced by the concept of a mind-body dichotomy that we cannot conceive of mind as body. Crick did so, however, relating everything we think we are to neurons firing and connecting. That is what I mean by *primal*. I'm trying to avoid the abstract, if that is possible when using words—to concentrate on conscious existence. Buddhism teaches that there is no inner and outer—only *is*. Postmodernism has tried to call attention to this idea by disrupting the supposed tight logic of the scientific method, modernism, realism, and reason. But postmodernism falls short of its goal, enmeshing itself in its own conundrum of the personal subjective (Best & Kellner, 1991). Therein, however, lies this *primal* to which I refer—at once core to the system and only a small part of the system. Postmodernism loses itself in its false focus on the symbolic as similitude. These so-called symbols are what *is* as much as what they supposedly stand for—they are as real as anything else. And they are not just manifestations—they *are*.

For example, consider the fictional television character of Murphy Brown—fictional, yet influential enough to lead politicians to blame her for the rise in unwed pregnancies. Yet she *is*—what some would call a symbolic form—a constructed entity representing the 1990s professional woman. Consider for a moment that Brown is real—as real as anyone is real—a construction, yes, as we all are, and who lives in a constructed world, as we all do—and simultaneously a creator of her own life, of a way of living. She came to be as part of our system of living, and she disappeared into the system. If the visual is constructed via our brains, and brains are real, then the visual must be made of organic entities that are as real as our bodies. We simply have not made the connection because we are so stuck on what we assume to be humankind's ability to communicate on a symbolic level. We keep trying to distinguish ourselves from other organisms, when that effort in and of itself is a construction of hierarchical ways of thinking. The visual is not merely symbolic—it *is*. Any symbol we create *is*, just as much as anything else *is*, as real as anything else. Consider the words on this page—the ink is tangible, as is the paper. Our minds see the words, and neurons fire, causing us to react, to remember, to respond. Focusing on the visual as representation subverts the opportunity to experience anew in present consciousness.

This is what "the loss of experienceability of the world" really means. Focusing on symbolic meaning diminishes our experience of that meaning. Consider Orlan, for example, a human being who pushed bodily experience into a new level of reflexive intensity (Dodd, 1998; Fulfs, 1999). As part of Orlan's performance art a surgeon sculpted her body into a unique form (*Synthetic pleasures*, 1996). Determined to exercise her conscious will over her body rather than allow it to succumb to the will of others, Orlan moves painfully and acutely within the present (Orlan, 1999). Consider also how we learn to become more conscious of the present: through meditation, visualization, looking inward. The present *is*.

■ ■ ■

Once upon a time 60,000 years ago, Human thought her first thought. Maybe she remembered the warmth of the sun on her face or the rabbit hopping behind a tree. She knew no difference between thought and the warmth, or between her memory's image and her sighting the rabbit. She thought, she imagined, envisioned, and acted. Her self and body, mind and eye worked in reflexive tandem, smoothly transferring information to keep her alive and to give her pleasure.

This chapter draws heavily on the concept of a vision instinct—the perceptual mechanism for knowing via the observable and the imagined. Scientists and philosophers, theologians and mythologists, poets and painters have for centuries explored, discovered, and imagined what sight is and does. And for those who, for whatever reason, cannot gather light rays from outside their bodies for their brains to interpret, the vision instinct still operates—for the instinct is about far more than the body's response to external visual stimuli. The vision instinct is about the primordial ability of human creatures to see within their own bodies, to live within and without, to dream without seeing outside the body, to imagine the not visible and to make it so, to create the uncreated and to create again.

A central thesis of this chapter is that seeing is the intersection of consciousness, the place where the body's physical responses to the unique explosion of energy without and within meet as thought. A corollary thesis is that thought itself is visual, that even words have their roots in images and would not exist had the mind not created them from visual response to light, sound, motion, touch, and smell. A second corollary is that the traditional split between verbal and visual symbols is a hegemonic construction that neatly supports a dichotomous understanding of the rational and the intuitive. This construction has been fostered by Western modernism and dominant systems that distrust and discount anything not clearly explainable or controllable. The word *vision* is at once ambiguous and inclusive, encompassing physical seeing as well as imaginative seeing and insight (which, according to Crick, is also physical). *Instinct*, too, is a key word in its inclusive relating of an involuntary aspect of human perception. So, the vision instinct can be defined as a human creature's ability to perceive external stimuli, as well as to create new stimuli within. For the sighted, this means observing the observable—as with one definition of light, the visible part of the electromagnetic spectrum—and using those experiences to imagine in the mind's eye. For the nonphysically sighted (can we come up with a better word that does not operate as a negative in relation to sight?), it means experiencing physical stimuli with means that are not dependent on light (Gregory, 1979).

The ecology of the visual frames human visual activity as an integrated cultural/physiological system, that is more primal in the sense of being core than it is symbolic, and that is evolutionary in nature. Consider this suggestion from Ronell (1994):

> It would be hardly sufficient to assimilate television to the Frankfurt School's subsumption of it under the regime of the visual, which is associated with mass media and the threat of a culture of fascism. This threat always exists, but I would like to consider the way television in its couple with video offers a picture of numbed resistance to the unlacerated regimes of fascist media as it mutates into forms of video and cybernetic technology, electronic reproduction, and cybervisual technologies. (p. 313)

The 19th and 20th centuries were a time of visual exploration and extension. If thinking is being ... seeing (in the broad sense of the word) is being and being is seeing. The images we create and to which we respond are one way we process the emotions and ideas exploding along the neural pathways and immunological viaducts of our beings. As the earth spins 1,000 miles per hour, as it travels around the sun, as both spiral through space, so spin the cells in our bodies throughout a resonating system of corporeality. While we pine nostalgically for a more naive, nonreflective state that supposedly was more experiential and less simulative, we are, via our visual systems, simultaneously embracing the primordial intuitive, lifting it once again to the surface of consciousness. We are in the process of seizing our evolution from centuries of nonreflexive marking of time (Ornstein, 1991) toward another level of Enlightenment. Now is the time for theory that employs inclusive, empowering paradigms set forth as potential locations for human actualization. Rather than condemn the developments of the 19th and 20th centuries to dark criticism and hyperbolic nay-saying, we can forge ahead, considering an ecology of the visual as an integrated cultural/physiological system that focuses on the prevailing inventiveness of the human spirit.

WHAT IS THE ROLE OF PHOTOJOURNALISM IN AN ECOLOGY OF THE VISUAL?

Visual reportage is a complex extension of the human instinct to scan our environments for survival, for information, and for expression. Photojournalists play various roles in this regard: eyewitnesses, watchdogs, voyeurs, storytellers, artists, participant observers, visual social scientists. They gather visual artifacts with cameras for dissemination to others, who, in turn, survey the artifacts, using them for survival, for information, and for expression. The artifacts then take on their own physicality. The following section uses visual ecology to examine the making and use of a particularly disturbing image of photojournalism.

ON BECOMING AN ARTIFACT IN A VISUAL SYSTEM

When I boarded the plane that would take me to Arlington, Texas, a number of years ago, I thought I was prepared for what I would see: images of death, human suffering, war … the typical—for lack of a better term—award-winning images of photojournalism. But when I saw "Photojournalism Since Vietnam," an exhibition of work by Contact Press photographers (1992), I was far from prepared for the lightning bolt that would strike my personal perception of visual reality.

When I walked into the gallery, a place for viewing art, the large size of the images on the walls, the colors of blood and sunshine, the juxtaposition of life celebrations with acts of dying jarred my senses. I was particularly awed by several images:

- The grimace of a charred man—his teeth … eyes … skull … the visceral communication of bodily remains, of a life gone, his body left to communicate to those still living.
- A woman soaking half a leg in a pan.
- A man thrusting his blood-draped hands toward the camera.
- A girl's eyes staring from her death trap.

I had to look. I had to look again. I had to turn away.

I felt indignation at the violence and at the violation of human life. I felt that indignation on several levels—on the level of the event itself, on the level of making the photograph, and on the level of violating life still further by putting such images on a gallery wall for us to view while partaking of wine and cheese.

I wished the captions carrying words of time and place, and sometimes names, were not there, for I found myself reading the words rather than the images, and that act itself somehow took away from the significance of the human forms held in horror or glory within the borders of the photographs.

A short time after viewing the exhibit, I heard photojournalist Kenneth Jarecke (1992) tell his story of covering the Gulf War. Jarecke spoke of taking his by-then-well-known picture (Jarecke & Cervenka, 1992) of the incinerated Iraqi soldier and of his determination to get the image into print because of his conviction that the world needed to see what he himself had seen. The integrity of Jarecke's heart struck my own heart like lightning and enabled me to see the image as a kind of consecration of the life of the person it documented, rather than a photographic violation. As Lindaman said, "One of life's most fulfilling moments occurs in that split-second when the familiar is suddenly transformed into the dazzling aura of the profoundly new" (as cited Burnham, 1990, p. 231).

Jarecke's photographs (1992) and words transformed what had become a familiar personal philosophy into a profoundly new understanding of visual reportage. Those who regularly face the dangers of that "other world out there"—the world of war, death, famine, poverty that is so huge and is usually "out of sight, out of mind" to those of us who live within our comparatively comfortable U.S. culture—may think me horribly naive. I can hear some of them saying, "Why else would we do this?" But for someone who has for years wrestled with the rationale underlying photojournalism, the issues involved had been irreconcilable. I began thinking of several contradictory terms: *literal* and *abstract, identification* and *anonymity, real life* and *life represented, death* and the *representation of death, news* and *art, violation* and *sanctification*. Each word—although expressed with an opposite—describes the image. All are true.

Consider the words and their meanings (*Webster's*, 1967):

- *Literal:* Adhering to fact, exact, verbatim.
- *Abstract:* Disassociated from any specific instance, expressing a quality apart from an object, theoretical, impersonal.
- *Identification:* Evidence of identity, sameness in all that constitutes the objective reality of a thing.
- *Anonymity:* Having no name, of unknown or unnamed source or origin.
- *Real:* Genuine, actual.
- *Representational:* Serves as a sign or image of, to typify, standing or acting for another.
- *Death:* The permanent cessation of all vital functions, the end of life.

- *Life:* The quality that distinguishes a vital and functional being from a dead body or purely chemical matter; the sequence of physical and mental experiences that make up the existence of an individual; spiritual existence transcending physical death; a vital or living being, specifically: person; an animating and shaping force or principle; animation, spirit.
- *News:* A report of events.
- *Art:* The conscious use of skill, taste, and creative imagination in the production of aesthetic objects, also, works so produced; a branch of learning.
- *Violation:* Infringement, transgression, an act of irreverence or desecration, profanation, interruption, disturbance, ravishment, rape.
- *Sanctification:* To devote to a purpose with deep solemnity or dedication, to make inviolate or venerable.

Applying these terms to the image takes the analysis further around the ecological circle. The incinerated man in Jarecke's noted photo was a literal being who had existed; his body was real and genuine. His visual equivalent still exists. In its realism, the photograph seems to identify—indeed, the image does have the detail to identify the human gesture of agony. But we do not know the human's name. In the translation from living human to dead body through the process of war and from body to image equivalent through the process of reportage, a man became an icon.

The body itself shows a human form after death, transfixed at the moment of death. The body so convey a living person in fear and agony that we also see—or intuit—life.

The image was taken as reportage. Humans also made it art.

The violation? The killing was a violation.

Taking the picture was a violation.

The publication and exhibition were violations.

We furthered the violation by staring at the image and by objectifying it in lectures and essays.

Yet the picture preserves, helps us remember the value of a human life—and in so doing the picture sanctifies.

The key to whether the photograph violates or sanctifies or both is in the act of beholding—in the hearts, minds, eyes of the witnesses—be they voyeurs or beholders. How we look, how we use, edit, view, store the image of the creature who once was human, how we act—or do not act—on what we see, whether we see and feel ... or merely stare with curiosity, with vulture eyes, or, maybe worse, with empty eyes for the sake of looking itself—determine whether the photograph violates or sanctifies.

How can an image both violate and sanctify the person who reflected light? Thinking in the context of an ecology of the visual, begin a circle of thought with the death of the soldier—a violation of human life.

Certainly, most people can agree about the inappropriateness of this man's death. Evans (1992), the first editor to publish the photograph, even took some responsibility for the death, saying that in a way he had willed the man dead by supporting the Gulf War.

Move now to questioning the appropriateness of taking the photograph of his remains. A camera and lens are pointed and what remains of a body reflects light onto film. What right does any person have to the image of another? Journalists assume that right, take that right. I question the right as a given. On one level, taking the picture was a further violation of this human being and of anyone who cared about him.

Continue to follow the ecological circle through the process of news photography. The film is developed and the image is digitized and transmitted from the Middle East to the western world. The image appears on a computer monitor in pixilated form. Editors discuss whether to publish the image. They decide against it. The image is too grotesque. It will be months before the world casts eyes on the soldier's image.

Then, finally, England saw him. And then the United States. And then the man's image was printed in magazines and newspapers, again translated into black-on-white or four-color dots to be viewed with respect—or horror or disgust or disdain, or, perhaps the worst of all, cool, quick observation and dismissal before it was tossed into the recycle bin or used to wrap the garbage.

I also question the appropriateness of publishing the photograph on the cover of the brochure highlighting an exhibition. I question the appropriateness of exhibiting works of reportage in an art gallery with an opening reception at which wine and hors d'oeuvres are served. And I especially abhor the practice of putting the image on a large screen for glib or esoteric talk, as it was during the opening symposium, and as it was during my own lecture closing the exhibition.

The image will always be the image of what remained of a human life, and in that sense it has become the remains of that life and should be respected as such.

But here is where you can begin to close the circle of thought.

Not being seen is a violation. To have died such a death and be unseen is like another death, akin to having never existed.

Furthermore, is *any* site appropriate for viewing such an image? An art gallery is in some ways a far more appropriate place to show this image than a newspaper or magazine. Viewers generally hold a measure of respect for work on gallery walls and often take time to contemplate the work. Sometimes the pictures in a gallery are so large that it is difficult to avoid the reality trapped within them. A brochure promoting an exhibition also calls necessary attention to viewing the images in a serious, reflective manner.

But newspaper and magazine pages can be appropriate sites for viewing, too. Images in the newspaper and magazine may come to us whether or not we want them with our coffee. And many more people see them—whether or not they want to. At least publishing the images increases the possibility that more people will care about others in the world.

The photograph itself, the newspaper page, and the gallery wall further violate human life by translating that life into a form that can be tossed aside.

But the body itself gives a *person* visible form. Published or exhibited images can do that, too. They can sanctify even as they violate. We have the power to sanctify if we look as beholders, or to violate if we look as voyeurs. What gives the viewer—whether photographer, editor, curator, or reader—such awesome power in a simple act of looking? The astounding power to sanctify or violate comes from the fact that the pictures convey something of the essence of the being who lived—and we can either connect with that life or not.

Photographs can convey the spirit, something of the immaterial entity of the person, as Elizabeth Barrett noted: In photographs we find "the very shadow of the person lying there fixed for ever!" Barrett said the "very sanctification of portraits" made her prefer a photograph of a person she loved to "the noblest artist's work ever produced" (letter to Mary Russell Mitford, 1843, cited in Gernsheim, 1962, p. 28). Gernsheim further noted that "the intimacy of the actual image of life was its chief attraction" (p. 28).

I went to the Contact Press exhibition with my long-held conviction that respecting human life and the human individual means respecting the human image. I had always agreed that there are pictures we must see, horrible pictures, but I had regularly questioned the need to photograph and to see dying or dead human beings as a general practice of photojournalism. I left Arlington, Texas, that fall with new-found convictions that photojournalists have an obligation to take, publish, and exhibit such pictures, and that the images are transformations of human beings that can communicate to living viewers.

Critical to remember is that through the process of photojournalism, a three-dimensional body becomes a two-dimensional equivalent that will be reproduced over and over and over again. Surviving through the photographic image may very well be the ultimate sacrifice—life laid forth for all to see— and for all to ignore—to pass by—to throw away—to forget?

Now, complete the ecological circle.

Images of death can lead to a cynical acceptance of death, to the erosion of human connectedness rather than the communication of respect for life and outrage at the ultimate disrespect for life—the taking of life.

Or they can lead to recognition of life itself.

A common theme in contemporary media criticism is the idea that people can no longer believe their eyes because of the erosion of image authenticity through misuse and technological alterations. But lack of credibility is not the most significant issue here. Challenging the credibility of visual reportage is a dodge: If we do not believe an image, we do not have to deal with its message. The problem is not the lack of credibility, but the sheer visibility of human cruelty. The issue is the erosion of compassion, the proliferation of human disconnection—even as we think we are connecting, albeit safely. How else can we explain the fact that we can view the image of a starving child and do nothing but throw it away as tomorrow's refuse? The irony is that the pictures are made so we can see what happened to people—but we glance and perhaps talk sadly about the individuals and then we walk away. We convert what happens to people into pixels and dot patterns, call it news, and reward it in competitions. We put the images in galleries and call them art. We put them on a big screen and make erudite remarks.

There is something truly horrible in all this—a second, and maybe even a third or fourth, slaying, with our eyes, and with the translation of human bodies into images for discussion.

But there is also something potentially redemptive in all of this: In a context of compassion, viewers can choose to connect with human beings they would never know except through the process of visual reportage.

When you look at images of human beings, particularly of human beings in pain, at the point of death, or who have died, you can choose to ponder for a moment the life you see before you. Remove the context of memory, words, and time, when you can, and let the images speak. Connect with the life preserved—even within death itself. Let the human souls preserved or kidnapped, reflected and attached by other human beings, speak forth, spring forth from the images that hold them forever.

Consider this dictionary definition of *photography*: "the art or process of producing images on a sensitized surface by the action of light or other radiant energy" (*Webster's*, 1979).

Images of human beings in pain or death can violate those persons if we discard our own humanity by turning away from theirs. But those images can sanctify life if we assume our full power as sentient beings connecting with others. Then the issue becomes a most appropriate one: how best to *act* on those connections. Therein lies the burden of *viewing* truth.

SUMMARY

The role of photojournalism in mediating reality becomes easily lost within the morass of the visual in contemporary life. Thinking of the visual ecologically, as an interdependent system of human visual activity, provides a framework for analyzing components of behavior. One can argue that humans are evolving toward increasingly sophisticated use of their most powerful sense—vision. As a component of a vast system, photojournalism's mandates to guard visual truth and to facilitate human connection and appropriate action become clearer. The next chapter presents a way to clarify further the analysis of visual reportage.

VISUAL DOCUMENT OR VISUAL THEFT? Tía María passes the afternoon near the front door of a furniture store, greeting customers as they come in from the heat. While working on a long-term documentary project in northern Mexico, I visited with Tía María every day on my way to buy a cold soda. Eventually, I took this candid of her sitting beneath a defenbachia. I knew the moment to be characteristic because I had seen it repeatedly. But when I showed Tía María the photograph, she was horrified, pointing to her felt houseshoes, her rolled-down stockings, the trash can, and her knitting as negative elements. As I began to look at the photograph more critically, I noticed my omniscient point of view from overhead. So, I asked her if we could make a photograph that documented her as she saw herself. See page 130 for the second portrait. (Photo by Julie Newton.)

CHAPTER 10

Translating the Visual

A major hindrance to any analysis of visual communication is the lack of appropriate terms to describe that which is not verbal. This chapter presents a continuum of human visual behavior to facilitate discussion of human visual interaction, particularly in regard to the behavior typical of photojournalism. Although the typology uses words, along with visual symbols, for human actions that are primarily visual, the attempted translation is necessary to facilitate understanding. The typology exemplifies ecological interpretation of the visual.

CHAPTER 10

Translating the Visual

Consider this scene.

An elderly woman sits in the same chair in the same storefront in a small town in Mexico at the same time every afternoon. She busies herself with knitting and with greeting customers as they enter the store.

A photographer passes by her every afternoon on her way to buy a soda. The photographer has lived in the area for two months by this time, and has taken few candid photographs in her effort to establish trust and good faith between herself and the community she has come to observe.

One afternoon, the photographer thinks to herself that she has established rapport with the elderly woman, that she knows the woman's activities are genuine, and that it is time to make a photographic record of her activities. So she snaps a picture with the woman unaware.

A few days later, the photographer returns with a print for the elderly woman to see. Much to her amazement, the woman is upset.

"But you sit here every day like this. I know this is what you always look like in this situation," the photographer tells her subject.

VISUAL EMBRACE OR VISUAL THEATER? Tía María assumes a pose with which she is more comfortable. She located herself on this couch, directly behind the site of the earlier photograph, in her family's furniture store. Tía María felt this photograph represented her more accurately (or at least more appropriately), portraying her as the proud matriarch of a wealthy family. Comparing this photograph with the first, I noticed that my point of view also had changed—for the second photograph, I positioned myself to look Tía María directly in the eye, a much more egalitarian interaction. But is this a visual document, as we might call the first photograph of Tía María? Is it a visual embrace between Tía María and me? Or is it visual theater by a now-aware subject? The image is all three. At the very least, the photograph documents how Tía María wants to be seen, a part of her personal character I probably would never have known otherwise.

The woman grimaces and says,

"But look, I'm wearing my houseshoes, and my stockings are rolled down, and I'm knitting and don't have on a nice dress, and I'm sitting by a trashcan."

"Yes, I see," says the photographer, suddenly noticing that her photographic point of view was from above the woman, looking down on her. "How would you like to be photographed?"

"I want to put on a nice dress and fix my hair and sit somewhere else," the woman says.

"Okay," says the photographer. "Let's meet here at 2 o'clock Tuesday, and you can show me how you want to be photographed."

Tuesday arrives and the two meet. This time, the elderly woman is adorned—in a new dress and shiny new stockings and shoes, and with carefully styled hair and makeup. She seats herself on a large couch, pulls her body up to its full sitting height, raises her chin proudly, and looks straight into the camera. This time, the photographer's gaze meets the woman's and they exchange a moment of time—and a visual record of the moment is made.

The resulting photograph (shown on p. 130) could hardly be more different than the first. Same woman—different person. And this time, she is pleased with the picture.

What has happened during these scenarios and what do the pictures mean? In the first photo, one can argue that the photographer recognized and captured an authentic moment, a visual document—or that the anthropologist had assumed the role of omniscient observer, along with the power to possess, dominate, construct how a person would be imaged. In the second photo, the woman has assumed more authority over her image, engaging in a visual embrace with the photographer—or did the two conspire to construct an inauthentic moment of visual theater? Documentary historian William Stott (1973) would argue that the second photo is just as authentic as the first, perhaps even more so, because it is evidence of how the woman sees her best self and wants to be seen, rather than evidence of someone else's view of her. But if both photos are authentic—or if both photos are highly manipulated during the picture-taking event—how do we discuss them, use them, read them? What we need is a means for discussing that which is not verbal or discrete, but rather, visual and evocative.

This chapter proposes a typology for analyzing human visual behavior. The typology draws on behaviors occurring in photojournalism, documentary photography, and visual social science—because of their intended relation to the real—to ground normative and practical issues in visual interaction. One goal of the typology is to facilitate the study of visual behavior by offering visual and verbal shortcuts to aid the analysis of visual behavior. A second goal is to further the discussion of visual interaction as a form of behavior with consequences beyond representational issues. The typology therefore locates human visual behavior along a continuum of communicative action ranging from visual embrace through visual suicide.

The typology exemplifies how an ecology of the visual can be developed by working through certain kinds of visual behavior as part of an overall system. A key part of a visual ecology is how people interact visually; photojournalism is a highly public form of visual interaction that can be hauntingly intimate or coldly impersonal.

Important to note at this point is that observer–observed practices and "reality-type imaging" of human beings regularly occur—in everyday life, in media, and in visual social science. These activities continue, regardless of whether we agree on the nature of reality or the meaning of a photograph, or who is observing whom with what purpose and power, or even if an observation should occur at all. Further, these activities often create tangible evidence, via photographs, videotape, film, and digital forms, of the seemingly intangible behavior of human beings in interaction (Snyder & Allen, 1982; Wagner, 1979). The "evidence" is gathered, edited, preserved, and disseminated via such disparate means as family albums, news media, film, and scholarly publications. The selected images then invite interaction with readers and viewers, exponentially engendering various levels of visual communication. Although the evidence of the original interaction may be disseminated to mass audiences, human response is necessarily personal and interpersonal. Here the theory behind the typology begins, locating human visual behavior beyond the representational as its own form of interaction with identifiable patterns and effects.

HUMAN VISUAL BEHAVIOR

The concept of human visual behavior was introduced in chapters 2 and 3 as fundamental to this book. Chapter 9 discussed human visual behavior in terms of an ecology of the visual. This chapter examines the concept once more, focusing on ways to analyze the behavior. The term *human visual behavior* shelters this discussion for several reasons. Some are self-evident: *human*, as opposed to the visual behavior of other creatures of this earth; *visual*, rather than nonverbal; *behavior*, rather than communication. However, using the term *human* limits the types of visual behavior to be studied.

Although visual behavior of other living things may share characteristics with human behavior, and we know of at least one chimpanzee who has consciously made a photographic self-portrait (Patterson & Cohn, 1978), our focus on photojournalism emphasizes human activity. *Visual* is more difficult to argue. Communication studies typically use such terms as *nonverbal behavior* and *nonverbal communication*. As noted in chapters 2 and 9, gesture expert Jürgen Streeck (personal communication, 1994) suggested that the term *human visual behavior* replace *nonverbal behavior* in order to shift attention to the visual rather than to that which is defined via a negative relationship to the verbal. The term *visual* behavior also is preferable to the term *image acts*, because image is so readily associated with representational issues. Similarly, visual *behavior* is preferable to visual *communication* because behavior focuses attention on actions, whereas communication focuses attention on meaning. Note that human visual behavior can be external or internal, meaning that people can visually act on the basis of something outside of themselves, such as someone else or a photograph, or on the basis of interior visual activity, such as imagining or dreaming, that may not be observable to others unless acted on externally. Human communication is a form of human behavior.

Figure 3.1 presented a general model of a photographic event, which occurs between subject and photographer, and a viewing event, which occurs among subject, photographer, and viewer via the photograph. Note that context, which includes time, place, culture, and medium, is critical at all levels.

IDENTITY

Although I would like to position this discussion outside of the conundrum of postmodern debates regarding self and other, human visual behavior necessarily involves observers and observed. Significant to note, however, is that neither observers nor observed are "separate populations, one of producers and another of consumers, or one of objects and another of spectators," but rather parts of a dual self that is both "producer and consumer" (Bakewell, 1998, p. 28). Nor are they always oppositional, but are better served by examination as relational. The development of a concept of self as both actor and object (Cooley, 1902/1956; Mead, 1913, 1934) is perhaps best expressed in Blumer's (1969) articulation of symbolic interactionism, an approach to studying human group life and human conduct. Blumer argued that symbolic interactionism entails three premises: that people act toward things on the basis of the meanings the things have for them, that the meaning of such things is derived from social interaction, and that these meanings are negotiated through an interpretative process by people as they deal with things they encounter. *Things*, in Blumer's theory, can be anything a person might encounter: animate or inanimate, conceptual or structural. For the purposes of this volume, *things* could refer to either photographer or subject, editor or photograph, viewer or medium, and so forth.

Also key to the discussion here is Blumer's (1969) assertion that social interaction is "of vital importance in its own right" (p. 8). Blumer maintained that the process of social interaction forms human conduct rather than merely serving "as a means or a setting for the expression or release of human conduct" (p. 8). If, indeed, interaction between individuals is substantive, such behavior is significant, in and of itself, not merely as a manifestation of the interaction. And although Blumer argued for the existence of an obdurate, empirical world outside of the observer, and he believed the "world of reality" exists only in human experience and in the forms in which we see the world, "this does not shift 'reality,' as so many conclude, from the empirical world to the realm of imagery and conception" (p. 22). Blumer wrote, "One errs if he thinks that since the empirical world can exist for human beings only in terms of images or conceptions of it, therefore reality must be sought in images or conceptions independent of an empirical world" (p. 22).

Blumer's ideas can be applied to the current discussion by interpreting the interaction between a photographer and subject as substantive in and of itself, resulting still and moving images as meaningful bases for interaction, subsequent viewers or observers of the imaged person as both objects and actors engaged in visual behavior, and so forth. Such applications are supported by theoretical trends in both communication and anthropology. Carey (1988), a communication theorist, wrote that "media of communication are not merely instruments of will and purpose but definite forms of life: organisms, so to say, that reproduce in miniature the contradictions in our thought, action, and social relations" (p. 9). Carey asserted that technology itself is a cultural expression of "the very outlooks and aspirations we pretend it merely demonstrates" (p. 9). Further, Carey defined *culture* as the meaning people "discover in their experience" (p. 44). "What is called the study of culture also can be called the study of communications, for what we are studying in this context are the ways in which experience is worked into understanding and then disseminated and celebrated (the distinctions, as in dialogue, are not sharp)" (p. 44). Considering human visual communication a "form of life" inseparable from culture locates its function beyond representation within the realm of interactions among human organisms and also places it solidly within an ecological interpretation.

This relatively new understanding of communication is consistent with a growing perspective in visual social science. Ruby (1997), for example, wrote that visual anthropology itself deals "with all aspects of the visible world from the vantage point afforded by theories of culture and communication" (p. 3). What is needed, MacDougall (1997) argued, is to suspend "anthropology's dominant orientation as a discipline of words" and to rethink "certain categories of anthropological knowledge in the light of understandings that may be accessible only by nonverbal means" (p. 292). MacDougall (1997) called for the building of "an intellectual foundation for visual anthropology by enabling a shift from word-and-sentence-based anthropological thought to image-and-sequence-based anthropological thought" (p. 292).

Photojournalism is a form of visual anthropology. Photojournalists study humankind through their reportage; they are professional observers. Anthropologists may bristle at this assertion, arguing that journalists are not social scientists, but the best journalists are indeed social scientists. As noted in chapter 4, photojournalists observe, participate, record, analyze, immerse themselves in the culture of the observed, report what they find, and continue to observe.

Making the shift from the verbal to the visual as an intellectual base of one's studies is difficult—precisely because social scientists more often are well practiced in verbal analysis, rather than visual analysis, and because they continue to conceive of the visual as representational, rather than method or behavior. Many communication scholars also continue their research as if verbal communication were the most salient, even though popular media have shifted from verbal to visual as technology has transformed word-based media into forms whose power is rooted in the visual.

A personal vignette illustrates the point. During a meeting of journalism faculty who were examining scholarship criteria, a discussion of scholarship donations for print-based journalists arose. One faculty member insisted that "print-based" referred to newspaper and magazine writers and editors, even though print media clearly depend heavily on photographs, graphics, and even the basis of words—type design. He could not comprehend that photojournalism students were also print students. In his mind, photographs remained illustrative of stories and attention grabbers, rather than a powerful means of telling a story—more powerful, in fact, than words. Visual journalism, visual anthropology, and visual sociology often remain marginalized in academia, except by those who fully comprehend the role of the visual in human behavior and in the construction of knowledge.

So, in summary here, *human visual behavior* refers to human activity—both internal and external—that relies on seeing. Examples are gestures, artistic expression, photographic behavior, and imagination. The importance of such human activity shadows representational issues: The activity itself is fundamental to human life, substantive, and more significant in and of itself than anything its manifestation may be later said to represent. What we typically consider the manifestation is itself an act of visual behavior. Consider, for example, a photograph of someone. The photograph was created by human action. Though it may be read ultimately in terms of representational issues, even that reading is a form of human visual behavior in which the viewer or reader interacts with and interprets the person's likeness in some fashion. Most important here are the behavior and what the behavior means and does—not the resulting representation of the behavior. Representation then falls into place as a subform of human visual behavior. This allows us to step out of the intellectual trap of trying to verbalize issues regarding representations of reality and to focus instead on visual behavior as its own form of meaning and interaction.

At this point, I want to return to another realm of visual theory, photographic aesthetics, an area introduced in chapters 2 and 3.

EQUIVALENTS

Chapter 5 introduced Stieglitz's Theory of Equivalents, which the early-20th-century photographer and aestheticist proposed as a way to explain the translation of his ideas and feelings into images conveying concepts: "What is of greatest importance is to hold a moment, to record something so completely that those who see it will relive an equivalent of what has been expressed" (Stieglitz, in Norman, 1973, p. 161). Stieglitz said his photographs of the sky and clouds were "equivalents" of "'something already taking form within me'" (Calloway & Hamilton, n.d., pp. 24–25).

Although Stieglitz's theory of equivalents referred to ways form conveys meaning, as noted in chapter 5, the theory can be applied to human visual behavior. For example, a photograph that results from the interaction between people can be conceptualized as an equivalent of their communication. As with Stieglitz's photographs of clouds, such "equivalents" are "simultaneously abstract and real" in that they are both evocative and descriptive. For what Stieglitz came to understand was that photographic communication was not simply a description or record of the material world: "'I have a vision of life ... and I try to find equivalents for it'" (Stieglitz, in Calloway &

Hamilton, n.d., p 23). Hence, a photograph of someone becomes, in a way, his or her equivalent, not only carrying the person via imagery, but also "endowed" meaning (Newhall, 1964). The equivalent then enters the dialectic of popular or scholarly discourse, where it can take on new meaning through context or a viewer's interaction with the equivalent. The photograph may carry an equivalent for the photographer's feelings, or the subject's feelings, or the dynamic moment when the image was made, or eventually be the catalyst for viewer perceptions. In other words, a photograph of a person is a "thing" as defined in symbolic interaction theory, moving outward through time and space as its own action. In this manner, the photographic equivalent is substantive beyond representation, and concerns regarding the ambiguity of the photograph become secondary. Most important here is that an interaction between people occurs and a new basis for interaction is created via a photographic equivalent. The equivalent then enters other contexts for interaction with an editor, a social scientist, a casual observer, a media viewer, perhaps even the photographed person—and each subsequent viewer brings his or her own personality, experiences and cultural frames to each subsequent interaction.

Positioning visual behavior within equivalents theory helps to maintain our focus on issues grounded in humanism rather than representation. Contemporary applications of symbolic interactionism, particularly in the critical theory tradition, too often abstract the effects of individual conduct and experience in ways that sacrifice our connection to the human beings and cultures we are trying to understand—including even ourselves (Denzin, 1995). The proposed typology then can be applied as a continuum of human visual interaction, rather than a continuum of "merely symbolic" or metaphorical interpretations of the artifacts of interaction (Christians, 1996, p. 243).

A TYPOLOGY OF VISUAL BEHAVIOR

The heart of the problem is the difficulty of translating visual behavior into a manageable form for study. Although the translation can only approximate the behavioral interaction, there is something to be gained in trying—perhaps more clarity than we had before, and at least a relatively simplified, two-dimensional means for analyzing visual behavior. Much like the difficulty two people who speak different languages share in trying to communicate beyond basic gesture, the translation is somewhat crude—but it is a beginning.

As noted earlier, the typology is based on a model of photographic communication (see Fig. 3.1). Basic units are the person who is photographed, commonly called the subject, here defined as the individual reflecting light into the camera; the person using the camera, commonly called the photographer, here defined as the individual who is visually recording the interaction; and the context of their interaction, which is the situation, with its accompanying personal, temporal, spatial, and cultural influences. Each person brings to the situation his or her personality, experiences, and cultural orientation, participating in the photographic event with varying levels of power. *Power* is defined here as the level of influence a person has during the photographic event. Photographic event can vary from a split second in which a subject is "caught" photographically to an extended exchange. The primary goal of the event—a photograph—itself defines the event to some extent. The use of a "seeing mechanism" to record parts of the interaction, combined with the knowledge that a photographic equivalent and subsequent viewing events will result from the interaction, requires a unique form of analysis.

The typology (Fig. 10.1) is based primarily on process: how the observer approaches and interacts with the observed, how the observed approaches and interacts with the observer, and so on. The continuum uses terms of human visual behavior in which an action can be placed within a named category translated via visual symbol and verbal definitions. For example, when subject and photographer embrace, or make an intimate, reciprocal interaction, the resulting equivalent is a visual embrace. Other terms include visual gift, visual encounter, visual quote, visual document, visual theater, visual cliché, visual lie, visual theft, visual intrusion, visual assault, visual rape, visual murder, and visual suicide. The categories are not mutually exclusive, and may be used to analyze interactions from different starting points and different perspectives. The categories are not absolutes, but rather terms and symbols that can facilitate analysis of the resonating, synergistic forms of visual behavior. Although the categories are listed in a normative fashion, human behavior is rarely linear, but rather dynamically nonlinear, ebbing and flowing, and turning back on itself in the fashion of a Mobius strip. I have tried to translate human interactions into a typology that can evoke, at least partially, the emotive nuances of the behavior.

Note that the typology is not an exhaustive set of categories, but rather a base that can be extended to match the variety of human behavior. For example, in *Art on My Mind: visual politics*, bell hooks (1995) used such terms as "visual hegemony," "a revolutionary visual aesthetic," "visual interventions," and "visual journey" in her critique of societal representations of the Black male body. Remember, however, that human visual behavior effects fundamental, embodied consequences among people and that those consequences lie beyond the representational frames within which scholars often examine them.

Dimensions of the Typology

Definitions of each term and examples of its application along several dimensions follow. Note that each dimension can be applied to either the photographic event or the viewing event.

Perspective: From whose point of view is the behavior to be analyzed—that of the subject, the photographer, the viewer? From the perspective of the subject, the behavior may be voluntary submission, as in an embrace or gift of intimacy, or involuntary submission, as in assault or rape. From the perspective of the photographer, the behavior may be an open-armed reception of the subject, as in an embrace, or an aggressive action bent on taking a picture, as in assault or rape.

Direction: What is the direction of the action—from where to where and from whom to whom at the moment the behavior occurs? Direction can be intrapersonal, interpersonal, or mass. If the action is directed toward the subject, it might be an intrusion, a quote, or murder. Directed from the subject to the photographer, it might be a lie or theater. Directed from the subject's equivalent to the viewer, it might be a beckoning toward embrace. Directed from viewer to equivalent, it might be an encounter or an intrusion. Directed from subject to self it might be suicide, or from subject to society it might be a gift or a cliché. Direction can also be mutual and reciprocal, as in a mutual embrace or shared theater.

Intensity: Evocatory capacity of the behavior—the extent to which the behavior affects the observed or observer. Locating intensity in the behavior effect shifts the focus from the content of a photographic equivalent to the behavior it engenders. Stieglitz's clouds appear to be of low intensity in terms of representational content, but apparently can evoke intense behavioral response from many viewers.

The dimensions are only guidelines on which to base analysis of visual behavior. As with any human interaction or behavior, perspective, direction, and intensity shift along a Mobius strip of human communication.

Figure 10.1 presents the typology in simplified visual and verbal forms. Core definitions and references to how each behavior can be analyzed

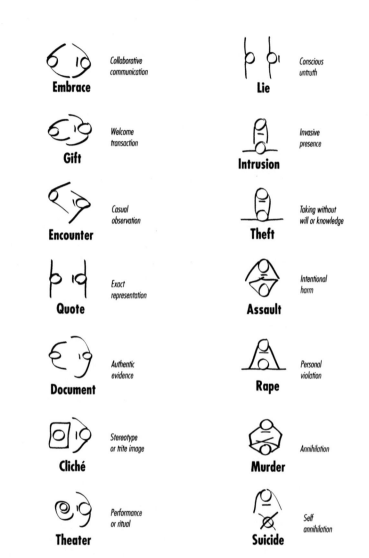

FIGURE 10.1 Typology of human visual behavior

along various dimensions follow. In some cases, the applications result from my own visual interactions. In a other instances, the applications described are those of others. Readers have their own responses and interpretations.

Visual embrace refers to collaborative, encircling or enveloping exchange between observer and observed. Curator Roy Flukinger (personal communication, 1987) noted that when street photographer Ave Bonar wants to photograph someone, she catches the person's eye and—with a kind of "visual embrace," implying consent and reciprocal interaction—makes a photograph with him. In such an application of the term, perspective and direction are mutual; intensity varies according to the level of connection achieved. For example, when photojournalist Eddie Adams and a frightened Marine visually embraced (Kobre, 1996), we can only imagine the intensity of their interaction. In that instance, Adams chose not to make a photograph, keeping a visual equivalent only in his memory. Had Adams made the picture, the photographic equivalent would evoke an intense embrace from me as a viewer only if I stopped long enough to look into the young soldier's eyes in the photo. It would be all too easy to refuse his embrace by quickly looking past him, reducing the interaction to an encounter.

Visual gift refers to a visual transaction in which something is voluntarily transferred from one person to another. For example, a visual gift can be the act of submission of the observed to the process of observation. The perspective can be that of the giver, the subject, or the photographer, to whom the image has been given; direction can go either way. Intensity varies according to the significance of the gift. In the example of Adams and the young Marine, the visual gift was the Marine's willingness to connect with Adams via his eyes. Adams' gift, one could argue, was connecting with the Marine but not taking the picture. Visual gift can also refer to a positive effect of observing someone. For example, photographer Mark Goodrich (personal communication, April 1995) noted that his family considered his photographic documentation of his grandfather at work in his barbershop an irreplaceable gift, especially after the grandfather's death. Goodrich's experience led him to suggest the term *visual gift*. In this case, one could apply the term visual gift to the visual self the grandfather gave to his grandson, to the photographic portrait the grandson gave to his family, and to the interaction both subject and photographer gave to their family via visual equivalents. Perspective and direction shift in each case. Intensity varied from a relatively mild level evoked as Goodrich photographed his grandfather at work and at home to deep grief after his grandfather's death, to celebration of his grandfather's life through the visual equivalents.

Visual encounter refers to situations in which the interaction between observer and observed is momentary, a mere brush of behavior. Photographing a person watching a parade or opening her umbrella would be a visual encounter, even if no eye contact occurred. Glancing at a photograph of someone in the newspaper without much consideration would be a visual encounter. In both cases, the encounter is not mutual, occurring only from the perspective of the photographer or viewer. Although visual encounter typically refers to low-intensity behavior, an encounter can also be momentarily violent, as in the visual equivalent of Jack Ruby shooting Lee Harvey Oswald.

Visual quote refers to an authentic record. Although "quoting" visually, the photographer tries to manipulate the moment as little as possible, given the subjective nature of human perception and communication. Photographer Ron Shulman used the term *film quote* to describe an image of photojournalism intended to accurately communicate a moment in time (personal communication, April 1995), and one that should not be altered. In such a scenario, the action moves from photographer to subject. Can a person viewing an image visually quote the person he or she is observing? Yes. If the observer seeks to accurately record the visual equivalent in memory, the observer is visually quoting. The level of intensity will vary according to the content and context of the quote. Eddie Adams's visual quote of the moment a Viet Cong soldier was executed is intense for all involved, including viewers who choose to ponder the event via the photographic equivalent. A photograph of a rose might have low intensity for someone who cares little for flowers, or high intensity for a woman whose lover regularly sends her roses.

Visual document applies to behavior that becomes evidentiary. A photograph may begin as a visual quote from an event, or even as a visual encounter, but become a visual document in time. The photograph of O. J. Simpson wearing a particular kind of shoes had little value until its documentary status became known. Perspective varies according to viewer use. Direction is most often from the document to the viewer, in that the document serves the viewer in some way. Intensity may be low if the document is being interpreted in a highly rational manner, or high if the document stirs someone to further action. Charles Moore's photographs of the civil rights movement began as intense visual quotes that evolved into visual documents used on the floor of Congress to argue for passage of the Civil Rights Act of 1964.

Visual theater refers to images created by photographers and subjects in a kind of conscious or unconscious ritual or performance. Examples of relatively unconscious visual theater might be "candid" wedding photographs or "candid" photographs of such public events as demonstrations or funerals. Examples of relatively conscious visual theater might be posed wedding photography, which also becomes a visual document, or Avedon's (1985) "silent theater" form of portraiture. One photojournalist's presence at a community event signaled legitimacy to those attending; over time he had become part of the visual theater of the community (Newton, 1984). Visual theater can appear to be a visual quote when it is not, especially in circumstances in which the observer asks the observed to reenact an activity for image-recording purposes. Such a practice used to be commonplace in photojournalism. A class assignment from the 1970s, for example, titled the "Posed/Unposed Portrait," was designed to teach students how to pose subjects so they looked unposed. Although now banned in photojournalism, except in the case of feature or illustration photography, visual theater for research purposes has an important function. Collier (1967), for example, wrote of a Peruvian hat maker who carefully reenacted for the anthropologists' eyes and cameras the correct process of making a hat—after seeing the process incorrectly recorded in photographs. In such a setting, visual theater produces visual documents. Perspective lies on either or both sides of the interaction, as does direction. Intensity varies according to the purpose of the theater.

Visual cliché categorizes behavior that has become trite or stereotypical. An example of a visual cliché in photojournalism is a picture of a child kissing a dog. Sadly, many horrid behaviors also have become clichés. For example, photographs of starving children looking pleadingly into the camera have been published so frequently that viewers quickly gloss over them as they review the day's news. The cliché can occur at any level. A behavior that is unique and intense to the subject, such as mourning at a graveside, may be a visual cliché with no intensity to a hardened public audience.

Visual lie refers to manipulative behavior by either observer or observed, or both, and then using the equivalent as if it were authentic. An example might be a staged photograph published as if the photographer caught the actual moment. The initial interaction may have been visual theater—or even a visual document—but the equivalent is used and perceived in such a way that it becomes a visual lie.

Visual intrusion occurs when someone pushes into a situation where he or she is unwanted. The tabloid press's pursuit of celebrities in intimate settings is an example of a visual intrusion. Another commonplace example is the funeral where photographers move in too close to record the tears of a mourner, or when photographers use a long lens to photograph people in a private moment on their own property. Increasingly, the courts are working to restrain such intrusions via "right-to-privacy" litigation (Sherer, 1990). Visual social scientists work hard not to be intrusive, although even their presence in a community can be just that.

Visual theft is taking something against the will of the observed, and often without the person's knowledge. The resulting equivalent is often one that a person probably would not want a photographer to take, such as the image of Princess Anne in which the wind is blowing her skirt above the waist, revealing her body through sheer underwear. Another example might be taking a photograph of a Native American who does not want to be photographed and feels the observer is "stealing his soul," or of a street person unknowingly photographed while digging through a trash can.

Visual assault takes intrusion to a more violent level, conducted with the intention to inflict harm. A visual assault can be executed with a camera, meaning the observer records an action while knowing that doing so can bring harm, either directly or through negligence, to the observed. For example, a photojournalist who is first on the scene of an accident and stops to photograph rather than give aid may be, via negligence, committing visual assault. The observer who records the image of an unwilling observer may, in effect, be assaulting that person. Consider the situation in which an individual photographs a dirty, barefoot child on the streets of Mexico without interacting with that child. In one sense, the photographer is assaulting the child, both stealing something from the child that she cannot protect—her image—and inviting others to view her in a pitying way. A pack of video and still photojournalists forcefully surrounding someone and obtaining images is another example of a visual assault.

Visual rape refers to the violation of a person through observation. Naggar (1990) used the term to describe how Muslim women were photographed without their veils and against their wills. Another example might be taking photographs of crime victims, thereby subjecting them to a second victimization, or forcefully intruding into someone's private domain in order to get a photograph. In one specific example, a mother was photographed writhing on the floor in hysteria on learning her daughter had been killed in a plane crash. She later commented that she felt raped by the cameras (Deppa, Russell, Hayes, & Flocke, 1993). I use the term *rape* here quite cautiously because of the brutally violent nature of a physical rape. However, I consider the term appropriate for expressing violation via dominating, intrusive visual behavior that cannot be successfully refused.

Visual murder refers to images that could result in the psychological or physical annihilation of the observed. Sontag (1973) maintained that the camera does not rape, but, rather, presumes, intrudes, trespasses, distorts, exploits, "and, at the farthest reach of metaphor, assassinates" (pp. 13–15). She added: "To photograph people is to violate them, by seeing them as they never see themselves, by having knowledge of them they can never have; it turns people into objects that can be symbolically possessed. Just as the camera is a sublimation of the gun, to photograph someone is a sublimated murder—a soft murder, appropriate to a sad, frightened time" (pp. 13–15). On one end of the visual murder continuum is the action of an observer who creates an image that so strips a person of dignity that nothing is left but bodily form or some other pitiable state. On the other end of the visual murder continuum is the observer who visually quotes a subject who is in mortal danger if identified. Meiselas (Meiselas & Rosenberg, 1981; Meiselas, personal communication, 1988) noted, for example, that she never photographed the Sandanistas unmasked because to do so would produce evidence that could be used to identify and kill them.

Visual suicide refers to the process in which an individual kills himself, either physically or psychologically, in front of the camera. A physical example is the act of a Buddhist monk setting himself on fire in front of photographers. A psychological example is a public figure behaving embarrassingly in front of photographers. The defining characteristic of visual suicide is that the observed individual commits an act of self-annihilation in which others can visually participate.

This list of terms and examples is a glossed beginning of the ways the typology can be used to analyze human visual behavior.

APPLICATION

For an example of how the typology can be applied, return to the photographs of Tía María at the beginning of this chapter. From my perspective, my conscious intention in photographing her candidly was to embrace a quiet moment with her doing something I knew to be a consistent behavior—a visual embrace and visual document. Not until I showed her the photograph did I realize that there might have been subconscious tendencies on my part to "look down on her" in more ways than literally. Of all the moments I had observed Tía María, why did I choose the one I did? In my effort to make a visual document in a manner I thought was visually embracing, I had committed visual intrusion and visual theft, according to

Tía María's perspective. Given the opportunity to participate in the photographic event, Tía María helped prevent my perpetuating a visual cliché and made instead a visual document of how she wanted to be viewed. Many would argue that the first photograph is the "true" visual document precisely because she did not know I was stealing her image. Although that is indeed one side of the observer–observed conundrum, it is only one side, and an arrogant one at that. The assumption that a photographer can discern the *real* person better than he can see himself is its own kind of visual assault; at the very least, it is presumptuous and arrogant. Was the second photograph more visual theater than visual document? It was both. At the very least, the second picture documents the way this woman sees her best self—and it was not a self that I had seen or chosen to document. The second portrait also shifted the *direction* of the photo from one of photographer to subject—and hence viewer to subject—to one of reciprocal viewing. At best, the two documents combined make a balanced, authentic portrait of this woman whom I set out to embrace visually. The *intensity* of the portraits also varies. The first photo usually evokes a mild, curious, perhaps even amused response—except from Tía María! The second photo evokes a stronger, more respectful response from viewers, who react with surprise to the differently imaged Tía María.

A visual shorthand for the preceding analysis might look like this:

If A = photographer

B = subject

E_1 = original image equivalent

> = to observe

V = viewer/observer

Then A > B = E_1

V > B via E_1 = E_2

If A embraces B = E_1 as visual embrace

Then V is more likely to visually embrace B when looking at E_1

Using the icons, if A ⟨⟩ B then it is more likely that V ⟨⟩ B via E_1 to create E_2.

The goal of the typology is to facilitate analysis of the complex array of human visual behavior.

DISCUSSION

A theoretical exploration of human visual behavior may seem insignificant compared with the effects of physical violence or benevolence. However, one irony of civilization is that increased facility for communication via technological advances has made possible visual dehumanization on an unprecedented scale. Much of today's global society considers itself civilized, yet still permits the oppression of women, people of color, and other nondominant groups through a hegemonic and often brutally intrusive visual system. Does this mean we should never look at someone or photograph him or her unless the person observed is uplifted via the process? No. This does mean, however, that if we can recognize the subtle-like-a-sledgehammer effects of visual behavior on individuals and societies, we are moving closer to comprehending human behavior in general and to raising the level of concern about how humans interact.

For photojournalists to determine appropriate "visual behavior," they must question what they do doing and why. What are the long-term effects of a person's "reflecting light onto film" or of viewing others superficially without concern for their welfare? Are we in the so-called civilized world playing out our emotional lives via visual behavior that has to a large extent replaced physical behavior? Or is visual behavior indeed its own form of human interaction? No one, no matter how well intentioned, can always avoid erring in interaction with those he or she purportedly observes—any more than any of us can always avoid hurting others in other kinds of human interaction. But perhaps the terms explored in the typology can be used to interrogate human visual interaction in new ways.

At the heart of communication, whether on the mass or individual level, is interpersonal communication. And at the heart of all interpersonal communication are the selves of those involved. This chapter has sought to demonstrate in a new way that human visual behavior is an enigmatic, meaningful interaction with consequences of varying magnitude. Visual behavior is distinct, in that the potential types and levels of interactions appear to vary infinitely in terms of perspective, direction, and intensity, and with implications reaching far beyond the universes in which a behavior originally occurred. If we can carefully and sensitively understand the powerful though often subtle characteristics of human visual behavior, perhaps we can move closer to understanding our visually interactive universes.

A MOMENT OF HORROR. On June 8, 1972, Huynh Cong (Nick) Ut, a combat photographer for the Associated Press, recorded "a moment so horrible the American people, dulled by an unending, remote war, are deeply moved" (Leekley & Leekley, 1982, p. 88). The person who touched so many individuals through her image was 9-year-old Phan Thi Kim Phuc, who ran naked down a South Vietnamese road, screaming in pain from her napalm wounds.

CHAPTER 11

The Problem
of Real People

The unique characteristic of images of photojournalism is that they are photographs of real people, people who exist outside of our minds. Many times the only way we know these people is through their images. Yet it is not uncommon to feel a bond with them. Relationships formed on the basis of viewer or reader perception of someone via mass media images, particularly images of photojournalism, push the boundaries of traditionally defined communication patterns. Exploring the sometimes intimate, sometimes public relationships that occur between persons who are photographed for publication and the photographer, as well as between the person and the mass of individuals who relate to him or her, is one route to understanding the way an imaged person becomes a part of mass society via media images.

This chapter explores photojournalism's ability to connect human beings via a photograph and demonstrates how to use the typology of visual behavior to articulate the ambiguous flow of relationships involving a media image of a real person.

CHAPTER 11

The Problem
of Real People

Thirty-three-year-old Kim Phuc stood weeping along with war veterans, a living symbol of many entities: a legacy of war, human endurance, and American shame, and the ability of one individual to communicate with masses of people in a manner so personal that many feel they know her. Yet most of that public came to know Phuc through one moment, recorded photographically, published worldwide, legitimized by a Pulitzer Prize, and preserved forever in books of history, photojournalism, media studies, and war. How is it that one person, whose photograph is disseminated via mass media, can affect large groups of individuals to the extent that they feel they have a kind of relationship with her? What are the *interpersonal* dimensions of this *mass* relationship? This chapter describes how images of photojournalism can act as visual equivalents of the imaged individuals, drawing sensitive viewers into a kind of *mass-interpersonal relationship* with the imaged individual.

Once again, our discussion is supported by symbolic interactionism, which provides a synthesis of self, object and meaning that can help explain the seemingly oxymoronic "mass-interpersonal relationship," and by photographic equivalents theory, which offers a way to explain this unique link between the physical and what some call the representational. Together, the theories focus on the ability of human perception to forge new ways of communicating among individuals.

For data, this chapter examines a photograph that falls into its own genre of mass media imagery of *real people:* visual reportage that becomes a historically significant document. The central argument is that authentic reportage blurs the physical and the representational into a form of communication employing both the interpersonal and the mass. Although one could place this discussion within parasocial and critical literatures, a more fruitful location is in new theory encompassing a continuum ranging from the deeply compassionate to the coldly dispassionate. Applying the interactive model of photography (see Fig. 3.1) and the typology of visual behavior (see Fig. 10.1) clarifies the relationship between Kim Phuc and the public. The chapter concludes that this kind of communication can be characterized in three ways: the commodification of the human interaction, or a highly evolved capacity of humankind to relate via representational forms—or both.

THEORY

As noted earlier, one theoretical approach to this area of study is the growing body of literature on parasocial relationships. *Parasocial relationships,* defined as one-sided relationships with media personae, often categorize interaction between viewers and a fictional media character or a media personality.

Consider one example. A number of years ago, the sitcom character Murphy Brown (played by Candice Bergen) became the object of public discussion beyond the entertainment realm. Brown, who was single, became pregnant and gave birth to a son in an ongoing series of sitcom episodes. Dan Quayle, then vice president of the United States, attacked Brown's decision to raise her child alone, using the television character's behavior as an example of the decline of family values in the United States. The incident raised a furor, making headlines in newspapers and magazines. In response to Quayle, a subsequent episode of *Murphy Brown* featured Bergen speaking directly to viewers as she introduced a variety of "real families" who differed from the traditional father–mother–children nuclear family idealized by Quayle. The fictional character's life choices had sparked public debate about real-life issues, which then were added to the sitcom's program as "real life."

The kind of images considered here, however, are those which begin as visual reportage of real people and events, often entering public consciousness via extraordinary visual content or via repeated publication. Florence Thompson, for example, unwittingly became an icon for the plight of migrant families during the Depression era in the United States. Thompson was photographed by Dorothea Lange while waiting with her three children for their broken-down vehicle to be repaired. Now, 60 years later, the photograph, titled "Migrant Mother," has become a defining icon for the Depression era. The real-life person in the photograph, Florence Thompson, died a bitter woman, angry that her state in the photo had been misinterpreted. Thompson maintained that she had not been a migrant worker staying at the camp—and that her image had been taken, publicized, and published innumerable times without her permission and with no compensation to her (Livingston, 1980). Yet the interpersonal appeal of a tired madonna gazing directly at viewers from a tent promulgated the image into its own constructed, historical reality and the person into the public eye and memory.

A recent example of a photograph that entered public consciousness is the controversial image of a fireman carrying the limp body of a young child from the Oklahoma City bombing wreckage in 1996. The photograph ran on the front pages and covers of newspapers and magazines nationally and internationally because, as one picture editor said, "I knew this was *the* photo of the event" (Newton, 1994–1999). The image of a uniformed fireman tenderly cradling a child victim of senseless violence quickly became the easily recognizable, primary visual equivalent of the bombing, engaging the public eye and heart.

Viewers throughout the world shared a distant horror at the thought that such a tragedy could befall an innocent child so close to home. My own first response to the photo was one of relatively dispassionate observation. But the process of looking at the image, reading the mother's grieving words, and seeing another photo of the same child when she was alive and smiling with curly hair and bright eyes moved me to tears. Within the time it took to read past the front-page photo I had formed a bond with the child, the fireman, the mother, and even the shared grief of a mass of unknown fellow viewers. Within days of the bombing, however, opportunists were selling t-shirts bearing a simplified form of the photograph, capitalizing on public recognition of the image and involvement in the tragedy. The photograph had rapidly evoked a wide range of responses—from crass commercialism to shared sorrow.

SYMBOLIC INTERACTIONISM

Symbolic interactionism (Blumer, 1969) provides an appropriate framework for examining the concept of a "*mass interpersonal relationship.*" Blumer advanced George Herbert Mead's ideas regarding the relationship between the individual and society through symbolic interactions. A review of his three main premises is useful here: (a) Individuals "act toward things on the basis of the meanings that the things have for them," (b) meanings arise out of social interaction, and (c) "these meanings are handled in, and modified through, an interpretative process used by the person in dealing with the things he encounters" (Blumer, 1969, p. 2). To understand the process by which we make meaning and determine actions, Blumer maintained, we must move beyond societal structures to focus on people's individual selves:

> Students of human society will have to face the question of whether their preoccupation with categories of structure and organization can be squared with the interpretative process by means of which human beings, individually and collectively, act in human society. … The question remains whether human society or social action can be successfully analyzed by schemes which refuse to recognize human beings as they are, namely, as persons constructing individual and collective action through an interpretation of the situations which confront them. (p. 89)

In this analysis, scholarly focus on the mass media and its mass audience can be considered a "category of structure" that obfuscates the process through which human beings construct their actions as they interpret situations in which they are involved. An individual viewing a photograph in a newspaper, for example, is not simply responding to a mass medium as a medium, but also to the content of the image, the meaning that content has for him, and any contextual material. Similarly, the individual responds with "self-indication," the process through which a person communicates with him- or herself. The individual may or may not have a sense of being part of a mass audience, although that sense of being part of a whole may grow through time. Furthermore, Blumer (1969) said:

> People—that is, acting units—do not act toward culture, social structure or the like; they act toward situations. Social organization enters into action only to the extent to which it shapes situations in which people act, and to the extent to which it supplies fixed sets of symbols which people use in interpreting their situations. (p. 88)

One might say that viewers act toward a situation in an image and toward the situation of their viewing; the social organization here may be the situation in which the subject acts, or the medium that shapes the situation in which the image will be viewed and interpreted by the "acting units," or viewers.

Blumer (1969) stressed looking at the process from the standpoint of the individual:

> To try to catch the interpretative process by remaining aloof as a so-called "objective" observer and refusing to take the role of the acting unit is to risk the worst kind of subjectivism—the objective observer is likely to fill in the process of interpretation with his own surmises in place of catching the process as it occurs in the experience of the acting unit which uses it. (p. 86)

Much of what is done in mass communication research is to impose one's "own surmises" on the processes studied, rather than to try to get inside the process as one human being interpreting situations as an individual. Although Blumer crystallized his theory 30 years ago, presaging contemporary fascination with personal perspective via literary criticism, postmodernism, and feminism, the resonance between his thinking and that of many contemporary theorists who advocate qualitative research is clear.

Particularly relevant is Blumer's discussion (1969) of the source of meaning. Meaning does not emanate "from the intrinsic makeup of the thing that has meaning," nor does it arise "through a coalescence of psychological elements in the person" (p. 4). Symbolic interactionism "sees meaning as arising in the process of interaction between people" (p. 5). Meanings are products created through the process of human interaction (p. 5). This would indicate, then, that the meaning of an image is created through the process of interaction between the image and the viewer, which is consistent with contemporary audience reception studies (Staiger, 1992). Can we take this line of thought so far as to propose that meaning is created through the process of interaction between the imaged person and the viewer? Is it conceivable that the visual image of a person in a still or moving mass medium becomes the visual equivalent for the person imaged, with the potential to serve as the imaged person's functional equivalent for someone viewing and interpreting the image? If so, this would help explain how intense feelings of connection develop between the image of a human being and millions of other human beings who meet only through an image, as well as feelings between the person imaged and an unknown mass of individual viewers.

VISUAL EQUIVALENTS THEORY

Return now to visual equivalents theory, which typically has been used to discuss representational issues related to form, abstract ideas and feelings. Stieglitz (Newhall, 1964) developed the theory to explain how a photograph of something—such as a cloud—could communicate his feelings about seeing the cloud because the image served as the visual equivalent of the cloud. Stieglitz wanted the photographic equivalent, which was created during his contemplation of the cloud, to stimulate a meaningful response in a person viewing the photograph (Calloway & Hamilton, n.d.). In effect, the imaged cloud then has become a functional equivalent to the physical cloud during the moment of interaction between viewer and image. If we apply the same line of thought to a human being, rather than to a cloud, we can conjecture that a photograph of a person becomes a visual equivalent of a person with the potential to become an interactive equivalent of that person when the image equivalent is encountered by a viewer.

Support for this argument can be found in visual perception theory, which offers empirical evidence that when the human brain comes to know something through its eyes, it tends to respond to that something as if it physically exists. For example, a baby placed on the edge of a precipice covered by clear glass will not crawl over the precipice because the baby instinctively understands the danger of falling into the precipice (Gregory, 1990). Carpenter (1975) noticed a similar response among people who had never seen themselves via photographs: They reacted with fear and self-protective gestures, as if they were looking at another self. Although they quickly learned to respond to the photographs as something other than another physical self, and certainly humans in mass-media societies have learned to deal with images as frequent, daily occurrences, is it not possible that those images that stop us and that become part of our memories, both individually and collectively, could evoke responses equivalent to those we might experience were we to have seen the imaged moment firsthand? If meaning is something we construct in the process of social interaction, then is not the meaning we construct when interacting with a photographic image as valid for discussion as the meaning we construct when interacting in the flesh? We are in the flesh. The person imaged was in the flesh, or he or she could not have reflected light into a visual recording device. The fact that the person is in imaged form is significant in terms of the characteristics of the medium, in terms of the objectification of human beings, and in terms of the ambiguity of the message interpretation. Yet each of those concerns is also a concern in face-to-face communication, where the medium is the human body, where a person can also be objectified by the one with whom he or she interacts, and where the ambiguity of shared meaning causes multiple problems. Framing the imaged person as an entity that is in some ways equivalent to the person offers promising insight into the nature of human communication, especially in this age of mass and virtual media.

The key to understanding mass communication as interpersonal communication is to consider the "mass" as "individuals who have selves" (Blumer, 1969, p. 83) who respond to the selves who are imaged. These selves relate to what they perceive to be personal selves within images as if they are relating to those selves face to face. Blumer maintained that "human beings have selves" in "that they act by making indications to themselves." So if we look at the photograph of 9-year-old Kim Phuc running from a napalm bombing in naked horror and pain, and we respond by feeling sick in the pits of our stomachs and empathy for the child, what is happening? What has occurred is a kind of interpersonal interaction between the viewer and the child—an interaction that has been facilitated by the action of a photographer, a mass medium, and the viewer's visual perception. Turn now to definitions of *mass* and *interpersonal* communication.

MASS COMMUNICATION

As McQuail noted in *Mass Communication Theory* (1994), defining mass communication is not as simple as it might seem. But therein lies a key point for our discussion: "Mass communication was, from the beginning, more of an idea than a reality" (p. 11). Though the term often is used to encompass a transmission model, in which groups use the press, broadcasting, recorded music, electronic media, and film to send magic-bullet-type messages to large audiences, the term has evolved to encompass an active audience characterized by response, sharing, and interaction (McQuail, 1994, p. 10). Cautioning that *mass communication* is not synonymous with *mass media*, which are "the organized technologies which make mass communication possible," McQuail noted:

> The same media that carry public messages to large publics for public purposes can also carry personal notices, advocacy messages, charitable appeals, situations-vacant advertisements and many varied kinds of information and culture. This point is especially relevant at a time of convergence of communication technologies, when the boundaries between public and private and large-scale and individual communication networks are increasingly blurred. (pp. 10–11)

McQuail further noted that "everyday experience with mass communication is extremely varied" (p. 11).

INTERPERSONAL COMMUNICATION

Chapter 3 introduced the idea that photographers and subjects enter into an interpersonal relationship during a photographic event. In their work on interpersonal deception theory, Buller and Burgoon (1996) offered a useful description of interpersonal communication. Consistent with Roloff and Miller (1987), Buller and Burgoon (1996) defined interpersonal communication "as the dynamic exchange of messages between two (or more) people" (p. 205). Although the communication may or may not be interactive, dyadic, face to face, unmediated, idiosyncratic, or "personal," Buller and Burgoon pointed to "dyadic, face-to-face exchange" as the benchmark for comparing communication formats: "When communicative transactions increase beyond two participants or shift from face-to-face to mediated formats, they become increasingly less interpersonal and interactive" (p. 205). According to Buller and Burgoon, interpersonal communication is characterized by six "critical attributes":

- Active participation by both sender and receiver.
- Dynamism.
- Multifunctional, multidimensional, and multimodal.
- Both strategic and nonstrategic.
- Governed by cognitive and behavioral factors.
- Involves judgment of communicator and message credibility (pp. 206–207).

Considering both mass and interpersonal approaches to the study of communication, we can discern the overlap. Both involve "social interaction through messages," as Gerbner (1967, in McQuail, 1994, p. 10) defined *communication*. Although theorists typically have defined *interpersonal communication* in terms of a dyad, and *mass communication* in terms of society, the lines increasingly are blurred (McQuail, 1994). As people spend more time interacting via technological media and less time interacting in person, new terms are needed to describe the interactions.

THE CASE OF KIM PHUC

Return to the photograph that opened this chapter. On June 8, 1972, Huynh Cong (Nick) Ut, a combat photographer for the Associated Press, recorded "a moment so horrible the American people, dulled by an unending, remote war, are deeply moved" (Leekley & Leekley, 1982, p. 88). The

AP/Wide World Photos

person who touched so many individuals through her image was 9-year-old Phan Thi Kim Phuc, who ran naked down a South Vietnamese road, screaming in pain from her napalm wounds.

Thirty-four years later, a *New York Times* reporter would write that the photograph embodied the "searing memories" of the Vietnam War (Schiolino, 1996, p. A1, caption). The effect of the photograph was so strong that many of those who met the adult Kim Phuc, in person, on November 11, 1996, in Veteran's Day ceremonies, "started bawling" when they "realized who she was," said a sergeant who had been with the unit that dropped the napalm (p. A8). Both a photograph of Kim Phuc taken by AP photographer Dennis Cook during the Washington, DC, ceremony (shown here), and Nick Ut's photograph from 1972 ran with stories in *The New York Times* (Schiolino, 1996) and *The Austin-American Statesman* (Gearan, 1997) as well as in many other newspapers throughout the United States. Viewers who had come to know Kim Phuc via her visual equivalent were riveted by the updated story of her survival and life.

Kim Phuc related to the earlier photograph of herself as a personal communication: "I wanted to share my experience with people so that they feel better," she said. "Behind that picture of me, thousands and thousands of people, they suffered—more than me. They died. They lost parts of their bodies. Their whole lives were destroyed, and nobody took that picture" (Schiolino, 1996, p. A8). The photograph of a young girl in pain not only established a relationship between her and countless viewers unknown to her, but went on to become a visual document that could instantly trigger a range of personal, ideological and political feelings within its viewers and those who had been associated with the Vietnam War. The photograph became a visual equivalent—for a specific human being and her personal experience of physical and psychological pain, for the anguish many people feel about acts committed during the Vietnam War, and for human suffering during any time of war.

Is the Communication Interpersonal?

The communication engendered by the photographic mediation of Kim Phuc's story does not meet the requirements for a dyadic, face-to-face prototype of interpersonal communication. However, the communication can be described as "the dynamic exchange of messages between two (or more) people" (Buller & Burgoon, 1996, p. 205). One way to approach this issue is to consider the idea that the body, particularly the face, is itself an equivalent of the composite life form within it. Why then would only physical face to face suffice as interpersonal? Is it simply that body to body or face to face is the closest communication human beings can experience in terms of physical proximity? If so, we are limiting human communication in terms of proxemics, rather than in terms of the sharing of meaning between individuals. Communication via photographic media is less interpersonal and less interactive than face-to-face communication and is indeed technologically mediated. But it is also interpersonal in the sense of one individual communicating with another—or with the other's visual equivalent.

In the photograph of Kim Phuc, the naked body of a severely injured girl is recorded. People viewing the photograph of Kim Phuc respond to the communication of her screaming mouth, nakedness, and fleeing form, as well as to the situation imaged: other people running from something and background smoke. The context of message creation could be described as face to face between the photographer and Kim Phuc. The message is then further contextualized via electronic or print media, almost always with words delineating the time, place, action, and persons involved. The visual equivalent of the original face-to-face moment continues to evolve through various forms of media until it is encountered image-face to physical-face by a viewer. The viewer in turn interacts with the image-face, casting it aside or absorbing it into his or her consciousness in another stage of meaning creation. The viewer's interpretation and any ensuing response then enters the dialectic of message exchange created with other viewers.

Does This Process Involve People in Varying Roles and Relationships to One Another?

Hartley (1993) noted two ways of considering roles and relationships in interpersonal communication. One requires authenticity and mutual caring. The other is more neutral, focusing on the intersection of personality, self-concept, and role. Applying the first approach to the photograph of Kim Phuc, I cannot imagine a moment that more clearly communicates with authenticity or that better demonstrates mutual caring, as well as terror. In terms of authenticity, other witnesses, including other media and military personnel, have confirmed the actuality of the event. Napalm was indeed dropped on a village, innocent people were horribly injured, and a photojournalist did record their flight from the scene on film. Although one could argue about the role of the photographer's point of view in the creation of the message, it would not negate the fact that the event occurred and the photographer responded interpersonally to the individual in the image. The issue of mutual caring is harder to argue, however. Although it can be readily agreed that the photographer cared for Kim Phuc and expressed his care through the photographic documentation, can it be argued that Kim Phuc cared about Nick Ut or about future viewers? Hardly. But one can argue that over time Kim Phuc came to care for Ut, for people viewing her photograph, and for others—both civilian and military—who also suffered because of the war in Vietnam.

Hartley's (1993) second approach suggested that the nature of relationship sharing is determined by social identity, whose components are personality, self-concept, and role. It is fairly easy to conjecture about the unique personality characteristics and self-concept that led Kim Phuc to react as she did, not only in the photographic moment, but also through ensuing years.

Although her role in the photograph was as a victim of war, her role in public consciousness about the war quickly took on global proportions, some positive, some negative.

Were Both Sender and Receiver Active?

Now applying Buller and Burgoon's (1996) criteria, the answer is, "Yes." The sender in the case of the original photograph of Kim Phuc was the girl herself. The primary mediator was Nick Ut, with secondary mediators being the mass media, military and government officials, and war veterans. Anyone viewing the photograph, no matter the medium, would be an active receiver, reading, viewing, interpreting, feeling, and reacting. We know that Kim Phuc and Ut were active participants in the communication, which affected numerous viewers, who in turn responded in various ways, often with direct feedback to Kim Phuc or to Ut. One problem is simultaneity; clearly the sender and receiver are not active simultaneously. If we stretch the equivalent metaphor, however, we can argue that the senders encode latent action in an image of photojournalism, which receivers might perceive as active and to which they can respond. Traditional caption style in photojournalism encourages such "presently occurring" perception by using the present tense to describe action.

Furthermore, the evidence suggests that some kind of lasting two-way relationship has been established between Kim Phuc and individuals who have viewed the photograph. The photographer reunited with her, people have followed her story through the years, and when she made an appearance during 1996 Veteran's Day ceremonies, she and numerous veteran onlookers were moved to tears. Kim Phuc, in turn, responded by agreeing to be photographed with her infant in a pose that showed her scarred back, by agreeing to appear at the Veterans Day event, by talking with reporters, and by continuing her friendship with Ut.

Was/Is the Communication Dynamic?

Yes. As Buller and Burgoon specified, behavioral patterns of Kim Phuc, Nick Ut, media, and viewers have fluctuated over time, ranging from neglect in the first year after the bombing to passionate concern and bitter resentment as the years went by. Another way of addressing this characteristic is to determine if the communication is an ongoing process rather than an event or series of events (Hartley, 1993). The picture "'that doesn't rest'" has continued to introduce Kim Phuc to viewers through the years in newspapers and magazines, in books, and via electronic media (Goldberg, 1991). But even more relevant to the discussion of the interpersonal versus the mass is the fact that public viewers have watched Kim Phuc grow up, have multiple surgeries, have a family, and announce that she had forgiven those who fought in the war (Schiolino, 1996). That process is the result of what can be termed multiple "mass-interpersonal relationships" between Kim Phuc and individuals who have known her through the images.

Was/Is the Communication Multifunctional, Multidimensional, and Multimodal?

Yes. Those involved with the photographic relationship with Kim Phuc have had multiple purposes—reporting, selling newspapers, war commentary, propagandizing, expressing pain and compassion, challenging historical frames; and multifaceted responses—horror, disbelief, empathy, loyalty, trust, apathy. They have sent and received communication in multichanneled ways—still photography and video images, television, newspapers, books, magazines, the Internet, public appearances, and so forth.

Was/Is It Both Strategic and Nonstrategic?

Buller and Burgoon (1996) noted that interpersonal communication can be conscious and deliberate or unconscious and unintentional. Hartley (1993) discussed similar concerns when he distinguished between informative behavior and behavior calculated to inform the observer. In the case of Kim Phuc and Nick Ut, one could argue that the girl's behavior was informative but not calculated to inform. Yet one could also argue that she purposefully sought refuge among the photojournalists and the soldiers present at the scene. Goldberg (1991) described seeing a videotape of the scenario in which Kim Phuc passed the videographer, revealing her charred flesh and running toward soldiers who poured water over her. Certainly Ut's behavior can be described as intentional communication. On assignment as a war photographer, Ut rushed to the scene specifically to record the event for people to see. The photograph was broadcast the same evening, June 8, 1972, via television news and "the next morning the picture of the naked girl was on every breakfast table and newsstand" (Goldberg, 1991, p. 242). On the evening of June 9, CBS broadcast the photograph again when they reported on her condition. The image subsequently was published in *Newsweek* and *Life* and repeatedly in newspapers (Goldberg, 1991). In 1973, Nick Ut was awarded the Pulitzer Prize for the photo, which has been reprinted frequently since that time (Goldberg, 1991).

Did/Does the Communication Involve Judgment of Communicator and Message Credibility?

Yes. The immediate response to the photograph and its message was horrified belief—that the war in Vietnam was so unacceptable that children were being killed and injured by a military that was supposed to be protecting them. This level of credibility was as much a product of the political times surrounding an increasingly unacceptable war as it was a product of generally accepted media routines. The era predated both manipulative digital imaging techniques and loss of public trust in journalism, and the photograph confirmed growing disillusion with U.S. involvement in Vietnam.

Further underscoring the credibility of the image was the fact that journalists other than Ut witnessed the scene and recorded it on videotape,

Joe McNally/LIFE Magazine © Time, Inc.

which also was broadcast the evening of the bombing. The still photograph, disseminated to newspapers by the Associated Press, quickly became a powerful symbol of why the United States should not support the war. Another truth-establishing process occurred when the photograph was nominated for the Pulitzer Prize. Before a photograph qualifies for the prize, its authenticity is carefully verified by witnesses and even subjects, when possible. Although some viewers questioned whether Kim Phuc had actually been burned because her skin appears unblemished in the photograph, videotape documenting the wounds to her back set doubts aside (Goldberg, 1991). Nevertheless, a U.S. general tried to discredit the photograph. In 1986, retired General William C. Westmoreland told a group of Florida business people that "an investigation determined Kim Phuc had been burned in an accident involving a hibachi, an open grill." When questioned later, he said, "My God, if she was hit by napalm, she would not have survived. I said it was told to me that she was burned by a hibachi." The military found no records of the investigation (Goldberg, 1991, p. 245).

As time went on, Kim Phuc's story was followed by the media and a concerned public audience. As noted earlier, in October 1996, *Life Magazine* published both the 1972 photo and the 1996 photograph by Joe McNally (see p. 164) clearly showing burn scars on Kim Phuc's arm and back. And in November 1996, Kim Phuc placed a wreath at the Vietnam War Memorial.

The photo's role as interpersonal and mass communication does not end there. Although the photograph was credited as being one of a few key images that helped turn public opinion against the Vietnam War (Goldberg, 1991, p. 244), the photo also has been blamed for misleading the public about culpability for the bombing (Timberlake, 1997). Timberlake, a Vietnam veteran, felt the need to investigate the origins of the photo. Acknowledging that the picture became an icon for peace, he pointed out that by the time the photo was taken, "almost all U.S. Ground forces had already been brought home from Viet Nam" (p. 3). Timberlake added:

By March of 1973, after the signing of the Paris Peace Accord, all U.S. combat forces were out of Viet Nam.

The photo was embarrassing to the U.S. government, but extremely damaging to the South Vietnamese government. It was a great propaganda tool for the Communists, and may have done more than any other photo to prevent the U.S. Congress from allowing assistance to the South Vietnamese government when North Viet Nam launched the full scale invasion of that country, in 1975. (p. 3)

Timberlake (1997) noted that Kim Phuc did not try to correct the assumption that the United States was responsible for her injuries: "All veterans have to see her pain, and feel her pain, and know that the people of their own country, and the people of the world, are once again being told, erroneously, that they are the ones who did that terrible deed" (pp. 4–5).

Timberlake and others (Irvine & Goulden, 1998) suggested Kim Phuc and "her handlers" had motives other than forgiveness for appearing at the 1996 Veteran's Day ceremony: "The new surge of publicity helped Kim Phuc as well, and in November 1997 she was named a good will ambassador by UNESCO" (Irvine & Goulden, 1998, p. 1).

Freund (1996), a columnist for *Slate*, noted that the photograph was used as propaganda for the North Vietnamese, but concluded, "The political manipulation of imagery doesn't delegitimize its content. The pain here is only too real; Kim still suffers from her wounds" (p. 3).

The debate continues, further evidence of the impact of one image of photojournalism.

In summary, using Buller's and Burgoon's criteria (1996) for describing interpersonal communication, we have established interpersonal dimensions related to a photograph distributed by the mass media: "Children Fleeing Napalm." The photograph and its protagonist have stirred multiple and varying individual relationships via mass media, a kind of "mass interpersonal relationship" that has become commonplace in this era of mass communication.

THEORETICAL IMPLICATIONS

The subject of this chapter can be approached in various ways. Are we talking about the interpersonal relationship that can develop between a photographer and subject as part of the mass media construction of reality? Are we talking about a politician's authentic effort (is that an oxymoron?) to connect with voters via television? I am specifically concerned about three locations with "interpersonal dimensions" within the mass communication process:

- The human being whose image is recorded and distributed in mass form to mass audiences.
- The human being or beings who record and distribute the image.
- The human beings who view and respond to the image.

Interpersonal communication, once considered only to occur between two persons face to face, has been effectively extended via mediating technology and global culture. As we have come to understand the construction of personal identity as integrally linked with social interaction, and as our means for extending human communication beyond face-to-face interaction has expanded exponentially, we must recognize that the nature of interpersonal communication has expanded to include communication between individuals who may never meet in physical form. Their meeting occurs as one individual is photographed for a news story and then is introduced throughout the world via television, newspapers, and the Internet. Acting as primary mediators, or facilitators, are the still and video photographers who must be physically present at the scene, which must be occupied by a physically real subject.

Secondary mediators are the editors and producers who select specific images and clips for the mass introduction. For the photographers, the interaction often is interpersonal as traditionally defined: two people communicate face to face. Their interaction can fall anywhere on a continuum from a quick encounter, such as that between an accident victim and a news photographer, to an extensive, long-term exchange, such as that between a documentary photographer who spends months developing a trusting relationship with a drug addict. Just as in any interpersonal communication, the resulting dialogue, whether verbal or visual, can be perceived as negative or positive by either person. Power, also, can reside on either side of the dialogue. Although often we think of photographers as having more power because of their assumed authority as conveyors of visual truth, certainly many subjects exert enormous power and control over their images, manipulating photographers into recording supposedly real, but actually pseudo activities.

After the initial person-to-person encounter, the photographer takes or sends his or her film or videotape to the news distribution point. This transfer can be handled personally, as with local newspaper photographers, or via couriers. A degree of discussion about the best report of the photographed individual and event may or may not occur, depending on the daily structures of the news organization. Important to our current discussion is that the interaction between the photographer and the imaged person may be reduced to one photograph or to a short video clip, and that visual equivalent of the person, in turn, may be viewed once or many times by a relatively small audience or by a mass, global audience.

Now move to the other side of the communication: the viewer, reader, audience, who can ignore, briefly view, stare, repeatedly view, and exhibit varying responses to the image of the original human being. Here is the heart of this chapter: In that viewing, in which the original person has agency only through the image, the seeds of a relationship with interpersonal dimensions may be planted. Although we must consider the process of image construction, distribution, and viewing a holistic process, it is important to understand the interpersonal dimensions involved in the way viewers and individuals who are imaged relate via a visual equivalent. These relationships are interpersonal because they are composed of two human beings, both of whom are real and one of whom communicates via his or her visual equivalent. The completion of the relationship occurs as the person who is imaged receives feedback from viewers in some form. The person then may respond with additional imaged nuances of communication about him- or herself, as he or she relates to a mentally imaged equivalent of the mass "other." And the loop continues, as demonstrated in the case of Kim Phuc.

SYMBOLIC INTERACTIONISM
AND VISUAL EQUIVALENTS THEORY

Return now to the theoretical bases for this discussion. Symbolic interactionism offers a useful framework in which to analyze the issue of mass-interpersonal communication. Those involved in a process of communication, such as those involved with the photographs of Kim Phuc, have acted on the basis of the meaning the photograph has for them. That meaning, in turn, was derived from social interaction on various levels. And the meanings derived were dealt with through an interpretative process unique to each person involved.

Visual equivalents theory helps to explain a phenomenon of visual perception that allows the mass-interpersonal communication to occur with a photographic stimulus. Images disseminated through the mass media can evoke interpersonal-like responses from viewers, establish feedback loops, and invite responses from the imaged persons. The communication requires exchange of meaning between two or more individuals via a dialogic moment accomplished through the mass media.

One way to articulate what happens in a mass interpersonal relationship is to apply terms from the typology of visual ethics presented in chapter 10. The typology, a dynamic, normative, and resonating continuum, begins with the concept of visual embrace. Applied to "Children Fleeing Napalm," one can argue that Nick Ut visually embraced Kim Phuc in her moment of terror, wrapping his eyes around her via his camera. At the same time he secured a visual quote from the moment, a quote that has become a visual document, and in some ways, a visual gift to Kim Phuc, in that public involvement in her tragedy has helped to improve her life since the event occurred.

Approaching the communication from another interpretation, one can argue that Ut visually raped Kim Phuc: She had no choice but to participate in the photographic moment during which she was as vulnerable as a person can be except at the point of death. Broadcasting her naked image could be termed a visual assault, further victimizing the 9-year-old girl by objectifying and commodifying her agony. So much of what people do during a communication event is interpreted through their own perceptual filters that the photograph cannot definitively be labeled visual embrace or visual rape. It is both. Even though we have come to know Kim Phuc through mass communication forms, individual interaction, as part of a collective, is the key to understanding the overall communication process.

PROPOSITIONS OF MASS-INTERPERSONAL COMMUNICATION

1. Making a photograph constitutes an event in which the photographer and the subject are participants.
2. The event of making a photograph involves a relationship between the photographer and the subject that can be interpersonal.
3. The relationship requires the photographer and subject to make conscious and unconscious decisions affecting their behaviors.
4. Those behavioral decisions are based on such factors as personal emotion, personality differences, gender, and conventions of photographic practice, as well as the interaction itself.
5. Both the photographer and the subject can exercise varying amounts of power in the relationship.
6. The resulting photograph reveals something about the subject, about the photographer, and about the relationship between the subject and the photographer.
7. Viewing a photograph constitutes an event in which the photographer, subject, and viewer are participants.
8. The quality of the event interaction occurring during the making of a photograph can affect the quality of the interaction during the viewing event.
9. The viewer brings his or her own set of personal interaction variables to the viewing event.
10. The event of viewing a photograph involves a relationship among the photographer, subject, and viewer.
11. Communicating via realistic imagery that is presented as an authentic equivalent involves an exchange of information and control between a photographer and subject and among a photographer, subject, and viewer. This exchange, which begins as an interpersonal relationship, can also be considered interpersonal as it continues, one-on-one, at mass levels.

Figure 3.1 presented a visual model of the interactive process of photojournalism. In the model, several key terms deserve explanation. First, *self:* Self refers to a human being, a sentient entity with feelings, thoughts, personality, and physiological characteristics, and possessing and using various degrees of power and interaction behaviors. As noted in the model, the person being photographed or videotaped is the "subject self," or the "person reflecting light." Note that this description is constructed as neutrally as possible, so as to avoid the inference that the individual is "subject to" the photographer or viewer, as well as to avoid the assumption that the "subject" is objectified via the interaction. A continuum of agency is essential to the definition: The "person reflecting light" can exhibit a range of behaviors from passivity to aggression. On the other side of the primary interaction is the "photographer self," or the "person recording the light." Typically, this individual describes his or her actions in aggressive terms: "I'm *shooting* the President this afternoon," "I'm here to *take* your picture." Ideally, the interaction between the two selves, which is mediated to some extent by the camera, or recording device, allows each individual to respond to equal degrees. However, as literature in interpersonal communication demonstrates, the power balance between a photographer and subject can vary widely, with one or the other behaving in a more or less powerful manner. Key to our discussion is the fact that the image or images that result from their interaction also can be considered a form of data, a visible record of interpersonal communication. Yet another factor, also discussed extensively in interpersonal literature, is the context of the interaction, the situation in which the subject and photographer communicate.

The next level of the model, the level of the image itself, should be interpreted as a visual equivalent of the interaction. The photographer, however, is no longer visible—except through the latent implication that someone looked through a camera lens at the individual imaged and recorded light reflected from that person as he or she moved or talked or stared back at the photographer. Although we know the photographer selected the frame, the moment, perhaps even the individual to record, these factors are seldom considered as we focus on the individual in the photograph. The resulting image, which is the visual record of an interpersonal communication, translates the body of a human being into a form to which editors, producers, and, ultimately, viewers can respond.

Another term applied at this level of the communication process is *context*, which now refers to its own multilevel set. Context can be the physical and ideological frame in which the image is created or the package of words, pictures, and sounds that accompany the image on its voyage through the media. Context includes the ultimate form of presentation to a viewer, whether an electronic medium, with its screen, or a print publication, with its page.

The third level, that of the "viewer self," must be understood in terms of the first two levels, and both level two and level three are grounded in the

FIGURE 11.1 Ecology of an Image of Reportage

first. For the first level is where the image begins—within the interpersonal dynamic between two people. Although the image they created together has entered multiple mediation arenas, an authentic, arresting piece of visual reportage carries at least part of its own meaning throughout time. Figure 11.1 details the overall multilevel process as an ecology of the visual.

A great deal of contemporary theoretical literature emphasizes ideas of the subjectivity of audience reception, "the other," subjective construction of reality, the powerlessness of the individual, and the hegemony of global media. However, although all such factors expressed in critical and cultural literature do potentially influence the creation, use, and reading of the image, the fact is that in visual reportage the image began with a human who reflected light. That human may have been exuberant or dead, in the throes of grief or the jubilation of birth. That person existed and something happened. The event in which the person participated may have been accidental (a plane crash), intentional (war), or fabricated (parade). But the event occurred in some real-life form that could be recorded on film or videotape and shown to a world of individual viewers. It is important to distinguish this real-life event of a real person from the majority of media images, in which the image of the person reflecting light can be so purposefully and carefully constructed that even the *person* may be fictitious. As discussed in chapter 9, that construction also is, or exists as an entity. Nevertheless, such images confuse our abilities to distinguish between the real and the fantastic, obfuscate our responses to images of real people is real situations.

The answer to this dilemma is to increase visual literacy of media users, empowering them to discern visual truth from visual fiction.

CONCLUSION

As people's abilities to communicate have diminished the necessity for physical interaction, mass–interpersonal relationships have become commonplace. By broadening the conception of interpersonal communication to include *face-to-image* communication, communication scholarship can acknowledge an existing phenomenon facilitated by visual reportage and begin to study it for what it is. Is it not possible that in the midst of our concern about the "loss of experienceability of the world" (Ronell, 1994), we are evolving to a higher plane of interaction in which the visual equivalent of a person can evoke our deepest human responses?

NAVA CHRISTMAS EVE. Doña Margarita with her great-granddaughter on a Christmas Eve in Mexico. (Photo by Julie Newton.)

CHAPTER 12

The Future

Changes in the practice of photojournalism have accompanied each new technological shift: from glass plates to film, from large-format to 35 mm, from film to video, and from film/video to digital. What has not changed is the need to understand and to know about the world around us and about those who share that world with us. This chapter reviews the major themes of this book within the context of one question: Is there a future for photojournalism and for visual truth?

CHAPTER 12

The Future

The great Wilson Hicks, a pioneer in photojournalism, was among the first to recognize that words plus pictures equaled something more than either alone. As with the theory of relativity, a simple equation expressed a complex phenomenon—this one known as the principle of the Gestalt. When visual elements are read as part of a whole, the message perceived is greater than—and different from—the sum of any of those elements read separately.

The classic idea "the whole is greater than the sum of its parts" encapsulates the complexities of understanding truth in visual reportage. A newspaper page, for example, comprises several kinds of visual symbols: words and images arranged on an underlying grid or skeleton. Words, of course, comprise letterforms that are associated with sounds, all of which, when combined in certain patterns, mean something to the human mind—if that mind has learned to decode the words and if the words are in a language that mind understands. Images, whether photographs or graphic designs, comprise shapes and tones that represent animate and inanimate entities carved out of a multidimensional world in unique frames, which, when combined in certain patterns, mean something to the human mind. And when the words, with all their letterforms, are combined with images, with all their shapes and tones, as parts of a single page or a single screen, we see them in relation to one another—as parts forming the pattern of a whole page with one and many meanings.

But just as seeing the whole page is different from reading one headline, so is truth more than any one part. Journalism is at once a construction and real. Word and visual reporters go out into the world to gather information to the best of their abilities. They represent what they find in stories, or verbal compositions, and in pictures, which are visual compositions. Reportage began as a simple, vital necessity for human survival. As humans have evolved, so have their capacities for gathering, disseminating, and interpreting information. What once was communicated by guttural sounds and silent gestures, or perhaps by a responsive action, is now communicated in newspapers, magazines, books, print publications of various kinds; on television and via computers; in film and new media. Although *journalism* as a term was coined to refer to journal reports, the term now includes reportage disseminated via a variety of media.

What we knew as photojournalism during most of the 20th century meant print photographs accompanied by words and intended to depict reality. New practices have occurred with each new technological shift: from large-format to 35 mm, from still to film to video, and from film/video to digital. The shift from the 4 × 5 Speed-Graphic to 35-mm camera format enabled photographers to shoot more quickly and discretely. The shift from gelatin-silver film processes to digital processes has enabled photographers to transmit images instantly to their newsrooms from the scene of an event. As readers have come to expect color in their newspapers, even *The New York Times* has changed its classic "good, gray" front-page design to incorporate color (although muted) pictures. The ease of using videocameras has enabled amateur witnesses to assume a larger role in mass media reportage, as in the cases of John F. Kennedy's assassination and Rodney King's beating, and people can use one camera to make both still and moving images. Digital imaging, in tandem with Internet communication, has made possible the immediate updating of news accounts via the Web. Satellite technology has made possible a worldwide, real-time audience for any activity that can be recorded visually. Awareness of a media connected global citizenry made watching television reportage of turn-of-the-millennium celebrations uncannily poignant.

But has the substance of photojournalism changed? Will photojournalism continue to mean reporting with still and video cameras? What is its relationship to reality TV, magnetic resonance imaging (MRI), and satellite surveillance? Is a new term, such as *visual journalism*, or *visual reportage*, or *digital journalist* (Halsteadt), in order? Can photojournalism continue its quest to produce uncompromising visual reportage? How will future technological advances affect the production, content, use, and perception of photojournalism? Will words and pictures continue to merge into increasingly sophisticated media forms until they are indistinguishable from the manner in which human beings express themselves without technology? Or does the body comprise the machines it makes and uses, extending itself via ever-growing tentacles? Does technology itself comprise the body as well as the machines the body makes? Changes in human communication that we cannot yet imagine will be in place by the year 2100. Will photojournalism continue to play a role in mediating visual truth? Will we even continue to pursue an ideal of visual truth?

STATUS OF PHOTOJOURNALISM

A few years ago, a panel of journalism educators addressed the question: "Photojournalism: Are We Beating a Dead Horse?" The question was posed in light of advances in digital imaging that challenged the authority of the photograph. Responses ranged from "teaching photojournalism is a good way to teach students to be good observers and to think critically," to "photojournalism remains invaluable in and of itself." People predicted the demise of art with the advent of photography, the demise of radio with the advent of television, the demise of newspapers with the advent of the Internet. Photography freed hand art from the burden of realistic representation, opening the door to new forms of visual expression and personal reflexivity. Although television captured the so-called mass audience, radio became a requisite part of an automobile culture and developed in-depth global reporting strategies. Newspapers are adapting to Internet forms, while continuing print forms. Digital imaging, which many predicted spelled the demise of photojournalism, has freed visual reportage from the time-consuming and physical constraints of wet, gelatin-silver processing. Photographic processes now refer to a variety of 19th- and 20th-century methods, as well as to styles ranging from straight, or unmanipulated, photographs, to nonrealist, pictorialist, photo-montage, and highly constructed works.

More important than technique, process, or style, however, is the rationale driving the image production. Technologies come and go, adapt, and mutate. But the rationale for doing good photojournalism has only clarified with each new advance. It is as if each new level of capability for producing images has heightened our awareness of the human capacity for molding what we perceive to be real. The need for good visual reportage has not lessened—it has increased. We still need reliable visual records and reports of events and people from around the world in order to comprehend contemporary life and to make decisions about how best to live our individual and collective lives. Some form of the visual must remain dependably honest and nonmanipulative. Visual reportage remains the only form of mass, multimedia practice that strives to communicate via accurate and fair imagery. Newspapers, television, magazines, and the Internet continue to rely on visual reportage to communicate what cannot be articulated verbally and to draw reader or viewer attention to the news. What remains to be seen is the extent to which visual reportage will be used and the extent to which it will be believed.

VISUAL TRUTH

This book has examined various components of photojournalistic practice: photographer, subject, editor, viewer, society, visual perception, and human visual behavior. Each component affects what ultimately becomes thought of or known as truth. Technologies of reportage change, practices change, and human understanding of the nature of reality and truth changes. But the pursuit of understanding continues. Visual reportage maintains a delicate relationship with truth. Many people believe we cannot really know reality, we cannot really know truth, and therefore that we cannot really know. Yet we continue to rely on visual truth. We believe X-rays when they show us a broken bone, ultrasound when it reveals the moving form of a fetus, the Hubbell telescope when it transmits photographs from space. Each of those technologies requires human mediation to some extent. So, why would we not believe the images of trained seers, the visual journalists, many of whom are willing to die in order to show us what is happening in our world?

At any given moment, each of us is seer and seen, manipulator and manipulated, mediator and judge, authentic and inauthentic. The shift is both as powerful and as subtle as the shift from seeing figure to seeing ground—and back again to seeing figure and then to seeing ground. Sometimes we become stuck viewing only figure and cannot discern ground as its own truth. And sometimes we are so embedded in ground that we cannot rise to see the figure we do not want to see. If we can but hold the notion of *the shift itself* as the constant in our perceptions and experiences of the real—as in the old saw, "the only thing that's certain is change itself"— we may approach the mature vision that is possible in this new century.

Photojournalism is the perfect metaphor—and the necessary method— for tending this shift. It at once beckons our focus toward human's organic existence, refusing to enable the preference for seeing only what one wants to see, and suspends subjective perceptions of existence in a medium through which we can ponder them and learn from them—if we will. Photojournalism stops a bit of time so that people can consider the whole of time. The burden of visual truth falls on the shoulders of all travelers through the labyrinth. But all travelers cannot be present in all places and times. We need the eyes of others to perceive and record their visions for us to view when we can. We have never needed them more. And that is the burden of the visual journalist—and of visual truth. We can theorize the origins, the effects, the ethics, the practice of photojournalism; the encoding and decoding of a photograph; and the use and misuse of images. But theorize as we will, without a caring person behind a camera at a scene— whether war or peace—we would not know as much as we do about the world, the people who inhabit it, or about ourselves as members of the human species.

What is the alternative? The worst-case scenario is that no one will believe anything. The best-case scenario is that people will be able to believe anything that is supposed to be true. The likely case is that people will continue to believe some images. So, how do we increase the likelihood that images of photojournalism will be credible?

WHAT CAN WE DO?

The effects of the visual on human life, culture, and behavior, and vice versa, are profound. Few would deny the need to improve the practice and use of visual reportage, and thereby to improve comprehension of visual truth. It is always easier to suggest that something needs to be done than it is to figure out how to do it—or to do it. The process of image-making and image-understanding is hardly something to marginalize or ignore. We can start in several ways.

1. Think in terms of an ecology of the visual that increases awareness of the impact of visual behavior on everything else humans know and do.

2. Require visual training from preschool through higher education as a significant part of the general preparation of a free, self-reflective person who can participate consciously, appropriately, and fully in contemporary society. We can emphasize values-based teaching, learning, and research that focus on respect for others, respect for oneself, and respect for the process of interacting with others.

3. Increase the opportunities for communication professionals to become aware of the relationship between images and visual truth via journalism and mass communication education based on an integrated visual and verbal curriculum.

4. Extend research into perception and visual communication across disciplines and into the forefront of priorities.

5. Extend the appropriate use of visual methods throughout all research processes.

6. Continue to extend the photojournalistic eye wherever needed while respecting the privacy of an individual wherever possible.

A photographer might begin with a series of questions: Do I need to take (or make or co-create) this photograph? Why? What will this image communicate? Is it as fair and truthful as I can make it? Will this image invade someone's privacy or invite harm to come to him or her? If so, what justifies the act of photographing this—if anything?

A visual journalist/social scientist should consider six basic concerns: subject, community, project purpose, society, science, and self (Newton, 1983, 1984). Thinking through an observing situation at each of the six levels of concern can help a visual journalist/researcher enter a setting as an individual who has established his or her own ethical system for behaving fairly, honestly, and in a caring, responsible manner. Such a process of self-study can maximize the opportunity for conducting work ethically, in terms of both how one goes about the investigation (process), and how the results of the investigation are used (meaning).

Professionals can design journalism routines that acknowledge the subjective nature of visual truth while striving to produce reasonably accurate visual images. New routines might include structuring caption information to cite the subjective role of photojournalism in reporting news; regularly using more than one exciting image to communicate a story; showing the same moment from different points of view; noting when a particularly compelling image is not necessarily representative of a story, person, place, or event; and regularly including visual and media literacy lessons through examples published in journalism media.

Viewers can develop ways to make image critique an ongoing part of their interpretation of images. Recalling Eco's suggestion that people launch semiological guerilla warfare, Eldridge (1993) called for better education of media users as "a response to the technological imperatives of the mass media and a form of resistance to the elusive, sometimes anonymous power which produces and suffuses the media" (p. 348). Viewers can discuss significant pictures, help their children learn to critique media images, and challenge sources that disseminate inauthentic material.

Consider the potential impact of some of these actions on a reading of the news. Instead of looking at news through a kind of mindless, what-is-the-world-coming-to filter, people might stop to ponder context, stereotype, point of view, and editorial concerns. Idealistic. Yes, indeed. But as I have argued throughout this book, if we do not strive for the best possibility we can imagine, we are likely to settle for much less—or to settle for no possibility at all. Visual truth is the most authentically seen information humans can discern, and it is worth the search.

IN CONCLUSION

The 20th century began with a new world of imaging waiting ahead, 100 years in which human visual behavior would expand via technology into the body, into what were thought the smallest particles of matter, and around and beyond the earth. Much as the 16th-century discovery that the sun was the center of the solar system shifted humans' perceptions of their role in existence, so did 20th-century visual exploration shift human understanding of the very nature of perception itself. We left the century with the fear than we could understand, or truly know, nothing.

Just the opposite is true. The more we understand about the limitations of perception and knowledge, the more we can know. Photojournalism exemplifies this concept. The ability to catch bits of time from different points of view has shown us how variable our perceptions can be. Armed with that knowledge, 21st-century humans have the unique opportunity to see more clearly than anyone before them. We know now that technology can not solve perceptual problems for us simply by recording light reflected from the real world and conveying that visual record. We know now that a photograph can lie by showing us only part of the whole, by showing us only one angle, by showing us a bit of time out of an hour. We know now how easily a person can manipulate what is seen by manipulating real-world action, by manipulating the frame put around part of that action, or by later manipulating the resulting image and its use.

So what? The fact that we know that people can lie and fake behaviors does not mean we have to stop believing everything all people say and do. We can, however, develop the perceptual abilities to distinguish lie from truth. The same is true of photojournalism. It is mostly a matter of shifting our assumptions. We can shift the assumption that a photograph is true because it looks real to the assumption that what we know from an image is the product of perception. The authenticity of an image's content depends on the authenticity of the subject, the photographer, the editors and publishers, society, and one's own abilities to see through personal and public filters.

The tricky part is that some parts of our bodies may still be operating on the assumption that seeing is believing, even if other parts know better. Therein lies the burden of visual truth. For the photojournalist, the burden is seeing as clearly and authentically as one can. For the source or subject of information, the burden is being as authentic as one can. For the editor and publishers, the burden is disseminating the most authentic information possible. For the viewer, the burden is stopping to think about what one sees and demanding authenticity in images that are intended to be true. For society at large, the burden is creating an educational and media structure that teaches the power and limitations of visual knowing.

The critical task for visual reportage in the coming century is to guard vehemently the real within the culture of the virtual. Photojournalism traditionally has been known as still photography, using wet labs and gelatin-silver technology. The New Photojournalism crosses media:

- Still—film and digital.
- Video.
- Internet.
- Multimedia.
- Information companies.

But we have come to understand that photojournalism is more than a medium or technological application. Photojournalism is visual journalism, the guardian of the real. In that function, visual reportage acknowledges that reality is constructed, but applies well-considered methods to record and interpret real occurrences in people's lives in as authentic a manner as possible for others to see.

In that role, those who practice visual reportage must consider the significance of ethics to their being and, in turn, the significance of their being to how they navigate the world and how they work as journalists.

Real ethics is made of the subtle moments of living and dying. The burden of truth is composed of those decisions we make, in every moment we live. Those moments, in turn, make up the whole of our lives and our realities.

Law is what society decides people *have* to do. Ethics is deciding what is *right* to do. For visual journalists, editors, and disseminators of images, that means maintaining the right to take pictures, to protect their pictures, and to freely express themselves via their pictures. But they also have responsibilities:

- To respect human beings.
- To report clearly what they see.
- To be fair, accurate, and honest.
- To use images fairly.

Subjects, in turn, have the right to privacy of space and place, of time and moment, to say "no," and to protect themselves and their images. They also have responsibilities:

- To be nonmanipulative.
- To be truthful.
- To understand their role in the collective imagery of humankind.
- To respect the idea of a free press as ultimately being in everyone's interest.

For viewers, that means having the right to expect conscientiously obtained, reasonable truth from all forms of news media. But they also have responsibilities:

- To pursue and promote visual literacy.
- To read images with concern for the individuals and messages within them.
- To think critically about visual messages.
- To challenge misleading or untruthful reportage.
- To demand authenticity where appropriate.

Are these goals unobtainable? Yes. But the burden—and the truth—are in the seeking.

AFTERWORD

If I am true to what I have said about ethics and reality, I must tell you about who I am, for all that I am has influenced everything you have read in this book. I have relied on a rational process to study and analyze the status of photojournalism and visual truth. I used both quantitative and qualitative methods to obtain data and test my ideas. But my intuitive sense of what people are about prompted the study, and at the heart of the ideas is human emotion, things we often cannot rationally explain. My work is the compilation of many feelings, thoughts, and conversations with others.

Without going through "It all began in… " I will tell a few important things about myself. Both of my grandfathers were preachers, and both of my parents were missionaries. I grew up in a self-conscious world, in which people were almost always concerned about (even driven to) helping other people. My grandmother gave me my first camera when I was 9, and people in my family have been recording my image since I was born. It probably is important that I am female, tall, was born in Texas, and have no idea what my IQ is. My gut feeling is that I really started living a conscious life when I was about 34. Until then I was living the life I thought I was supposed to live. I have a son who sometimes refuses to let me take his picture and two step children who think nothing at all of being photographed. My husband is a photographer and often makes images of me at unexpected times.

My husband and I once spent an hour photographing an event that will not happen again for 20 to 25 years—an eclipse of the sun. I could not help but wonder about the nature of our lives—so dependent on a bright light 400 million miles away. We had to view the eclipse projected through a small hole onto a piece of paper. I thought of Aristotle viewing the crescent-shaped image of the same sun through a leaf 2,400 years ago, and I wondered if Rick and I would photograph the next solar eclipse together.

Isn't it interesting that we could not look directly at something so vital to our lives without being blinded? We had to look at an image of the sun in order to see it. That seems extremely important: If we look directly at some things, we become blind. Looking at images instead enables us to see.

—J.N.

REFERENCES

Adorno, T. W. (1989). Lyric poetry and society. In S. E. Bronner & D. M. Kellner (Eds.), *Critical theory and society: A reader*. New York: Routledge.

Agee, J., & Evans, W. (1960). *Let us now praise famous men*. New York: Ballantine Books. (Original work published 1940)

Alabiso, V., Tunney, K. S., & Zoeller, C. (Eds.). (1998). *Flash! The Associated Press covers the world*. New York: The Associated Press in association with Harry N. Abrams.

American Society of Media Photographers. (1998). *Code of ethics*. Available: *http://www.monsterbit.com/asmp/ethics.html*

Americans' view of the press. (2000). *Frontline*. Available: *http://www.fiej.org/research_centre/research_news/index.html*

Arnheim, R. (1969). *Visual thinking*. Berkeley: University of California Press.

Arnheim, R. (1974). *Art and visual perception: A psychology of the creative eye* (rev. ed.). Berkeley: University of California Press.

Arnett, P. (1998). Introduction. Eyewitness to history. In V. Alabiso, K. S. Tunney, & C. Zoeller (Eds.), *Flash! The Associated Press covers the world* (pp. 15–22). New York: The Associated Press in association with Harry N. Abrams.

Aultschull, J. H. (1984). *Agents of power, the role of the news media in human affairs*. New York: Longman.

Avedon, R. (1985). *In the American West*. New York: Harry N. Abrams.

Bakewell, L. (1998). Image acts. *American Anthropologist, 100*(1), 22–32.

Barry, A. M. (1997a, May). *Digital manipulation of public images: Local issues and global consequences*. Paper presented at the annual meeting of the International Communication Association, Montreal.

Barry, A. M. (1997b). *Visual intelligence: Perception, image, and manipulation in visual communication*. Albany: State University of New York Press.

Baudrillard, J. (1994). *Simulacra and simulation* (S. F. Glaser, Trans.). Ann Arbor: University of Michigan Press.

Bazin, A. (1967). On the ontology of the photographic image. In *What is cinema?* (H. Gray, Trans., Vol. 1, pp. 9–16). Berkeley: University of California Press.

Bechara, A., Damasio, H., Tranel, D., & Damasio, A. (1997). Deciding advantageously before knowing the advantageous strategy. *Science, 275,* 1293–1295.

Becker, H. S. (2000). *Visual sociology, documentary photography, and photojournalism: It's (almost) all a matter of context.* Available: *http://www.lsweb.sscf.ucsb.edu/depts/soc/faculty/hbecker/visual.html* (Original work published 1995)

Bellman, B., & Jules-Rosette, B. (1977). *A paradigm for looking: Cross-cultural research with visual media.* Norwood, NJ: Ablex.

Beloff, H. (1985). *Camera culture.* Oxford: Basil Blackwell.

Benjamin, W. (1969). The work of art in the age of mechanical reproduction. In H. Arendt (Ed.), *Illuminations* (H. Zohn, Trans., pp. 219–253). New York: Harcourt, Brace & World.

Berger, J., & Mohr, J. (1982). *Another way of telling.* New York: Pantheon Books.

Berger, P. L., & Luckmann, T. (1967). *The social construction of reality: A treatise in the sociology of knowledge.* New York: Doubleday. (Original work published 1966)

Best, S., & Kellner, D. (1991). *Postmodern theory: critical interrogations.* New York: The Guilford Press.

Blumer, H. (1969). *Symbolic interactionism, perspective and method.* Englewood Cliffs, NJ: Prentice Hall.

Bolton, R. (Ed.). (1989). *The contest of meaning: Critical histories of photography.* Cambridge, MA: MIT Press.

Brown, C. (1995, August). *Listening to subjects of photojournalism.* Paper presented to the Visual Communication Division, Association for Education in Journalism and Mass Communication National Convention, Washington, DC.

Bryant, G. (1990). Ten-Fifty P.I.: Emotion and the photographer's role. In P. M. Lester (Ed.), *NPPA special report: The ethics of photojournalism* (pp. 20–22). Durham, NC: National Press Photographers Association.

Buell, H. (1999). *Moments, the Pulitzer-Prize winning photographs, a chronicle of our time.* New York: Black Dog & Leventhal Publishers.

Buller, D. B., & Burgoon, J. K. (1996). Interpersonal deception theory. *Communication Theory, 6*(3), 203–242.

Burgin, V. (Ed.). (1982). *Thinking photography.* London: Macmillan Press.

Burnham, S. (1990). *A book of angels.* New York: Ballantine.

Buss, A. J. (1980). *Self-consciousness and social anxiety.* San Francisco: Freeman.

Calloway, S. G., & Hamilton, J. (no date). *Alfred Stieglitz, photographs and writings.* New York: National Gallery of Art.

Capra, F. (1996). *The web of life: A new scientific understanding of living systems.* New York: Anchor Books.

Carey, J. W. (1988). *Communication as culture, essays on media and society.* Boston: Unwin Hyman.

Carlebach, M. L. (1992). *The origins of photojournalism in America.* Washington, DC: Smithsonian Institution Press.

Carpenter, E. (1975). The tribal terror of self awareness. In P. Hockings (Ed.), *Principles of visual anthropology* (pp. 452–461). The Hague: Mouton.

Carter, B. (2000, January 13). CBS divided over the use of fake images in broadcasts. *The New York Times,* pp. C1, C2.

Chapnick, H. (1994). *Truth needs no ally.* Columbia: University of Missouri Press.

Christians, C. G. (1996). Common ground and future hopes. In P. M. Lester (Ed.), *Images that injure: Pictorial stereotypes in the media* (pp. 237–243). Westport, CT: Praeger.

Christians, C. G., Fackler, M., & Rotzoll, K. B. (1995). *Media ethics: Cases & moral reasoning.* White Plains, NY: Longman.

Coles, R. (1997) *Doing documentary work.* New York: Oxford University Press.

Collier, J. (1967). *Visual anthropology: Photography as a research method.* New York: Holt, Rinehart & Winston.

Contact Press. (1992). *Photojournalism since Vietnam.* Exhibition presented at the Center for Research on Contemporary Art, University of Texas at Arlington.

Cooley, C. H. (1956). *Two major works: Social organization and Human nature and the social order* (rev. ed). Glencoe, IL: The Free Press. (Original work published 1902)

Cooper, T. (1998). New technology effects inventory: Forty leading ethical issues. *Journal of Mass Media Ethics, 13*(2), 71–92.

Craig, R. T. (1999). Communication theory as a field. *Communication Theory, 9*(2), 119–161.

Crick, F. (1994). *The astonishing hypothesis: The scientific search for the human soul.* New York: Scribner.

Dates, J., & Barlow, W. (1990). *Split image: African-Americans in the media.* Washington, DC: Howard University Press.

Debord, G. (1967). *The society of the spectacle* (D. Nicholson-Smith, Trans.). New York: Zone Books. (Original work published 1967)

Denton, C. (1994). *Graphics for visual communication.* Dubuque, IA: Wm. C. Brown.

Denzin, N. K. (1984). *On understanding emotion.* San Francisco: Jossey-Bass.

Denzin, N. K. (1995). *The cinematic society: The voyeur's gaze.* Thousand Oaks, CA: Sage.

Deppa, J., with M. Russell, D. Hayes, & E. L. Flocke. (1993). *The media and disasters: Pan Am 103.* London: Fulton.

Derrida, J. (1993). *Memoirs of the blind: The self-portrait and other ruins* (P.-A. Brault & M. Naas, Trans.). Chicago: University of Chicago Press.

Desfor, D. M. (1979). *The meaning that photographs depicting four different family units have for respondents*. Unpublished doctoral dissertation, United States International University, San Diego, CA.

Dodd, A. (1998, September 4). *Queen of the operating theatre*. Available: http://www.mg.co.za/art/fineart/9809/980904-orlan.html

Dondis, D.A. (1973). *A primer of visual literacy*. Cambridge, MA: MIT Press.

Duncan, D. D. (1951). *This is war! A photo narrative in three parts*. New York: Harper.

Duncan, D. D. (1958). *The private world of Pablo Picasso*. New York: Ridge Press.

Duncan, D. D. (1961). *Picasso's Picassos*. New York: Harper.

Duncan, D. D. (1969). *Self-portrait, USA*. New York: H. N. Abrams.

Duncan, D. D. (1970). *War without heroes*. New York: Harper & Row.

Duncan, D. D. (1974). *Goodbye Picasso*. New York: Grosset & Dunlap.

Durham, M. G. (1999). Girls, media, and the negotiation of sexuality: A study of race, class, and gender in adolescent peer groups. *Journalism & Mass Communication Quarterly, 76*(2), 193–216.

Dyer, R. (1993). *The matter of images, essays on representation*. London: Routledge.

Eldridge, J. (Ed.). (1993). *Getting the message. News, truth and power*. London: Routledge.

Evans, H. (1992). Facing a grim reality. *American Photographer 1*(4), 48.

First Amendment Center. (1999). *State of the First Amendment 1999*. Nashville, TN: First Amendment Center. Available:*http://www.freedomforum.org*

Foster, H. (Ed.). (1988). *Vision and visuality*. Seattle, WA: Bay Press.

Foucault, M. (1973). *The birth of the clinic: An archaeology of medical perception* (A. M. Sheridan Smith, Trans.). New York: Pantheon Books.

Foucault, M. (1977). *Discipline and punish* (A. Sheridan, Trans.). New York: Pantheon Books.

FOX Network. (1996, September 22 Channel 7, Austin, Texas). *This week*.

Freund, G. (1980). *Photography and society*. Boston: David R. Godine.

Freund, C. P. (Nov. 21 1996). Vietnam's most harrowing photo: From guilt to grace. *Slate*. Available: *http://www.slate.com/BigPicture/96-11-21/BigPicture.asp*

Fulfs, P. (1999). *Science and nature, beauty and the grotesque: Orlan and the embodiment of monstrosity*. Unpublished manuscript, The University of Texas at Austin.

Fulton, M. (1988). *The eyes of time*. Boston: Little, Brown.

Galassi, P. (1981). *Before photography: Painting and the invention of photography*. New York: Museum of Modern Art.

Gearan, A. (1997, April 13). Quieting the screams of war, soldier who gave bombing order meets girl in photo. *Austin-American Statesman*, p. A23.

Gernsheim, H. (1962). *Creative photography*. New York: Bonanza.

Gilman, S. L. (Ed.). (1976). *The face of madness, Hugh W. Diamond and the origin of psychiatric photography*. New York: Brunner/Mazel.

Goffman, E. (1967). *Interaction ritual.* New York: Pantheon Books.

Goffman, E. (1969). *Strategic interaction.* Philadelphia: University of Pennsylvania Press.

Goffman, E. (1973). *The presentation of self in everyday life.* Woodstock, NY: Overlook Press. (Original work published 1959)

Goffman, E. (1974). *Frame analysis.* New York: Harper & Row.

Goldberg, V. (1991). *The power of photography: How photographs changed our lives.* New York: Abbeville Press.

Goldberg, V. (1992, October). *Photojournalism since Vietnam.* Paper presented at a symposium, University of Texas at Arlington.

Gombrich, E. H. (1961). *Art and illusion, a study in the psychology of pictorial representation* (rev. ed.). Princeton, NJ: Princeton University Press.

Gombrich, E. H., Hochberg, J., & Black, M. (1972). *Art, perception, and reality.* Baltimore, MD: Johns Hopkins University Press.

Graber, D. A. (1990). Seeing is remembering: How visuals contribute to learning from television news. *Journal of Communication, 40*(3), 134–155.

Gregory, R. L. (1970). *The intelligent eye.* New York: McGraw-Hill.

Gregory, R. L. (1990). *Eye and brain, the psychology of seeing* (4th ed.). Princeton, NJ: Princeton University Press.

Gross, L., Katz, J. S., & Ruby, J. (Eds.). (1988). *Image ethics, the moral rights of subjects in photographs, film, and television.* New York: Oxford University Press.

Hagaman, D. (1996). *How I learned not to be a photojournalist.* Lexington: University of Kentucky.

Hale, L., & Church, D. (1996, December). *News Photographer,* pp. 22–25.

Hall, S. (1973). The determination of news photographs. In S. Cohen & J. Young (Eds.), *The manufacture of news: A reader* (pp. 176–190). London: Constable.

Hammersley, M. (1995). *The politics of social research.* London: Sage.

Harper, D. (1979). Life on the road. In J. Wagner (Ed.), *Images of information: Still photography in the social sciences* (pp. 25–42). Beverly Hills, CA: Sage.

Harper, D. A. (1982). *Good company.* Chicago: University of Chicago Press.

Harper, D. (1993). On the authority of the image: Visual methods at the crossroads. In N. K. Denzin & Y. S. Lincoln (Eds.), *Handbook of qualitative research* (pp. 403–412). Thousand Oaks, CA: Sage.

Hartley, C. (1981). *The reactions of photojournalists and the public to hypothetical ethical dilemmas confronting press photographers.* Unpublished master's thesis, University of Texas, Austin.

Hartley, C. (1990). Ethics in photojournalism: Past, present and future. In P. M. Lester (Ed.), *NPPA Special report: The ethics of photojournalism* (pp. 16–19). Durham, NC: National Press Photographers Association.

Hartley, P. (1993). *Interpersonal communication.* London: Routledge.

Henderson, L. (1988). A selected annotated bibliography. In L. Gross, J. S. Katz, & J. Ruby (Eds.), *Image ethics, the moral rights of subjects in photographs, film, and television* (pp. 273–379). New York: Oxford University Press.

Herman, E. S., & Chomsky, N. (1988). *Manufacturing consent: The political economy of the mass media.* New York: Pantheon Books.

Herman, E. S., & McChesney, R. W. (1997). *The global media: The new missionaries of corporate capitalism.* Washington, DC: Cassell.

Holmes, N. (1994, August 12). *The future of visual design.* Lecture presented to the Visual Communication Division, Association for Education in Journalism and Mass Communication, Atlanta, GA.

hooks, b. (1995). *Art on my mind: visual politics.* New York: New Press.

Innis, H. A. (1951). *The bias of communication.* Toronto: University of Toronto Press.

Irvine, R., & Goulden, J. (1998). *Energetic Vietnam veteran exposes a big war lie.* Available: *http://www.opinioninc.com/aim/1998/011598.html*

Ivins, W. (1978). *Prints and visual communication.* Cambridge: MIT Press. (Original work published 1953)

Jarecke, K. (1992, October 16). *Photojournalism since Vietnam.* Exhibition and symposium, Center for Research in Contemporary Art, University of Texas at Arlington.

Jarecke, K., & Cervenka, E. (1992). *Just another war.* Joliet, MO: Bedrock Press.

Jay, B. (1984). The photographer as aggressor. In D. Featherstone (Ed.), *Observations, essays on documentary photography* (pp. 7–23). Carmel, CA: Friends of Photography.

Jaynes, J. (1990). *The origin of consciousness in the breakdown of the bicameral mind.* Boston: Houghton Mifflin. (Original work published 1976)

JEB (Joan E. Biren). (1981). Lesbian photography—Seeing through our own eyes. *Studies in Visual Communication, 9*(2), 81–96.

Kelly, J. D., & Nace, D. (1994, Winter). Digital imaging & believing photos. *Visual Communication Quarterly, 1,* 4–5, 18.

Knapp, M. L., & Hall, J. A. (1997). *Nonverbal communication in human interaction* (4th ed.). Fort Worth, TX: Harcourt Brace.

Kobre, K. (1996). *Photojournalism: The professional approach* (3rd ed.). Boston: Focal Press.

Kozol, W. (1994). *Life's America—Family and nation in postwar photojournalism.* Philadelphia: Temple University Press.

Lasswell, H. D. (1948). The structure and function of communication in society. In L. Bryson (Ed.), *The communication of ideas* (pp. 32–51). New York: Harper.

LeDoux, J. (1986). Sensory systems and emotion. *Integrative Psychiatry, 4,* 237–243.

Leekley, S., & Leekley, J. (1982). *Moments, the Pulitzer Prize photographs, updated edition: 1942–1982.* New York: Crown.

Lester, P. M. (Ed.). (1990). *NPPA Special report: The ethics of photojournalism.* Durham, NC: National Press Photographers Association.

Lester, P. M. (1991). *Photojournalism, the ethical approach.* Hillsdale, NJ: Lawrence Erlbaum Associates.

Lester, P. M. (1995). *Visual communication: Images with messages.* Belmont, CA: Wadsworth.

Lester, P. M. (Ed.). (1996). *Images that injure: Pictorial stereotypes in the media.* Westport, CT: Praeger.

Lippmann, W. (1922). *Public opinion.* New York: Harcourt Brace.

Livingston, K. (1980). Migraine mother. *American Photographer, 5,* 9.

Logan, R. (1986). *The alphabet effect: The impact of the phonetic alphabet on the development of Western civilization.* New York: William Morrow.

Lutz, C. A., & Collins, J. L. (1993). *Reading National Geographic.* Chicago: University of Chicago Press.

Lyon, D. (1994). *The electronic eye.* Minneapolis: University of Minnesota Press.

MacDougall, D. (1997). The visual in anthropology. In M. Banks & H. Morphy (Eds.), *Rethinking visual anthropology* (pp. 276–295). New Haven, CT: Yale University Press.

Maharidge, D., & Williamson, M. (1989). *And their children after them,* New York: Pantheon Books.

Martin, E. (1990). The rights of those pictured. In P. M. Lester (Ed.), *NPPA Special report: the ethics of photojournalism* (pp. 28–34). Durham, NC: National Press Photographers Association.

May, W. F. (1980, February). Doing ethics: The bearing of ethical theories on fieldwork. *Social Problems, 27,* 358–370.

Mayo, B. (1989). Note 2 to T. Adorna, Lyric Poetry and Society. In S. E. Bromer & D. M. Kellner (Eds.), *Critical theory and society: A reader.* New York: Routledge.

McChesney, R. W. (1997). *Corporate media and the threat to democracy.* New York: Seven Stories Press.

McChesney, R. W. (1999). *Rich media, poor democracy: Communication politics in dubious times.* Urbana: University of Illinois Press.

McCombs, M. E., & Shaw, D. L. (1972). The agenda-setting function of mass media. *Public Opinion Quarterly, 36,* 176–187.

McCombs, M. E., & Shaw, D. L. (1993). The evolution of agenda-setting research: Twenty-five years in the marketplace of ideas. *Journal of Communication, 43*(2), 58–67.

McLuhan, M. (1951). *The mechanical bride: Folklore of industrial man.* New York: Vanguard.

McLuhan, M. (1964). *Understanding media, the extensions of man.* New York: McGraw-Hill.

McLuhan, M., & Fiore, Q. (1967). *The medium is the message.* New York: Random House.

McLuhan, M., & Powers, B. (1989). *The global village, transformations in world life and media in the 21st century.* New York: Oxford University Press.

McLuhan, T. C. (1994). *The way of the earth.* New York: Simon & Schuster.

McNally, J. (1996, October). Photograph, no title. *Life Magazine,* p. 102.

McQuail, D. (1994). *Mass communication theory.* London: Sage.

Mead, G. H. (1913). The social self. *Journal of Philosophy, 10,* 374–380.

Mead, G. H. (1934). *Mind, self and society.* Chicago: University of Chicago Press.

Mead, M. (1956). Some uses of still photography in culture and personality studies. In D. G. Haring (Comp. and Ed.), *Personal character and cultural milieu* (3rd ed. pp. 78–105). Syracuse, NY: Syracuse University Press.

Mead, M., & Bateson, G. (1977). Margaret Mead and Gregory Bateson on the use of the camera in anthropology. *Studies in the Anthropology of Visual Communication, 4,* 78–80.

Media History Project. (1996). *Timeline.* Available: *http://www.mediahistory.com/time/timeline.html*

Meiselas, S., with Rosenberg C. (1981). *Nicaragua, June 1978–July 1979.* New York: Pantheon Books.

Messaris, P. (1994). *Visual literacy: Image, mind and reality.* Boulder, CO: Westview.

Messaris, P. (1997). *Visual persuasion: The role of images in advertising.* Thousand Oaks, CA: Sage.

Milgram, S. (1974). *Obedience to authority, an experimental view.* New York: Harper & Row.

Milgram, S. (1977a). The image-freezing machine. *Psychology Today, 10,* 50–54, 108.

Milgram, S. (1977b). *The individual in a social world, essays and experiments.* Reading, MA: Addison-Wesley.

Miller, M. C. (1996). Free the media, *The Nation, 262*(22), 9–15.

Mitchell, W. J. T. (1994). *Picture theory: Essays on verbal and visual representation.* Chicago: University of Chicago Press.

Moore, T. (1992). *Care of the soul: A guide for cultivating depth and sacredness in everyday life.* New York: HarperCollins.

Moriarty, S. (1996). Abduction: A theory of visual interpretation. *Communication Theory, 6*(2), 167–187.

Morris, W. (1978). In our image. In *Photography: Current perspectives, The Massachusetts Review,* pp. 6–7. Rochester, NY: Light Impressions.

Muybridge, E. (1887). *Animal locomotion: An electro-photographic investigation of consecutive phases of animal movements, 1872–1885.* Philadelphia: University of Pennsylvania.

Naggar, C. (1990, Early Summer). The unveiled: Algerian women, 1960. *Aperture*, pp. 2–11.

National Press Photographers Association. (1950). *Complete book of press photography*. New York: National Press Photographers Association.

National Press Photographers Association. (1998). *Code of ethics, Application for membership*. Available: *http://sunsite.unc.ed/nppa/nppa_app.html*

Newhall, B. (1964). *The history of photography*. New York: Museum of Modern Art.

Newton, J. H. (1983). *The role of photography in a social science research project in Northern Mexico: A matter of ethics*. Unpublished master's thesis, University of Texas, Austin.

Newton, J. H. (1984, Spring). Photography and reality: A matter of ethics. *Photo-Letter, 5,* 36–44.

Newton, J. H. (1990). Why ethics? Every photograph is a metaphor for a part of life. In P. M. Lester (Ed.), *NPPA special report: The ethics of photojournalism* (pp. 6–9). Durham, NC: National Press Photographers Association.

Newton, J. H. (1991). *In front of the camera: Ethical issues of subject response in photography*. Unpublished doctoral dissertation, University of Texas, Austin.

Newton, J. H. (1994, August). *The other side of the camera: Emotion and personality as factors in subject response*. Paper presented to the annual meeting of the association for Education in Journalism and Mass Communication, Atlanta.

Newton, J. H. (1994–1999). [Field notes and photographs]. Unpublished raw data.

Newton, J. H. (1998). Beyond representation: Toward a typology of visual ethics. *Visual Anthropology Review, 14*(1), 58–72.

Nichols, B. (1994). *Blurred boundaries: Questions of meaning in contemporary culture*. Bloomington: Indiana University Press.

Norman, D. (1973). *Alfred Stieglitz: An American seer*. New York: Random House.

Nottingham, E. (1978). *From both sides of the lens: street photojournalism and personal space*. Unpublished doctoral dissertation, Indiana University, Bloomington.

Okrent, D. (2000). *Editorial: The death of print?* Available: *http://www.digitaljournalist.org/issue0002/okrent.htm*

Orlan. (1999). Me, my surgery and my art. Available: *http://www.terminal.cz:80/~blackice/digissue1/media/orlan.html*

Ornstein, R. (1991). *The evolution of consciousness*. New York: Prentice Hall.

Ornstein, R. (1997). *The right mind: Making sense of the hemispheres*. New York: Harcourt, Brace.

Patterson, F., & Cohn, R. H. (1978). Conversations with a gorilla. *National Geographic, 154*(4), cover, 438–465.

Potter, R. F., Bolls, P. D., & Dent, D. R. (1997, May). *Something for nothing: Is visual encoding automatic?* Paper presented to the annual meeting of the International Communication Association, Montreal.

Random House Webster's College Dictionary. (1995). New York: Random House.

Reaves, S. (1995a, Winter). Magazines vs. newspapers: Editors have different ethical standards on the digital manipulation of photographs. *Visual Communication Quarterly*, pp. 4–7.

Reaves, S. (1995b). The vulnerable image: Categories of photos as predictor of digital manipulation. *Journalism & Mass Communication Quarterly*, pp. 706–715.

Rogers, E. M. (1998, July). Anatomy of the two subdisciplines of communication study. In University of Haifa Department of Communication (Ed.), *The blurring of boundaries between mass and interpersonal communication.* Preconference proceedings, annual convention of the International Communication Association, Haifa, Israel.

Roloff, M. E., & Miller, G. R. (1987). *Interpersonal processes: New directions in communication research.* Newbury Park, CA: Sage.

Ronell, A. (1994). *Finitude's score: Essays for the end of the millennium.* Lincoln: University of Nebraska Press.

Rosenblum, N. (1984). *A world history of photography.* New York: Abbeville Press.

Ruby, J. (Ed.). (1982). *A crack in the mirror, reflexive perspectives in anthropology.* Philadelphia: University of Pennsylvania.

Ruby, J. (1987). The ethics of image making. In A. Rosenthal (Ed.), *Documentary challenge* (pp. 7–13). Berkeley: University of California Press.

Ruby, J. (1997). *What is visual anthropology?* Available: *http://www.temple.edu/anthro/ruby/jayruby.html*

Ruskin, J. (1904). *Modern painters. Vol. 111. Containing Part IV, Of many things.* In E. T. Cook & A. Wedderborn (Eds.), *The complete works of John Ruskin* (Vol. 5, Part 2). London: George Allen. (Original work published 1856)

Sargent, S. L., & Zillmann, D. (1999, May). *Image effects on selective exposure to news stories.* Paper presented to the International Communication Association annual convention, San Francisco.

Schele, L., & Freidel, D. (1990). *A forest of kings, the untold story of the ancient Maya.* New York: William Morrow.

Schiller, H. (1996). *Invisible crises: What conglomerate control of media means for America and the world.* Boulder, CO: Westview Press.

Schiolino, E. (1996, November 12). A painful road from Vietnam to forgiveness. *The New York Times*, pp. A1, A8.

Schneider, G. B. (1999). *Culture jamming: an active audience's response to media culture.* Unpublished master's thesis, The University of Texas at Austin.

Schramm, W. (1988). *The story of human communication. Cave painting to microchip.* New York: Harper & Row.

Schultz, M. (1993). *The effect of visual presentation, story complexity and story familiarity on recall and comprehension of television news.* Unpublished doctoral dissertation, Indiana University, Bloomington.

Severin, W. J., & Tankard, J. W. (1997). *Communication theories: Origins, methods and uses in the mass media* (4th ed.). New York: Longman.

Sherer, M. (1985, August). *Photojournalism and the infliction of emotional distress: A question of conduct.* Paper presented to the Association for Education in Journalism and Mass Communication, Memphis, TN.

Sherer, M. (1990). Bibliography of grief, Ethical issues in photographing private moments, and Photographic invasion of privacy: Pictures that can be painful. In P. M. Lester (Ed.), *NPPA special report: The ethics of photojournalism* (pp. 10–15, 23–27, 35–41). Durham, NC: National Press Photographers Association.

Shlain, L. (1991). *Art & physics: Parallel visions in space, time & light.* New York: William Morrow.

Shoemaker, P. J. (1996). Hard-wired for news: Using biological and cultural evolution to explain the news. *Journal of Communication, 46,* 32–47.

Shoemaker, P. J., & Reese, S. D. (1991). *Mediating the message, theories of influences on mass media content.* New York: Longman.

Shoemaker, P. J., & Reese, S. D. (1996). *Mediating the message: Theories of influences on mass media content* (2nd ed.). New York: Longman.

Snyder, J., & Allen, N. W. (1982). Photography, vision, and representation. In T. F. Barrow, S. Armitage, & W. E. Tydeman (Eds.), *Reading into photography, selected essays, 1959–1960* (pp. 29–75). Albuquerque: University of New Mexico Press.

Sontag, S. (1973). *On photography.* New York: Dell.

Sperry, R. W. (1973). Lateral specialization of cerebral function in the surgically separated hemispheres. In F. J. McGuigan & R. A. Schoonover (Eds.), *The psychophysiology of thinking* (pp. 209–229). New York: Academic Press.

Squiers, C. (1990). *The critical image.* Seattle WA: Bay Press.

Stafford, B. M. (1996). *Good looking: Essays on the virtue of images.* Cambridge, MA: MIT Press.

Stafford, B. M. (1997, June). Educating digiterati. *Art Bulletin,* pp. 214–216.

Staiger, J. (1992). *Interpreting films: Studies in the historical reception of American cinema.* Princeton, NJ: Princeton University Press.

Stott, W. (1973). *Documentary expression and thirties America.* London: Oxford University Press.

Synthetic pleasures. (1996). Retrieved February 12, 2000, from: *http://www.caipirinha.com/Film/spcontent.html*

Tagg, J. (1988). *The burden of representation: Essays on photographies and histories.* Basingstoke: Macmillan Education.

Timberlake, R. N. (1997). The myth of the girl in the photo. *Vets with a mission.* Available: *http://www.vwam.com/vets/myth/html*

Toffler, A. (1990). *Powershift: Knowledge, wealth, and violence at the edge of the 21st century.* New York: Bantam.

Tuchman, G. (1978). *Making news, a study in the construction of reality*. New York: The Free Press.

UT engineer works to help cameras interpret images. (1998, March 20). *Austin American-Statesman*. Section B, Metro & State, pp. 1, 3.

Wagner, J. (Ed.). (1979). *Images of information, still photography in the social sciences*. Beverly Hills, CA: Sage.

Warwick, D. P. (1977, December). Social sciences and ethics. *Special Supplement to Hastings Center Report*, 7, 8–10.

Weber, R. (1974). *The reporter as artist: A look at the New Journalism controversy*. New York: Hastings House.

Webster's new collegiate dictionary. (1979). Springfield, MA: G&C Merriam.

Williams, R. (1995). *Beyond visual literacy: Course guide, J310K* (University of Texas Department of Journalism). Austin: Longhorn Copies.

Williams, R. (1999, Autumn). Beyond visual literacy: Omniphasism: A theory of balance, (part one of three). *Journal of Visual Literacy*, *19* (2), 159–178.

Wilson, E. O. (1992). *The diversity of life*. Cambridge, MA: Belknap Press of Harvard University Press.

Wilson, E. O. (1998). *Consilience: The unity of knowledge*. New York: Knopf.

Winick, C. (1956). *Dictionary of anthropology*. New York: Philosophical Library.

Worth, S. (1980). Margaret Mead and the shift from "visual anthropology" to the "anthropology of visual communication." *Studies in Visual Communication*, *6*, 15–22.

Worth, S. (1981). *Studying visual communication* (L. Gross, Ed.). Philadelphia: University of Pennsylvania Press.

Worth, S., & Adair, J. (1972). *Through Navajo eyes: An exploration in film communication and anthropology*. Bloomington: Indiana University Press.

Zelizer, B. (1992). *Covering the body: The Kennedy assassination, the media, and the shaping of collective memory*. Chicago: University of Chicago Press.

Zelizer, B. (1998). *Remembering to forget: Holocaust memory through the camera eye*. Chicago: University of Chicago Press.

CREDITS AND PERMISSIONS

Kim Phuc running from napalm attack, by Nick Ut, The Associated Press, was used with the permission of AP/Wide World Photos.

Phan Thi Kim Phuc at 1996 Veterans Day ceremony, by Dennis Cook, The Associated Press, used with permission of AP/Wide World Photos.

"Kim Phuc showing her scarred back and arm," by Joe McNally, was used with the permission of LIFE Magazine©Time Inc.

Parts of chapter 1 were originally published as "Visual Truth: The Role of Photojournalism in Mediating Reality," *Visual Communication Quarterly,* Fall 1998, Vol. 5 (4), pages 1, 3–8.

An early version of chapter 2 was presented as a juried paper, "The Vision Instinct,"Visual Communication Division, International Communication Association, Acapulco, Mexico, June 2000.

Earlier versions of parts of chapter 4 were published in a review of *Doing Documentary Work* in *Spot Magazine,* Fall 1997" and were presented as "Visual Embrace or Visual Assault: Moral Implications of Photojournalistic Seeing," Twelfth Annual Visual Communication Conference, Winter Park, Colorado, June 1998.

Earlier versions of parts of chapter 5 were included in a panel presentation, "Stealing/Steeling the Soul: Identity and Media," AEJMC, Anaheim, 1996; and as a guest lecture, "La Etica y la identidad," NAFOTO II International Month of Photography, São Paulo, Brazil, 1995.

Earlier versions of parts of chapter 9 were originally published as "On Sanctification and Violation of the Human Image," Contact: Photojournalism Since Vietnam Exhibition and Symposium, Center for Research in Contemporary Art Research Subscription, 1992–93, pp. 13–14; a juried paper, "Toward an Ecology of the Visual," International Communication Association, San Francisco, May 1999; and a juried presentation "Body and Soul: Everyday Murders of the Spirit," International Conference on Violence in the Media, New York, New York, 1994.

An earlier version of chapter 10 was published as "Beyond Representation: Toward a Typology of Visual Behavior," *Visual Anthropology Review,* Vol. 14 (1), Spring-Summer 1998, pages 58–72. Figure 10.1 was adapted from Figure 3, p. 62. Figure 3.1 was adapted from Figure 4, p. 64. *Visual Anthropology Review* is a peer-reviewed publication of the Society for Visual Anthropology, a unit of the American Anthropological Association. An earlier version was presented as a juried paper, "From Visual Embrace to Visual Murder," International Communication Association, Sydney, Australia, 1994.

An earlier version of chapter 11 was selected for presentation as "Interpersonal Dimensions of Mass Media Imagery: The Problem of Real People," International Communication Association Pre-Conference, Haifa, Israel, July 1998.

AUTHOR INDEX

A

Adair, J., 34.
Adorna, T. W., 50, 53
Agee, J., 39–40, 43
Arnett, P., 49, 75
Arnheim, R., 84
Aultschull, J. H., 99, 101
Avedon, R., 143

B

Bakewell, L., 133
Barlow, W., 36
Barry, A. M., 27, 84, 111, 112, 113
Bateson, G., 34, 70
Baudrillard, J., 36, 83
Bazin, A., 21
Bechara, A., 22, 111, 112
Bellman, B., 34
Beloff, H., xiii, 34, 38, 39, 63, 65
Benjamin, W., xiii
Berger, J., 87
Berger, P. L., 8, 88, 96, 111, 14
Best, S., 115
Black, M., 20
Blumer, H., 54, 111, 114, 133, 134, 154, 155, 157
Bolls, P. D., 27
Brown, C., 34

Bryant, G., 41
Buell, H., 96
Buller, D. B., 158, 160, 161, 162
Burgoon, J. K., 158, 160, 161, 162
Burnham, S., 120
Buss, A. J., 69

C

Calloway, Sarah G., 136, 156
Capra, F., 8, 111
Carey, J. W., 134
Carlebach, M. L., 17
Carpenter, E., 34, 65, 156
Carter, B., 85
Cervenka, E., 119
Chapnick, H., xiii, 95, 98
Chomsky, N., 75
Christians, C. G., 34, 37, 71
Church, D., 52
Cohn, R. H., 133
Coles, R., 54–57
Collier, J. 34, 143
Collins, J. L., xiii, 36, 103
Cooley, C. H., 133
Cooper, T., 108
Craig, R. T., 108
Crick, F., 22, 24, 64, 115

D

Damasio, H., 22, 111, 112
Damasio, A. R., 22, 111, 112
Dates, J., 36
Debord, G., 36, 83
Dent, D. R., 27
Denton, C., 25
Denzin, N. K., 68
Deppa, J., 144
Derrida, J., 36
Desfor, D. M., 35
Dodd, A, 116.
Dondis, D. A., 84
Duncan, D. D., 54
Durham, M. G., 89
Dyer, R., 36

E

Eldridge, J., 183
Evans, H., 55, 122
Evans, W., 39–40, 43

F

Fackler, M, 34
Flocke, E. L., 44
Foucault, M., 18, 83
Freidel, D., 22
Freund, C. P., 165
Freund, G., xiii
Fulfs, P., 116
Fulton, M., xiii

G

Galassi, P., 20
Gearan, A., 159
Gernsheim, H., 123
Goffman, E., 8, 27, 42, 69
Goldberg, V., xiii, 24, 42, 90, 163, 165
Gombrich, E. H., 20, 84
Goulden, J., 165

Graber, D. A., 88, 90
Gregory, R. L., 27, 117, 156

H

Hagaman, D., xiii
Hale, L., 52
Hall, J. A., 113
Hall, S., xiii
Hamilton, J., 136, 156
Hammersley, M., 55
Harper, D. A., 34, 41
Hartley, C., 34, 41
Hartley, P., 160–163
Hayes, D., 144
Henderson, L., 34
Herman, E. S., 75
Holmes, N., 110
Hooks, b, 138.

I

Innis, H. A., 88
Irvine, R., 165
Ivins, W., 8, 84

J

Jarecke, K., 55, 119
Jay, B., 43
Jaynes, J., 112
JEB (Joan E. Biren), 38, 39
Jules-Rosette, B., 34

K

Kellner, D., 115
Kelly, J. D., 27
Knapp, M. L., 111, 113
Kobre, K., xiii. 42. 50, 141
Kozol, W., xiii

L

Lasswell, H. D., 23, 97

LeDoux, J, 111, 112, 113
Leekley, J., 148, 158
Leekley, S., 148, 158
Lester, P. M., xiii, 34, 36, 84
Lippmann, W., 99
Livingston, K., 153
Logan, R., 88
Luckmann, T., 8, 88, 96, 111, 114
Lutz, C. A., xiii, 36, 103
Lyon, D., 23

M
MacDougall, D., 135
Maharidge, D., 40
Martin, E. 39
May, W. F., 36
Mayo, 50, 53
McChesney, R. W., 75
McLuhan, M., 83, 88, 95–96, 99,
    110–114
McLuhan, T. C., 88
McQuail, D., 79, 97, 99, 102, 157–159
Mead, G. H., 133
Mead, M., 34, 70
Meiselas, S., 145
Messaris, P., xiii, 84
Milgram, S., 35–36, 39, 67
Miller, G. R., 35, 39, 158
Miller, M. C., 75, 76
Mitchell, W. J. T., xiiii, 83
Mohr, J., 87
Moore, T., 64
Moriarty, S., 111, 112
Morris, W., 3
Muybridge, E., 84

N
Nace, D., 27
Naggar, C., 42, 144
Newhall, B., 65, 137, 156

Newton, J. H., 12, 34, 36–39, 42, 70,
    102, 153
Nichols, B., 90
Norman, D., 136
Nottingham, E., 34, 39

O
Orlan, 116
Ornstein, R., 111, 112, 118

P
Patterson, F., 133,
Potter, R. F., 27
Powers, B., 83, 96, 111, 114

R
Reaves, S., 8
Reese, S. D., 8, 45
Rogers, E. M., 108
Roloff, M. E., 35, 39, 158
Ronell, A., 110, 118, 171
Rosenberg, C., 145
Rosenblum, N., 66
Rotzoll, K. B., 34
Ruby, J., 34, 135
Ruskin, J., 49
Russell, M., 144

S
Sargent, S. L., 34
Schele, L., 22
Schiller, H., 75.
Schiolino, E., 159, 162
Schneider, G. B., 101, 108
Schramm, W., 22
Schultz, M., 88, 90
Severin, W. J., 79, 97
Shaw, D. L., 99
Sherer, M., 34, 41, 144
Shlain, L., 21

Shoemaker, P. J., 8, 22, 23, 45, 11, 112
Snyder, J., & Allen, N. W., 132
Sontag, S., 34, 144
Sperry, R. W., 111, 112
Squiers, C., 36
Stafford, B. M., 111, 114
Staiger, J., 87, 155
Stott, W., 43, 131

T
Tagg, J., 24, 36
Tankard, J. W., 79, 97
Timberlake, R. N., 165–166
Toffler, A., 95
Tranel, D., 22, 111, 112
Tuchman, G., 8

W
Warwick, D. P., 41
Weber, R., 8, 50
Williams, R., 84–85
Williamson, M, 40
Wilson, E. O., 111–113
Worth, S., xiii, 34

Z
Zelizer, B., xiii
Zillmann, D., 34

SUBJECT INDEX

A

Abstract, defined, 120
Acoustic Age, 83
Adams, Eddie, 141, 142
Advertising, 89, 90, 109, 157
Aesthetic, 108, realism, 50
Aesthetics, photographic, 136
African-Americans, 89, see also People of color, 147
Agee, James, 40, 56
Agence France Presse, 51, 100
Agenda-setting, 99
Ake, David, 51
American Society of Media Photographers, 71
American-Statesman, Austin, 159
Anne, Princess, 144
Annihilation, psychological, 144–145
Anthropology, 44
    theory, 134
    see also Visual anthropology
AP, see Associated Press
Art, 179, defined, 121
Artifacts, 101, 118, 137
Artist, 50, 53
ASMP, see American Society of Media Photographers
Associated Press, 24, 49, 78, 99, 148, 159, 164

Audience 97, 165, 167
    active, 157
    reception, 87, 155, 171
    mass, 98, 132, 154
    see also Media users, Viewer
Authenticity, 8, 164, 182
Authority, 68, 89, 167
Avedon, Richard, 37, 143

B

Barrett, Elizabeth, 123
Behavior 19, 132, 158
    conscious and unconscious, 42
    defined, 115
    meaning of 136
    photographic, 35, 44, 67, 70
    photojournalism, 131
    visual as, 108, 135
    visual social science, 131
    see also Visual behavior
Behavioral system, 118
Beijing, 25
Being, 118
Bergen, Candice, 152
Black Star Photo Agency, 98
Body 121, 123, 157, 170, 181
    as equivalent, 160
    mind as, 115
Bonar, Ave, 141

Bouju, Jean-Marc, 24
Boundaries between public and
    private, 158
Brain
        right hemisphere of, 112
        left hemisphere of, 112
Brown, Murphy, 116, 152
Bryant, Jennings, 109
Burden of truth, 183
Burden of visual truth, 4, 125, 179,
    181, 184–185

C
Camel, Joe, 109
Camera, 38, 43, 168
        as mediating device, 170
        presence of, 67, 169
        as seeing mechanism, 138
        as weapon, 144, 145
Candid photos, 43, 143
Capitalism, 101
Caption, style of 162
Cartier-Bresson, Henri, 38
CBS, 85, 163
Chapnick, Harry, xiii, 98
Civil Rights Act, photojournalism's
    effect on, 142
Code of ethics, see Ethics
Codes, visual, 108
Cognition, defined, 115, 118, 86
Cognitive, the, 57
        system, 118
Co-image-makers, 39, see also Event,
    Observer, Observed, Photographer,
    Subject, Viewer
Commodification, 103, 152, 153, 168
Communication, 132, 147
        defined, 158
        personal, 157, 158, 159
        photographic, 138

theory, 108, 134
    see also Convergence, Face to
        face, Face to image,
        Interpersonal
Consciousness, 22, 64, 89, 115, 116,
    117, 153, see also Public
Consent, 34
Construction of reality, 165
Constructionism, 176
Contact Press, 100, 119
        exhibition, 123
Content, 34, 45, 182
        mass communication, 79
        transparency of photographic, 84
Context, 160, 170, 181
        defined, 138
Convergence of communication
    technologies, 158
Cook, Dennis, 159
Copyright, 41
Covenantal ethic, 36
Credibility, ix, 27, 90, 124, 158, 163
Critical theory, 97, 103, 137, 172
Cultural system, 117
Cultural theory, 103, 172
Culture jamming, 101, 109
Culture, 108
Curriculum, integrated visual and
    verbal, 182

D
Dallas Morning News, 75
Death, defined, 120
Depression era, 153
Designer, 76
Diamond, Hugh, 35
Diana, Princess, x
Digital imaging, ix–x, 38, 46, 163, 176,
    179
Digital journalist as a term, 179

Direction, as typology dimension, 139
Document, 152
Documentary
behavior, 131
dilemma of, 56
work, 56
Dole, Bob, 51
Dreaming, 133
Duncan, David Douglas, 54

E
Ecological niche, defined, 115
Ecology, 111
defined 114, 118
deep-ecology paradigm, 111
of an image of reportage, 171
of the visual, 132, 142,181,
chapter 9
Economic interests, 96, 101, see also
Capitalism, Commodification
Editor, 44, 122, 137, 167, 184–185
burden of, 184
see also Picture editor, Public
Editorial concerns, 181
Education, see Curriculum,
Photojournalism, Media literacy,
Visual literacy
Effects, intensity of behavior on
observer or observer, 139
Eisert, Sandra, 75, 78
Emotion, 41, 57, 68,169, 187, see also
Subject feelings
Emotional distress, 41
Emotional response, 153
Enlightenment, 118, paradigm, 55
Environment, defined, 115
Epistemology, 36
Equivalent, 146
body as, 160

functional, 155, 156
photographic, 139
Equivalents, Theory of, 65, 151,
156,167
Erikson, Erik, 56
Ethical right, 41
Ethics, x, 11, 57, 80, 180, 193
codes of, 71
law and, 41
see also Covenantal ethic, Ethical
right, Photojournalism ethics,
Ethnography, 39
Evans, Harold, 55, 122
Evans, Walker, 40, 43
Event
picture-making 39, 169–172
picture-taking, 76
see also Photographic event
Evidence, 24, 100, 101, 131, 142
Evolution, 112
Experience, 70, 96, 134
Experienceability, 110, 116, 172
Experiment, see Method
Eyewitness, 24, 27, 49, 68, 100, see also
Witness

F
Face to face, 160
communication, 157, 158, 166
Face to image communication, 172
Feature photograph, 80, 143
Feelings, 68, see also Emotion, Subject
feelings
Female, see Gender
Figure-ground theory, 109
as metaphor, 180
Film, 52
First Amendment, 71, 85, 100
Flukinger, Roy, 141
Fourth Estate, 18, 85, see also Press

Frame analysis, 27
Funeral, 143

G
Galela, Ron, 41
Gatekeeper, 75, 76, 100
Gaze, 38, 131, see also Glance
Gazes, intersection of, 103
Gender issues, 169
    girls, 89
    women, 36 42, 46, 144, 147
    men, 42, 46
    see also Sexual orientation
Gerbner, George, 158
Gestalt, 87, 175
Gesture, 121, 136, 156, 178
Glance, 38, see also Gaze and Gazes
Global culture, 166
Global media, 170,
Goodrich, Mark, 141
Government, 96, 101
Gulf War, 55, 78, 100, 119, 122

H
Hard-wired, 29, see also Physiology
Hawthorne effect, 69
Hegemony, 24, 117, 172
Heyward, Andrew, 85
Hicks, Wilson, 177
Higgins, Chester, Jr., 30
Hubbell Telescope, 101
Human
    being, 51, 57
    visual behavior, 132, 183
    see also Behavior, Humanism
Humanism, 34, 51, 132, 137

I
Icon, 121, 153
Identification, defined, 120

Identity, 38, 86, 166
Ideological issues, 45
Illustration, 143,
    photograph as, 80
Image, 37, 135, 175
    act, 133
    content of, 37 ,98
    disseminators of, 185
    meaning of, 37
    power of, 97
    see also Illustration, Pictures,
        Photographs
Images and identity, see Self-identity
Imagination, 136
Individual, 151, 154
    and society, 154
Instinct, 20
Intensity, as typology dimension,
    139
Interaction, 39, 155, 168
Interactive process of photojournalism,
    169
Internet, 101, 166, 176, 177, see also
    Online publications
Interpersonal communication, 37, 39,
    67, 147, 151, 157, 158, 160, 165,
    166, 169–170
Interpersonal deception theory,
    158
Interpersonal relationship, 167
Interpersonal, as direction for typology
    of visual behavior, 139
Interpretative process, 168
Intrapersonal, 67, as direction for
    typology of visual behavior, 139
Intuition, 20,117, 185

J
Jarecke, Kenneth, 55, 119
Journalism, as a term, 176

education, 182
New, 8
Journalists, 39, 54, see also
    Photographer, Photojournalist,
    Reporter
Judgment of communicator,
    158

K
Knowing, 87, 90, 96

L
Lambert, Ken, vi
Lange, Dorothea, 56
Langer, Ralph, 75
Law, 41, 183
Lee, Nancy, 30, 72
Lewis, Oscar, 56
Liebovitz, Annie, 37
Life Magazine, 163, 165
Life, defined, 120
Light table, 30
Limited effects, 97
Literal, defined, 120
London Times, 55

M
Magazines, 9, 11
Magic bullet, 97, 157
Magnum, 100
Mass, 139, 151
    audience, see Audience
    communication, 79, 164, 166
        education, 180
    as individuals who have selves,
        157
    -interpersonal communication,
        168
    -interpersonal relationship, 151,
        Chapter 11, 166, 171

media, 154, 157, 181
    relationship, 151
McLuhan, Marshall, 83, 110
McNally, Joe, 165
Mead, George Herbert, 154
Mead, Margaret, 6
Meaning, 88, 132, 133, 134, 151, 154,
    155, 156, 160, 168, 172
    negotiation of, 95, 134
    of photojournalism, 182
    see also Photograph
Media, 113
    education, 181
    literacy, 183
    new social theory of, 102
    powerful, 97
    users, 172, 181
Mediation of image, 170–172
    human, 180
Meiselas, Susan, 145
Memory, 7, 26, 34. 67, 87, 88, 96, 141
Men, see Gender
Method, visual as, 135
Methodology, 36, 185,
    social science 41
    experiment, 67, 70
    visual, 135, 182
Mexico, 129
Migrant Mother, 153
Milgram, 35, 36, 67, 68
Mind's eye, 19, 21, 86
Mind-body dichotomy, 115
Minorities, 89,
Mobius strip
    human behavior as, 138
    of human communication, 139
Modernism, 117
Mogadishu, 96
Mohin, Andrea, 46
Moore, Charles, 142

Muse, 38
Myller, Corinne, 72

N
National Enquirer, 27
National Geographic, x, 85
National Press Photographers
    Association, 49, 71
Native American, 144
NBC, 85
Neutral camera, ix, 6
New York Times, 27, 30, 38, 46, 83, 159,
    178
News Photographer, 33 35, 51, 52
News photographer, see
    Photojournalist
News, 181, defined, 120
Newspaper page, 175
Newspapers, 9, 10, 11, 24, 99, 142, 154,
    163, 166, 179
Newsweek, 163
Newswork, 99
Newton, Matt
Nineteenth century, ix, 43, 83, 84, 118
Nonverbal behavior, 19, 35, 113, 135
        as visual nonlinguistic
            communication, 113
NPPA, see National Press
    Photographers Association

O
O'Connor, Margaret, 72
Object, 151
Objectification, 156, 168, 169
Objective observer, 155
Objective reality, 12
Objectivity, ix, 6, 8
Observed, 36, 38
        as victim, 39

see also Photographer, Viewer,
    Observer and, 58
Observer, 36
    dispassionate, 51, 54
    and observed interaction, 132,
        133, 138
    participant, 39
    see also Photographer, Viewer,
        and Observed, 45, 58
Oklahoma City, 96, 153
Onassis, Jacqueline Kennedy, 41
Online publications, 10, see also
    Internet
Orlan, 116
Oswald, Lee Harvey, 142
Other, 36, 57, 68, 133, 167, 172

P
Panopticon, 83
Paparazzi, x, 51
Parasocial relationship, 152
Penn, Irving, 37
People of color, 147, see also African-
    Americans
Perception, 21, 87, 97, 108, 117, 182,
    see also Visual perception
Personality, 137, 138, 161, 169
Perspective, 21
        as typology dimension, 139
        of subject, 139
        of photographer, 139
        of viewer, 139
        see also Point of view
Photograph, 138
        can lie, 184
        manipulation of, 184
        meaning of, 33, 35, 132, 143
        see also Candid, Content, Image,
            Pictures, Wedding

Photographer, 167, 169–170, 182,
    as artist, 53
    behavior, see Behavior, Visual
        behavior
    defined, 138
    feelings of, 137, see also Emotion
    intrusive, 43
    press, 40
    as reporter, 53
    self, 1690170
    as storyteller, 54
    and subject interaction, 35,36,
        146, 166
    as voyeur, 52
    as watchdog, 52
    see also Observer and Observed,
        Perspective
Photographic event, 138, 145, 168, see
    also Event
Photography
    defined, 6, 125
    as 19th-century process, 179
    as 20th-century process, 179
    see also Still photography
Photojournalism , ix–x, 67,181, 185
    behavior, 131, see also Behavior,
        Visual behavior
    as cultural practice, 44
    defined, 5
    education, xi–xii,177
    effects of, 95, 99
    ethics, 33, 57
    history, 17
    invention of, chapter 2
    methods, 57
    New, 4,182
    practice of, 19,28, 33, 45, 49, 57,
        123
        conventions of, 169

process of, 180
    as public visual behavior, 108
    rationale for, 178
    role of, 103
    status of, 179–185
    as 20th-century practice, 178
    as visual anthropology, 54, 135
    as visual interaction, 132
    see also Visual journalism, Visual
        reportage
Photojournalism Since Vietnam
    exhibition, 119, 122
Photojournalist
    burden of, 182
    rights and responsibilities of,
        183
    see also Digital journalist,
        Observer, News
        photographer, Photographer,
        Visual journalist
Phuc, Phan Thi Kim, 85, 148, 151,
    Chapter 11, 157–168
Physical, the, 151, 152
Physiological system, 117
Physiology, 87, 90, 108, see also Hard-
    wired
Picture editor, 72, 76, 77, 153
Pictures, 88, 170, see also Image,
    Photograph
Point of view, 183, see also Perspective
Polaroid, 65
Portrait, 44, 64,146
Pose, 43, 80
Postmodernism, 12, 22, 36, 83, 115,
    133
Power, 11, 35, 41, 58, 95, 97, 99, 101,
    114, 131, 135, 138, 167,183
        of visual knowing, 184
Powerlessness, 96,170

Press, 96, 99
  free, 98
  penny, 101
  photographer
  see also Fourth Estate,
      Magazines, Newspapers,
      Photographer, Photojournalist
Primal, the, defined, 114, 115
Print media, see Magazines,
  Newspapers, Press
Privacy, 144, 180
  invasion of, 34, 41
  right to, 144
  subject, 41
  see also Boundaries;
      Photographer, intrusive;
      Public
Producers, 166
Propaganda, 99,165
Proxemics, 160
Psychology, 86, 87, 108
Public, 41, 96, 97, 151, 157,
  168
  consciousness, 161
  as editors, 98
  eye, 153
  memory, 153
  -needs-to-know, 98
  opinion, 98, 101, 165
  as subjects and sources, 98
  see also Boundaries
Public's right to know, 41, 45
Publisher, 76, 184
Pulitzer Prize, 24,151, 163, 164
Pyramids, see *National Geographic*

Q
Quayle, Dan, 152
Quinlan, Jim 72

R
Radio, 179
Rape, see Visual Rape
Rather, Dan, 85
Rational, 117
Readers, see Media users, Observers,
  Viewers
Reading as visual behavior, 136
Real, 88, 116, 131, 166, 167, 180
  construction of, 116
  defined, 120
  journalism as,176
  life, 152, 172
  person, 43
  reality, 44
  self, 37
  subject, 44
  time 19, 176
  visual journalism as guardian of,
      184
  within the culture of the virtual,
      4
  world, 20,184
Reality, 35, 132,180
  imaging, 95,132
  representations of, 136
  separate plane of, 36
  world of, 134
Reasonable truth, 12, 86, 185
Reportage, 57, see also Visual reportage
Reporter, 6, 53
Reporting, defined, 5
Representation, 7, 36, 44, 85, 132, 136,
  137, 152, see also Content
Representational, defined, 120, frames,
  139, visual as, 135
Research 55, 143, 182
Response, psychological, 25
  physiological, 25

Responsibility, see Social responsibility, 122
Reuters, 51, 100
Right to know, see public's
Rock drawings, 22
Roosevelt, Franklin D., 96
Routines, 180, media, 45
Ruby, Jack, 142

S
Sanctification, defined, 121
Sandanistas, 145
Satellite, 101, 176
Schlein, Lonnie, 72
Screen, 176
Seattle Times, 80
See, 117
Seeing, 86, 107, 118
   as believing, 27, 86, 90, 184
   mechanism, see Camera
Self, 63, 89, 131, 133, 151, 169
   and other, 68, 69
   presentational, 69
   real, 37
   unmasked, 37
   viewer, 170
   see also Observer, Photographer, Mass, Selves
Self-annihilation, 145
Self-awareness, 69
Self-concept, 161
Self-conscious, 70
Self-consciousness, 38, 69
Self-identity, 89
Self-indication, 154
Self-portrait, 133
Self-protective gestures, 156
Self-study, 180
Selves, 154
Semiotics, 108

semiological guerilla warfare, 181
Sender and receiver, 158, 161
Sexual orientation, 36
Signification, 110
Silver-based, 38
Simpson, O. J., 101, 102, 142
Simulacrum, 83
Simulation, 110
Sixteenth century, 183
Slade, Margot, 72
Slate, 165
Smith, Eugene, 53
Social
   anxiety, 69
   construction of reality, 96, 114, 166
   constructionism, 22
   identity, 11
   interaction, 134, 154, 156, 166, 167
   responsibility, 10, 99
Social science, 19
   methods, 41, 44
   see also Visual social science
Society, 86, 95, 184
Sociobiology, 103, 112
Sociology, see Visual sociology
Soul, 25, 63, 64, 86, 144, chapter 5
South Vietnam, see Vietnam
Spectacle, 83
Stakeout, vi
Staged, 80, 153
   photos, 70
Stapleton, Sally, 75, 78
Stereotype, 24, 89, 103, 183
Stieglitz, Alfred, 65, 136, 139, 156
Still photography, 10, 27, 184
Streeck, Jürgen, 133

Subject, 38, 169, 184
    burden, 184
    defined, 138
    and photographer interaction, 35
    effects on, 67
    feelings, 34, 37, 137
    manipulating, 70
    not co-creator, 41
    self, 169
Subjective perception, 57, 84, 85, 170
Subjectivity, x, 8, 172
Subjects, 167
    rights and responsibilities of,
        185
Surveillance, 21, 23, 24, 101, 112,
    179
Survival, 176
Symbol, 151, 164
Symbolic, 108
    defined, 114, 115
    interactionism, 22, 114, 133, 137,
        154, 168
    object, 41
Symbols
    verbal, 117
    visual, 117
System, cognitive/behavioral, 118
Systems theory, 111

T
Technologies of reportage, 180
Technology, 134, 135, 147, 166, 177,
    183
Television, 11, 166, 179
Thompson, Florence, 153
Thought, 117
    anthropological, 135
Tía Marâ, 126, 130, 145
Time, x
Transmission model, 157
Truth, 25, 57, 95, 96, 180, 185
    controlling, 100

reasonable,12, 86, 185
    see also Visual truth
Twentieth century, ix–x, 30, 54, 55, 83,
    84, 97, 118, 176, 181
Twenty-first century, ix–x, 45, 49, 183
Typology of visual behavior, 131, 137,
    152, 168
    applying as shorthand, 246

U
Unisden, Betty, 80
Ut, Huynh Cong (Nick), 85, 159–168

V
Verbal, 110, 117
Victim, 39, 41, 144, 161
Video, 10, 88
Vietnam, 119, 159, 161, 163, 165
    South, 148
Viewer, 37, 87, 103, 122, 124, 137, 139,
    153, 155, 157, 160, 167, 169–170
    burden, 184
    self, 170
    and subject, 146
    see also Observer, Editor
Viewers, 44, 132, 170, 181
    rights and responsibilities of,
        185
Violation, 144
    defined, 121
Virtual, 88
    media, 157
    reality, 110
Vision , 20, 117
    instinct, 20, 29, 115, 117
Visual Age, 83
Visual anthropology, 34, 38, 41, 54,
    135
Visual assault, 144, 146, 168
Visual behavior, 19, 39, 111, 113, 132,
    137, 147, 181
Visual cliché, 143

Visual communication, 84
    as primary, 112
Visual criticism, 114
Visual document, 126, 130, 131, 142,
    145–146, 168
Visual ecology, 109
Visual education, 181
Visual embrace, 130, 131, 138, 139,
    141, 145, 168
Visual encounter, 142
Visual environment, 107, 109
Visual equivalent, 38, 44, 103, 121, 141,
    153, 155, 159, 160, 166, 168, 170,
    171
Visual fiction, 172
Visual gift, 141, 168
Visual interaction, 132
Visual intrusion, 143, 145
Visual journalism, 135, 182
    as guardian of the real, 184
    as a term, 179
    see also Photojournalism, Visual
        reportage
Visual journalist, 182, 185
    as trained seer, 180
    see also Journalist, Photographer,
        Photojournalist, Reporter
Visual literacy, 172, 183, 185, see also ,
    Curriculum, Education
Visual murder, 144
Visual perception, 22, 25, 27, 84, 109,
    110, 168
    theory, 156
    see also Perception
Visual quote, 168
Visual rape, 139, 144, 168
Visual reportage, 99, 103, 118, 172, 182
    as document, 152
    and identity, 89
    improving, 181
    as mass multimedia practice, 180
    practice of, 107

    See also Photojournalism, Visual
        journalism
Visual social science, 135, 144
Visual social scientist, 182
Visual sociology, 34,
Visual studies, 114
Visual suicide, 145
Visual system, 147
Visual theater, 130, 131, 142, 146
Visual theft, 126, 144, 145
Visual theory, 108, 111, 114, 136
Visual truth, 5, 7, 9, 10, 84, 85, 91, 101,
    102, 103, 167, 173, 179, 181, 183
    relationship between images and,
        182
    subjectivity of, 182
    see also Truth
Visual waste, 109
Visual, the, 107, 110, 132
Voyeur, 29, 52, 103

W
Washington Post, 51
Washington Times, vi
Watchdog, 51, 52
Web, see Internet
Wedding photographs, 143
Wells, Orson, 56
Westmoreland, Gen. William C., 164
White, Gov. Mark
Wilking, Rick T., 51
Will, 41, 42
Witness, 103, see also Eyewitness
Women, see Gender
Word editors, 76, see also Editor
Words, 18, 88, 135, 170, 175, see also
    Verbal

Z
Zines, 101